David Feherty

The Power of
Positive Idiocy

David Feherty is a golf commentator for CBS
Sports and a columnist for *Golf Magazine*. He
is the author of *A Nasty Bit of Rough*, *Some-
where in Ireland a Village Is Missing an Idiot*, *An
Idiot for All Seasons*, and *David Feherty's Totally
Subjective History of the Ryder Cup*.

Also by David Feherty

A Nasty Bit of Rough

An Idiot for All Seasons

Somewhere in Ireland a Village Is Missing an Idiot

David Feherty's Totally Subjective History of the Ryder Cup: A Hardly
Definitive, Completely Cockeyed, but Absolutely Loving Tribute to Golf's
Most Exciting Event

The Power of Positive Idiocy

A Collection of Rants and Raves

David Feherty

ANCHOR BOOKS
A Division of Random House, Inc.
New York

FIRST ANCHOR BOOKS EDITION, MAY 2011

Copyright © 2010 by David Feherty

All rights reserved. Published in the United States by Anchor Books, a division of Random House, Inc., New York, and in Canada by Random House of Canada Limited, Toronto. Originally published in hardcover in the United States by Doubleday, a division of Random House, Inc., New York, in 2010.

Anchor Books and colophon are registered trademarks of Random House, Inc.

All of the pieces in this book except for the foreword and introduction originally appeared in *Golf Magazine* and on www.golf.com.

The Library of Congress has cataloged the Doubleday edition as follows:
Feherty, David.
The power of positive idiocy / by David Feherty. —1st ed.
p. cm.
Compilation of essays by golf commentator David Feherty.
1. Golf—Anecdotes. 2. Golf—Humor. I. Title.
GV967.F39 2010
796.352—dc22
2010002752

Anchor ISBN: 978-0-7679-3231-8

Book design by Michael Collica

www.anchorbooks.com

Printed in the United States of America
10 9 8 7 6

For my f-troop, I love you like brothers (you sick bastards),
Rear Cardinal Kell, Lindsey, and Ziggy,
the worst beagle in Texas.

Contents

Contents

Foreword

The strangest thing happened to me since my last book was published. Actually, I find the mere fact that my last book *was* published strange enough, but since then I have sobered up, stopped taking narcotics as a hobby, and for the most part I've managed to get a handle on the clinical depression that has haunted me for many years. All of this has given me a new purchase on life (I don't believe in leasing) and a clearer view of how lucky I've been to go through all of this in these great united states of America. I am convinced that if I had been living anywhere else in the world, I'd have been planted before I reached 50, but here in America, mental illness and addiction are accepted much more as normal human phenomena, and therefore it is much easier to get help. Also, it's no surprise to me that my return to the real world coincided with my first USO visit to Iraq and my subsequent involvement with wounded American soldiers both in theater and here at home, in places like Walter Reed, Bethesda Naval Medical Center, and the Brook Army Medical Center at Fort Sam Houston in San Antonio. To say they have been an inspiration is the understatement of my life. Compared to them, I have no problems.

A great friend of mine recently told me that we all know *when* we are born, but only the lucky ever find out *why*. I am one of those lucky few, and apparently the men and women who serve this country in the five branches of its armed services are my reason. Every smile I put on their faces is a treasure to me, every minute I get to spend with them, an honor. They have been my most valuable therapy, and outside of my family, the most wonderful gift I have received. This book is dedicated to all of them, wherever they are, and my greatest wish is that they come home safely.

I hear and read it all the time, in newspapers like the *New York Times* and TV stations like CNN, that this has been an "unpopular war." Now, I may be an Irish person, and like A. A. Milne's beloved bear, "of very little brain," but I do not understand this statement. In fact, it makes me want to vomit. It's as if WW2 was a hoot, or Korea was one giant episode of *M*A*S*H*. Of course it's unpopular, you idiots, *it's a fucking war!* That's at least as stupid as saying we're having an unpopular recession, and I can't help but feel that the *New York Times* might report on the conflict in the Middle East a little more accurately if we could convince them that it's a camouflage fashion show. Perhaps someone at the Pentagon ought to take a shot at that— just a suggestion. I have spent considerable time in the Middle East, first playing professional golf, and more recently on USO-sponsored troop visits, where I have been amazed by the job American and coalition troops have done, and the difference between what I have seen with my own eyes and what I see on the news and read in our papers. It seems to me that the only time we see soldiers in the news is when something has gone wrong. Perhaps a soldier has snapped under the immense strain of operating outside the wire of the forward operating bases, or civilians have been killed. America holds its armed forces to an incredibly high standard, and what stands for justice must be seen to be served. The fact that we are at war becomes irrelevant unless the price of gasoline is $4 a gallon.

What these soldiers have endured in order to eradicate the kind of people who, in my opinion, have given up their right to be treated as members of our species, has not been properly reported, as apparently the average American does not have the stomach for it. Frequently, our troops find the remains of children who have been tortured to death in front of their parents. A child's head on a stick, stuck in the dirt outside a house, is often a reminder of what happens to those who are seen talking to or cooperating with American or other coalition forces. American armed forces are presently engaged in making sure that the type of people who engage in this subhuman behavior do not make it to American soil, for the cold truth is that this is what they would like to do to *our* children.

Every day, there are countless occasions upon which our troops display extraordinary skill, compassion, and restraint while performing their duties under the most difficult and stressful conditions. Yet we hardly ever hear about this. They fight an army that refuses to wear a uniform, but they are continuously criticized when civilians are killed. Again, America seems to forget we are at war, and once more for the record, I believe we are fighting enemies that have given up their right to be treated as members of our species. I don't know about anyone else, but when it comes down to it, if civilians *have* to die, I prefer them to be residents of another country.

So call me old-fashioned, but when one of our brave men or women comes home with an injury sustained in the act of protecting *this* great country, I believe it is the duty of every American resident, citizen or not, to do whatever is within their means to help. With USO supporters like Gary Sinise and Robin Williams (to name but a couple), we are making headway into the damage done to Vietnam vets by Jane Fonda and her ilk, but we still have a long way to go before our population truly understands how much they owe the men and women of our volunteer armed forces. Some may consider it to be the government's job to look after these people, but not I. Furthermore, although my Troops First Foundation is a registered 501c3, I do not consider it or the USO a charity. Supporting organizations like these is merely a way of paying a tiny part of the bill that we owe our armed servicemen and servicewomen for the protection they have given so much of themselves to provide. Our troops do not lose their lives or limbs, they give them, so that we and our children may continue to enjoy the freedom and quality of life that most of us take for granted.

I am not an American citizen yet, but I'm working at it. During the course of my studies for the entrance exam (which most Americans would fail), I have become somewhat obsessed with the third president of the United States, Thomas Jefferson. Sir Winston Churchill may have been the greatest man of the twentieth century, but the more I read Thomas Jefferson's words, the more convinced I become that he was the greatest human being ever born. It's a shame that every country didn't have a man such as he was. Jefferson's Virginia Resolution, which became the first amendment to the Constitution of the United States of America, is arguably the greatest piece of literature ever written, for it safeguards us all against the governmental cancer more commonly known as organized religion. Most of the original settlers of this country fled to these shores to escape religious persecution, and Jefferson was determined to ensure that they stayed escaped. He was among the first to recognize that religious leaders kept their power by keeping people ignorant and afraid, and therefore controllable. "History," he said in an 1813 letter to Baron Alexander von Humboldt (whoever the hell *he* was), "furnishes no example of a priest-ridden people maintaining a free civil government."

Not a damn thing has changed since those words were written. Jefferson understood that the key to a free society was education, and while the credit for the introduction of pragmatism (the only philosophy born in America) is given to

Charles Pierce in the late 1800s, I believe it belongs to Jefferson, who much earlier, when he was asked to support a motion
to build a series of churches to give Americans a place to pray
for those who were trying to make landfall along the danger-
ously rocky northeast coast, suggested that a series of light-
houses might prove significantly more helpful. I believe that
this was the moment when pragmatism was born. Praise the
Lord! Or *not*, as Jefferson might have added. . . . I mean, whatever keeps your boat afloat—that's what he was saying.

When we look at the countries whose populations profess to
hate us, it is evident that most, if not all of them, have a couple
of things in common. First, they had no one like Thomas Jefferson, and second, possibly as a result, their religion plays
waaaaay too big a part in running their country. As a consequence, their populations are badly educated and easily controlled. Forgive me for yet again paraphrasing my newfound
hero, but TJ said that the occupants of any given country need
only a modicum of education before they become intelligent
enough to know when their elected representatives speak with
forked tongue. *That*, my future fellow Americans is, in a nut-
shell, why America works, and the countries that hate us don't.

Jefferson was also a huge supporter of the armed forces. In
his own words: "Although our prospect is peace, our policy and
purpose is to provide for defense by all those means to which
our resources are competent." While his language was considerably more beautiful than mine, I believe that this is what he
meant: Cut whatever budgets you want, but give the military
what it needs. We might be able to survive a liberal government, but we are royally hosed if a soldier ever yells, "Hey,
Farouk! I'm tired of gunfire—it's really loud. How 'bout I come
over there and we just sing, 'I'd like to buy the world a Coke'?
Whaddaya say?" Hmmm . . . No, that wouldn't work, although
I'm thinking I'd like to see Sean Penn give it a try.

My f-troop, just like Shoebox greeting cards, is a tiny little
division (which may or may not exist) of the Troops First Foun-

dation (troopsfirstfoundation.org). Consisting of severely injured American servicemen, mostly but not all Special Forces
(they are all special to me), almost all f-troopers are amputees.
This year I will host six IEDs for them (improvised explosive
days). There will be two of golf, two of cycling, one of pheasant
hunting, one of skiing, and all of them will be hysterically funny.

I know, it's hard to imagine someone laughing at a group of
amputees as being anything other than an exercise in bad
taste, and trust me, it is. You see, when a soldier gives a limb in
the service of his or her country, it's not just an arm or a leg
that is lost. More important is the dignity. So when Green
Beret Major Kent Solheim gave his leg away in March, after
two years and umpteen surgeries in an attempt to keep it, I
traveled to Walter Reed for his amputation. It's not a spectator
sport, but when Kent came out of the ether, the first thing I
asked him was what they'd done with his old leg. When he
asked me why, I told him that while normally I was just an
arms dealer, in this crappy economy I'd try to sell anything. A
couple of nurses were momentarily horrified, but when Kent
blew a snot bubble and called me a sick bastard, everyone felt
better. That's my trooper, I thought. By making fun of him in
the time of his greatest sadness, I had offered him a chance, by
his reaction, to regain some of his dignity. I also called him a
total pussy for losing 15 pounds the easy way. For our first IED
of Cycling I had to match his weight loss within six weeks, or
I'd be riding with man breasts, which he told me was unaccept-
able. Another of my boys is Chris Burrell, who lost most of his
leg and part of a buttock. I tell him to look on the bright side—
now at least people can't call him a complete asshole. He
laughs, and because of his laughter those around him see more
than a physically handicapped man, they see the strength and
character of American royalty. You can call them heroes too,
but they are American royalty to me, and they should be
treated as such. F. Scott Fitzgerald once wrote, "Show me a

hero and I will write you a tragedy." Apparently, Mr. Fitzgerald never met anyone like my f-troopers.

I am an alcoholic, a clinical depressive, and an addict. It is no coincidence that the happiest and healthiest time of my life has been since my first USO visit to Iraq two and a half years ago. The time I have spent with the USO and my Troops First Foundation people has been the greatest gift I have ever received, for they do a thousand times more for me than I will ever be able to do in return. They have also made me keenly aware of how lucky I am to be allowed to live in the world's greatest country. I have been clean, sober, eternally grateful, and even if they all *do* come home, I will remain their humble civilian servant for as long as I live. And I'll be visiting Monticello as soon as possible, too. Thank you, TJ, you were the bomb!

Introduction

The author of perhaps the most famous self-help book ever written, *The Power of Positive Thinking*, was Norman Vincent Peale, a bigoted evangelical Protestant preacher who, when confronted with the imminent election of John F. Kennedy (a Roman Catholic) in 1960, declared, "Our culture is at stake," and openly worried that "our right to free speech may disappear." Maybe it's just me, but holy crap, that kind of thinking doesn't seem very positive. Despite the obvious fact that he was a pious and hypocritical old fartbox, in 1984 NVP was awarded America's highest civilian honor, the Presidential Medal of Freedom, by, you guessed it, Ronald Reagan. I can only surmise that this honor was for another of his gifts to literature from 1957, the magnificently titled *Stay Alive All Your Life*. The stupid son of a bitch must have been Irish.

It's been several years since my last book was published, and almost three since I quit drinking, narcotics, and believing I was indestructible. I've also turned fifty and become addicted to road biking, which, in an irony I didn't find at all comforting, nearly killed me a lot faster than the alcohol and painkillers. What's more, it really hurt. The only way I would have found anything remotely amusing about the experience was if the truck that ran over me had been *hauling* alcohol and painkillers. Now, I don't care who you are, that would have been funny.

I don't expect this book will help anybody a whole lot, but then again, according to mental health professionals (then and now), neither did Positive Norman's. But you never know. Laughing, or even smiling, can be at least as effective as expensive therapy in banishing negativity from a person's thoughts. I wonder how many people are thinking positively when they are swallowing all their sleeping pills, attaching their larynxes to exhaust pipes, or teetering on some pigeon-stained ledge. I suppose they might be positive that they're going to die, but I'm not sure that's what Norman was trying to get across.

At the depth of my bout with addiction and depression, I too considered grabbing my own hat and assuming room temperature more than once, but there was always something or somebody who did something that made the part of me that was still alive giggle a little and take a step back up from the bottom of my amygdala, which is the landing that sits in the middle of the emotional stairwell of our brains. (I know that because I had a lot of expensive therapy.) Sometimes it was one of my children, or Anita, my beautiful and long-suffering wife, but more often than not, it was one of my dogs. All of my life, I've looked at dogs and imagined what they were thinking. Why do they look at me, embarrassed, when they are snapping one off on my lawn? Willard, my elderly Schnauzenweiner cross, will stop in midsqueeze and wait for me to lose interest before he'll continue. In one dog-shit psychology experiment I counted five or six rest rings in his offering, which coincided exactly with my glances in his direction. What the hell does he want—for me to look the other way and whistle, like there's nothing to see here? There most certainly is: Apparently, I can sculpt dog turds using only my mind. I don't know about you, but I bet Sigmund Freud would have been deeply impressed.

So there is less about golf in this book, and more about scat and other similar material, like life in general, which is just other people's scat when you think about it, which you positively shouldn't. That's the whole point—sorry, Norm—positively don't think. Just get on with whatever it is you're doing and pay attention to the present moment. If you can forget the past and disregard the future, you're right here right now, which is lucky, because right here, right now, is all you ever have. It's that simple.

You idiot.

1.

Beaglemania

Golf Magazine, *10565493*, *November 2005*, *Vol. 47, Issue 11*

It was one of those spur-of-the-moment impulse buys that usually turns out disastrously. From a squirming cluster of beagle puppies in a roadside wire cage, tended by a nasty looking hillbilly with a wooden pickup truck, four teeth and a shitty attitude, I paid 350 bucks for the littlest one, a pitiful runt with a broken tail. He was no bigger than a hamster, weighing in at less than a pound, and when She Who Must Be Obeyed finally stopped yelling at me, we learned from our vet that the feeble grub was from a puppy mill in Oklahoma, chemically dependent and completely incontinent. Hey, I'm not from Oklahoma, but already we had a couple of things in common! We named him Ziggy, and I knew I would love this dog like no other.

We'd never had a beagle before, but we were prepared for psychotic chewing and howling trauma. Our resident househound, Willard the Wonder Mutt, was positively dog-smacked about the new arrival. He thought this was great, something that he could hump around the den, but once young Zigmoid got a little strength, the student-houndling became the master and—who's your daddy!—the humper became the humpee.

As far as I can tell, a beagle's human exists only to provide too much food and the kind of vigorous arse and back scratching that a beagle deserves simply because he's a beagle. If Ziggy goes missing in the house, there's an odds-on chance he's buried in the most expensive throw pillow, and not before he's given it a horrible trampling. If I drop an M&M anywhere in the house, Ziggy will find it within 45 seconds, and I swear if the rest of the packet were hidden in the house next door, he'd spend the night tunneling through hardwood floors and four feet of concrete slab to get at it, pausing only to kill several squirrels and bang the crap out of an apparently dead possum. Hey, if it's still warm . . .

I adore this dog, whose life's mission it is to be at the center of mine. He's under my feet, in my bed, on my lap in the car and down my throat after dinner. I used to be able to blame the occasional sly air-biscuit on old Willard, but now Ziggy heads straight for the source at the seat of my pants. He's up my arse like a DustBuster. He's like a tri-colored scratch 'n' sniff lie detector. If I had two of them, they might meet at my pancreas. But the thing I admire most about the little prince is that, in his own mind, he is obviously the highest form of intelligence on the planet, and yet he carries himself with the sweet humility and groveling gratitude that only a dog can possess. In any other creature, such behavior would be revolting.

And Willard, the simple wiener-schnauzer-gerbil-hound who used to be top dog, has been transformed from the Wonder Mutt into the Mutt That Wonders. I dole out chew sticks, one apiece, and Ziggy calmly takes his and buries it in a houseplant, underneath a sofa cushion, or in the suitcase that lies half-packed most of the time on my dressing-room floor. (Finding a slimy piece of rawhide in your underpants is a real beagle bonus in a hotel room.) Then he returns to the underdog, and with the efficiency of a turbo-charged wood chipper, he eats Willard's treat. Then he goes back to the houseplant, retrieves his own, and eats it, too. Willard is completely unperturbed, but then one of the reasons dogs are better than humans is because the losers among them are happy to follow.

My life is weird. I have a late flight here, a bad flight there, here a prop, there a jet, occasionally a bed wet, and waaay too many old McDonalds for dinner. It's hard to find anything consistent on the road, but I do know this: When I stumble in at 1 a.m. on a Monday from Memphis, or Detroit, or Milwaukee, or wherever, even if I'm still wearing golf shoes and plastered with sunscreen and stale sweat, there will assuredly be frantically wiggling bodies at the back door. Willard will try to lick me into a coma, and after Ziggy has rooted through my suitcase to make sure there isn't some rotten pig's ear he's forgotten, this 28 pounds of anointed hound will allow me the privilege of scratching every square inch of him before he burrows his way under the sheets and molds himself into the crook of She Who Must Be Obeyed's legs.

Yes, we adore this dog, but then again, as he constantly reminds us, we're only human.

Eire She Blows

Golf Magazine, *10565493, January 2004, Vol. 46, Issue 1*

Fourteen years ago, right here on the Old Course, I hit the greatest shot of my career—a horrifyingly hung-over long iron that won the Dunhill Cup for Ireland. Now, my pal Sam Torrance and his son Daniel were leading the Dunhill Links pro-am, so I was on a mission to get behind the 18th green to surprise them. My first obstacle was a wee Jimmy in a flat hat, who was savagely guarding the media-and-players-only crossing point at the Road Hole.

"Excuse me, sir, I'm David Feherty," I said. "And I need to get over there to meet my best friend, Sam Torrance. I don't have a pass, but I captained the Irish team that won here against the English in 1990."

"Certainly ye did. . . . F—— off!"

So I bought a ticket, ran up through the town and saw them win. Sam had played rubbish, but 15-year-old Daniel won him 50 grand. I gave Sam a slap on the back, which as we say is "only 18 inches from a kick in the hole."

Then to Ireland we went, the family and I, back to 93 Clifton Rd., Bangor, County Down, and the real reason for the trip—a hug from my mummy, who knows I'm famous. As always, she had a pot of cream of sheepskin soup on the stove. I felt better until I got to Bangor Golf Club, where the members had been charged £20 for the privilege of listening to a speech by the idiot child who, 27 years ago, dropped out of high school and turned pro with a 5 handicap. They'd only just stopped laughing about that, so it wasn't so hard to get them started again. Due largely to their heroic consumption of Cork Gin, I survived.

The next stop was my old high school, Bangor Grammar, which has a history of academic excellence and now a tradition of having truants back to speak at Speech Day. I said it was nice that a pupil didn't actually have to finish in the school to qualify for such an honor—a line that went down better with the boys than with the faculty. I told of how I used to sit in class, listening to the drone of lawn mowers outside, inhaling the smell of grass cuttings and Simon Mercer (who sat in front of me), dreaming of sweet swings with battered old clubs and Titleists with elastic hanging out. I told them I used to go to roll call, then sneak out to the club, where I'd spend all day in the pro shop, working with glue, solvents and naked flame. What an education!

After my speech they gave me a diploma and, more important, a schoolboy's cap with a gold tassel, which I told them would increase the pleasure of my evening spanking immeasurably—a statement that, strangely enough, the faculty seemed to enjoy more than the boys.

Now the Fehertys set off for Donegal and a few days at the Fort Royal Hotel in Rathmullan, a favorite spot of mine. It rained for three days, prompting the postmaster to say, "It's keepin' the dust down nicely." On my parents' 50th anniversary (at press time there was no clear leader in their 50-year argument), I loaded Mum and Dad into a rental rocket along with She Who Must Be Obeyed and Erin the Terrifyingly Beautiful Small Person. My sister Debbie and her long-suffering husband, Ian, piled into another car with Murphy the black Lab;

Kiva the 125-pound boxer; DJ, a moronic Irish fox terrier; and Bart the cat. To a casual observer, it looked like the pound had just been robbed by two mental patients. On the way, I saw their car swerve violently and later found out it was caused by a surreptitious fart from my sister (since denied), which was hideous enough to make DJ the terrier hurl on her lap, which in turn made Bart the cat crap all over the backseat. When poor Ian rolled down a window, Kiva the heavyweight boxer jumped at the opportunity to either escape or commit suicide. I used to share a room with my sister, and would have done the same.

We sped to Portnablagh, where the surf was pounding over the sea wall. I love that crap and pride myself on being able to read the waves. I trundled the car down the pier so we could feel the power of Poseidon. A swell burst over the concrete and produced a giggle or two, so I let my window down a bit. Four seconds later the alarm was blaring, the doors were locking and unlocking themselves, my mother's hair was plastered to her skull, and there was a little winkle in my underpants.

All in all, it was a normal outing for the Fehertys, down to the return of two rental cars, which we nicknamed "Shite and Briny." I'd taken the collision damage waiver on mine, and what with the collision damage being caused by a wave. . . .

I argued, but they didn't waver.

Feherty's Mailbag

Online—Published: January 22, 2004

David, I like reading your stuff in the magazine. You write well and I like listening to you on your television coverage. My question is, growing up on the Euro Tour, what is the attitude towards American golf and how the players are treated on the American tour? To me, it seems that the Americans are treated extremely well. Is this the way you are/were treated on the Euro Tour? Also, is it too much of a difference between playing in several different countries and playing in different conditions to compare the two tours? Thanks.

—Ed Barrett, Wixom, MI

Eddie Baby: (Always wanted to say that, but I've no friends named Eddie)

The PGA Tour in the U.S. and the European PGA Tour try to treat the players as well as possible since they want to make sure they play there. The title sponsors and host organizations on both sides of the pond want the strongest field they can get. That helps the gate and television ratings, which help the sponsors sell more of their stuff, which justifies the enormous expense of broadcasting this alleged sport.

In general, the U.S. tour is more comfortable from a player's standpoint. The travel distances are less and the airfare is cheaper; the language is at least consistent (although sentence construction and syntax is deplorable except for the deep South, where, regardless of the grammar, no one can understand a word anybody says); the food's decent, affordable and dependable if not imaginative; (except down South again, where the first question every waitress asks is, "How ya'll want that fried?"); there's a free gassed-up courtesy car at every stop and, best of all, if you finish well, you make a hell of a lot more money. Those are the primary reasons the Europeans beat the bejesus out of the Americans in the Ryder Cup every other year; they're just really pissed off.

While I do not wish you to say or write anything ill-willed toward Mr. Hal Sutton, I would like to know if you had any insight as to why he has been picked as the Ryder Cup captain for the American side. Couldn't we have someone a tad more jovial and light-hearted? This is not life and death, yet it seems that the quality that is most sought after is the ability to bleed red, white and blue when cut. If I might suggest a few slightly less Spartan-like candidates: How about Bill Murray (I know, he's not a PGA member), Peter Jacobsen or Gary McCord? Someone with a sense a humor and a passion for camaraderie.

—Tom Garvey, Chapel Hill, NC

Any relation to Steve? How many times have you been married? More than Hal?

To begin with, Hal Sutton ain't no Robin Williams. The PGA of America is a very somber group and it's way beyond their capacity to consider someone like McCord who, frankly, is a little light in the spikes for that assignment. If the entire U.S. team came out of the closet, McCord might have a chance.

By the way, if you think Hal's a little stiff, wait till you get a load of that madcap scamp Bernard Langer! What a cut-up

Herman the German is! The joint press conference before the event with these two leading the discussion will be a right barney.

What is your opinion on Broomhandle-putters? I just read an interview where Colin Montgomerie said long putters should be banned. I know you are using one, or at one time have used one. Any ideas?
—Pekka Loukkola, Oulu, Finland

Pekkapickledpeppers:

Let me tell you, Pekka, I miss just as many putts with the long putter as I ever did with the short one, hell, maybe more. I could have that thing bolted to one of my chins and attach it to a universal joint mounted on my not inconsiderable stomach for additional stability and still manage to leave every putt a foot short. It's not the arrows, bubba, it's the archer. Go back to your sauna.

You have a sick, twisted, and obviously perverted sense of humor. That must be why I think you are the funniest guy since Lewis Grizzard. If I could put together a fantasy foursome for a round of golf, you would be first on the list, right in front of Lee and Arnold. We might not do that much damage to par, but we could seriously deplete a stock of frosty cold Dos Equis dark beer and I'm sure we could sufficiently terrorize all who came in contact with us.

Thanks for the tip on the III Forks Steak House in Dallas. It is now my favorite pit stop when I come back to Texas to visit my family. I had the opportunity to meet Rick there, and I believe everything he told me about you. I don't know if you are a barbecue aficionado or not, but if so, take a drive down to Waco some weekend and try "Underwoods." It's a Texas tradition that is slowly dying out. Keep it on the short grass.

—Gerry Calk, Columbia, SC (grew up in Coleman, TX)

Did you invent that stuff I put around my windows every fall? You must be one wealthy son of a gun. Incidentally, I don't care where you grew up. What is it with Texans? Why are they compelled to tell everyone where they're from all the time? Who cares? By the way, I'm from here too.

Why would you put a Mexican, a Pennsylvanian and an Irishman together? Sounds like the beginning of a really bad joke. Thanks for letting me know about talking to Rick about my recommendation. I have a commission deal with him and I think he's been slow-playing me, if you get my drift. I'm going to check the register receipts against the list he sends me and I had better see your name or I'm gonna hit Rick so hard, he'll have to wash his underpants to clean his teeth. God, I'm starting to sound like a Texan. Thank God the season has started.

For the life of me, I can never figure out how the pairings are picked before a tournament starts. Alphabetical? Names in a hat? Straws? And how do they pick the pairings heading into the weekend?
—Adam P., Pristina, Kosovo

The first two days they are paired by money list into threesomes. A players play with A players, B players with B players and so on. They play the first two days with the same guys, only they reverse the order. (If a group played in the morning on Thursday, they'll play the afternoon on Friday.) Once the cut is made (top 70 and ties), they play according to finish. The players at the bottom of the field play early each day. The field plays in reverse order from bottom to top and is redone each day.

In your opinion, what weaknesses do you see in Tiger's game? I cannot find any—wondering what your thoughts are?
—Kevin, Chicago

Are you kidding me? The Tigers lost 119 games last season, Kevin. Christ, one more and they would have set a record for the most losses in a single season. They have no pitching, they can't hit . . . No weaknesses???

Huh? Oh . . . sorry, you mean Tiger Woods. You're right, he's pretty buttoned up, golfwise, I mean. He'll be fine as long as he maintains his self-discipline and doesn't "Kobe" up or get a gigantic tattoo on his face or something. I would advise him not to make too many more commercials with Charles Barkley, though—it might start rubbing off.

4.

Ad Addict

Golf Magazine, 10565493, February 2004, Vol. 46, Issue 2

I don't get to see commercials when I'm working on a golf telecast, but after a few months of thumbing my remote in the off-season, I feel I've got myself up to speed. I'm at a stage in my career (retired) when, unlike most golfers, I'm not really looking for something that's going to make me brilliant overnight. I just want stuff that helps me suck less.

As part of that search, I just signed an endorsement deal. While I shouldn't let my new sponsor's name slip, let me give a hint: I've been bitten by the brand.

In my quest for less suckage, I've been fascinated by the proliferation of quite obviously useless devices that are touted as handicap-cutting miracles, and the apparently infinite number of people who buy them—golfers with too much money and not enough sense. Does anyone else remember the warm-up baseball-bat thingy with the water in it? If you could make it burp at the top of your backswing, you were in the perfect position.

My favorite at the moment is that hinged club, which when waved at the ball will either get you to the middle of the green with a birdie putt or to the emergency room with stitches in your lid. What a concept: Swing right or die.

I'm big into informercials. There's one with me in it, looking like a tool-belted Turkish prison guard. I've been up and down through five pants sizes and 11 hairstyles since that ad was made, but it's still running on the Golf Channel every time I turn on the telly. Granted, it's not as bad as the one in which Bobby Clampett flogs gas heaters for golf carts. Dear God, I wish I'd been in on the storyboards for that one: Let me see, let's take some propane, put it in a moving vehicle with Clampett, give him a box of matches, and dive for cover. Cart rental: $32. Golf balls: $28. Greens fee: $85. Watching Bobby Clampett dive headfirst into a frozen lake because his hair is on fire: f——ing priceless. Now that's a commercial.

The other one I love is for the Perfect Club. Peter Kessler—who I believe is a 6-handicap vampire—is perfect for the job. I once saw a shot of him on Golf Talk Dead, walking past a mirror with Phil Mickelson. For an instant Phil was right-handed and Kessler was gone—too weird.

So I'm thinking that if anyone out there wants to market a knockoff of the Perfect Club, give me a shout. I may not be perfect, but I think I'm quite good. So we'd call it the Quite Good Club, and it could be used from almost anywhere to do nearly everything. The Quite Good Club might not get you completely out of the bunker, but it'd certainly get you right up there under the lip. The concept might need work, but I think I'm on to something.

I've always fancied myself something of an ad exec. You know the type—ponytail and bowling shirt, brainstorming around the cube farm with a half-eaten cigar and a crappy attitude. I would never have allowed Gary McCord to admit he plays with a soft Noodle. And when Charles Howell III and Scott McCarron were hitting buttons in that elevator, why didn't David Duval walk in last and punch 59? Someone answer me that! And then this: When Johnny Miller said that great shots were "better against Jack," why the hell didn't someone punch him? We need more gratuitous punching in golf advertising, and more reality, too. If I see a fat, sign-carrying kid in shorts sneaking around the locker room, sniffing articles of clothing, I'd like to see Ernie Els and Jesper Parnevik ganging up and forcing his cheerful, chubby self into a locker.

I also think Frank the headcover's eyes should pop out just a little now that Tiger's inserting a driver with a bigger head into him. That would have to sting a bit, no?

My favorite golf commercials are those with John Cleese, who is clearly over the Far Hills and far, far away. I couldn't watch that man open his eyes in the morning without bursting out laughing. But for sheer selling power, no one can compete with Tiger—who, incidentally, learned how to act from McCord and me. You read it here first: The kid learned it all from us, on our *Late Night Show,* before he got famous and started buying watches with his Amex and seeing dead people driving Buicks.

Like he's the only one who sees dead people driving Buicks.

5.

Feherty's Mailbag

Online—Published: February 13, 2004

Could you give us readers an idea of what a week is like as a commentator? Do you get to play the course before you commentate on it? Thanks.

—Jeffrey Formanczyk, East Lansing

Monday: Hopefully got in Sunday night if there wasn't a Goddamn playoff and I missed the flight home again. Sleep late. Have She Who Must Be Obeyed bring in two lightly boiled with crisp bacon, golden toasted scones with clotted cream, raspberry jam and piping hot café au lait right to the bedroom. Nap. Stumble out of bed around 2:30. Slip on smoking jacket and ascot, call McCord to hear report of how magnificent I was yesterday. After flicking their turds off my lawn and onto the neighbor's, take Sigmoid and Willard for walkies. Snifter or two of Ketel One and grapefruit. Dinner. Weak attempt at sex (with myself). Take two Ambien and collapse, hopefully in bed.

Tuesday: Carpool duty. Try to remain in check while picking up other rich people's offspring. Meet with Rory's teacher. Try to convince her he was only kidding about shooting up the gym class. Double the dose on the Ritalin. Lunch with financial planner. Call agent and demand more bookings, need more money. Drive to shotgun club. Shoot 400 rounds of 28 gauge, miss 30 percent. Nap. Dinner. Field-test new case of Napa Valley Silver Oak Cab.

Wednesday: Same as Tuesday, unless I'm doing cable. Then I leave for tournament.

Thursday: Same as Wednesday unless I'm on cable, then I eat breakfast in hotel, go to course, eat lunch in CBS compound. Nap. Go to booth and perform extensive preparation for broadcast, which consists of: sound check and nap. Go back to hotel, go to bar and run up huge tab. Go to dinner with producer Lance and Barrow and Kostis. Let Kostis pick wine if Lance is buying.

Friday: Same as Thursday.

Saturday and Sunday: After I get to CBS compound, get trussed up in diabolical RF harness and hang antennas off dubious appendages. Walk all 18 with leaders while making brilliant commentary and reading greens as if I played on them all my life. Sweating like a lifer meeting the parole board for his last shot at getting out. Gold Bond powder shooting out my nose. Bar. Dinner, if I am ambulatory.

Hi David! Nice Name! Just curious as to your opinion on Greg Norman's golf future and your thoughts on whether he will win again on the PGA Tour, the majors, etc. I have been an avid fan of Greg since the mid '80s and have really admired his game, as well as the class he displays not only in victory, but in defeat as well. Anyway, just some of your thoughts as you are around these guys to have some of the inside scoop. It is amazing to me the parity on the Tour and the bright, new upcoming players that can hit the ball a mile. Appreciate your reply and the nice job you do announcing. Make sure to give McCord a hard time. Have a great day!

—Dave Summitt, Champaign, IL

Greg's done winning on the PGA Tour and sure as hell the majors. Don't get me wrong, he still has a lot of game and could beat both of our asses with one arm, but win on the Tour? Hey, who knew Jake (Peter Jacobsen) would win last year at 49? It could happen, but I doubt it. His business career has really taken off the last few years. Between that and his family, I'm not sure he has the desire to spend the time it takes to get to the level he was when he was younger.

If you look at the top-50 players for the last few years, you'll realize there is not really as much parity as you may think. The percentage of players breaking into the top ranks are relatively few, and some are on the strength of one-time wins who fade as quickly as they came. What concerns me is the fact that a top-notch player could play in the majors, the near-majors (Players Championship, Muirfield, Colonial, etc.) and the World Golf Championships and earn enough money in just those events to make a season. That weakens the field for the week-in/week-out events, who have to recruit hard to get the highest-level player they can for their event. Let's face it, the fans pay to see Tiger, Michelson, Furyk, Love, et al. The Tour needs to address this issue and soon.

David, is there any substance to the rumor that Tiger's contract with the PGA requires that no one but he can wear a predominantly red shirt during the final round of a major? Unless, of course, he has missed the cut, which we all know won't happen before 2025 at the earliest.

—Mike Guillory, Oberlin, Louisiana

Where does this crap get started? In the first place, Tiger doesn't have a contract with the PGA Tour. He's a member of the Tour and shows on the weeks he wants to play and wears whatever the hell he wants. The players have a rule book they put out every year, and nowhere in there does it make any reference to what color apparel anyone wears. They do have references to the *type* of things they may wear, such as no shorts. If they didn't, Jesper Parnevik would show up in stuff you really couldn't bear to look at! Now, if Nike wanted to tell their players what color they could wear on Sunday, that's up to them, but the Tour has nothing to do with that.

Why has golf become so boring and monotonous? The "new kids on the block" simply do not have the charisma that Tiger Woods has. It has become very difficult to muster any affection for a bunch of spoiled, egotistical and often homely millionaires. Help! I need an enthusiasm transfusion. Do you think 2004 will be bearable? Maybe if there were PGA Tour Cheerleaders . . . or maybe if the players had more interaction with the fans . . . Please God, let me love golf again!
—P.A.J., Fort Worth, Texas

It seems like I hear this lament every year. In fact, I'm pretty sure I heard or read about it when Nicklaus was challenging Palmer and Watson was taking a run at Nicklaus, when Miller was winning everything in sight and now Tiger's the only exciting guy around. I think there's a lot to be excited about. What about Ben Curtis's win in the United Kingdom and Shaun Micheel in the PGA Championship? I think I may have heard the spoiled and egotistical charge before as well. Homely's a first, though. The good news for the ugly guys, however, is they can usually find a much-better-looking wife or girlfriend than you can, unless you just inherited 80 bajillion dollars. Now, Tiger's not a bad-looking guy, but do you think for one minute he'd be marrying Elin if he was "popping the rag" at the airport? (That's shining shoes in case you don't know.) Funny the way that works.

PGA Tour cheerleaders, huh? You might want to try laying off the wacky tobacky for a while, my man.

6.

I'm Marrying Tiger

Golf Magazine, 10565493, March 2004, Vol. 46, Issue 3

She Who Must Be Obeyed doesn't normally allow me to address the subject of marriage in this column (or anywhere else, for that matter), but given these extraordinary times, I have been granted 750 words. In my capacity as a newly ordained minister, I have been asked to perform the sacred rites of marriage between Tiger Woods and the unbearably lovely Elin Nordegren. Yes, my tiny flock, I am now Rear Cardinal of the brand-spanking-new Hasidic Presbycatholic Church of St. Arnold-on-the-Green (none of the fun, all of the guilt, but half the price). I ordained myself online last Thursday, my kit arrived today and I am sooo excited. I've got a two-foot-tall red conehead cap; an infallibility headcover for my oversized Cobra crosier; a skintight Sansabelt cassock with matching V-neck intarsia surplice; and a righteous indignation that would make Jimmy Swaggart stop crying and drop the collection plate.

Why have I been chosen? Privacy, of course. You could have gagged me with a hamster when that rotten gnu-herder at his tawdry little zoo in South Africa dropped a dime on T and E (Who Must Soon Be Obeyed). If I weren't a man of the cloth,

I'd wish a pox on the dirty bastard. Over the past few years, I have always done my utmost to protect the privacy of the world's greatest golfer, deliberately tripping Golf Channel cameramen, keeping my interview questions short and pointless. I've even avoided eye contact for fear of learning something about Tiger that might later be tortured out of me. Hell, I once kissed Roger Maltbie on the lips and held him firmly by his microphone to keep him away from Tiger. Greater love hath no announcer than he who tastes secondhand Marlboros and Michelob Ultra for his friend. Mine is a noble cause, and watching Tiger play has been, until now, my only reward. Due totally to the fact that I know absolutely nothing about him, I now regard myself as his closest friend in the media. Deep joy!

Naturally, every horrible hack has an opinion on how the ball and chain will affect Tiger's career, but I am not going to speculate. I'm not the average sports journalist who thinks people might actually give a rat's ass what he writes. I know better than that. I prefer to use my tried and trusted system: Wait and see what happens, then claim I predicted it. In fact, I forecast Tiger's wedding in these pages three months ago, in my "Fearless '04 Cast." OK, so I said he'd marry Barbara Nicklaus—I was close.

Elin's appearance on the scene was a challenge to my relationship with Tiger, but again I took the high road and chose not to be there. There was far too much risk that Elin might fall for me instead (she's only human), and as She Who Must points out (she's writing this bit), I already signed a scorecard on this one, don't want to die, etc. Fortunately, in order to maintain the special relationship between Tiger and me, I've gone out of my way not to meet his new bride.

Now, I can imagine the furor this news will cause among the scumbag paparazzi, but I can state quite categorically that they can all go photo themselves. The date of these historic nuptials—unspecified by Tiger and Elin—has been left up to me, and I would never tell. I've already forgotten. However,

I can let the location slip. Try getting your horrible little heli-copters to hover over a diving bell 300 feet below the surface somewhere in the South Pacific, media vermin! And don't think you'll catch sight of the Very Rev. Rear Cardinal, either. Respect-ing the privacy of his friends as always, he won't be there. The Church of St. Arnold-on-the-Green is a low-maintenance outfit, so I'll just leave the happy couple a note in Latin:

For Tiger and Elin, on their wedding day—
Icto alterno semper lude et nil desperandum (Always play alternate shot and don't let the bastards get you down).
Love, Cardinal Dave

7

Feherty's Mailbag

Online—Published: March 1, 2004

Hi D: What's with the fancy goatee? Your shaver break? Why don't you play anymore? I seem to remember you challenging back in the day. Didn't you even win one? It'd be great to see you and McCord coming down the 18th tied for the U.S. Senior Open. Oops, are you even 50? Last question. Why doesn't the PGA allow a more relaxed dress code? You know how gross it is to watch guys sweating like Shaq walk around my television screen? Yettch! How about nice dress shorts like the ladies wear? I bet the scores would even go lower with more comfortable attire. Take it easy. Love your ironic insight.

—Fred Rogger, British Columbia, Canada

Have you considered decaf? And don't address me as "D." Where do you live, in the bar scene from "Star Wars"? To answer your questions in order, the goatee hides one of my chins, I hate golf, I won 10, and the reason no one takes the U.S. Amateur seriously is because they're allowed to wear shorts. It looks like a high school event. Go get a bunch of paper towels and then imagine John Daly in a nice pair of dress shorts like the ladies wear. Yettch!

David, Now that John Daly has finally won again, do you think that he can win again this year? I have always been a big fan of John ever since he won the PGA Championship. Please express your thoughts.

—Bart Wynn, Doha, Qatar

How do you pronounce Qatar? Is it like when you hock a lugee? John is the best. Everybody knows he's had his problems and still has a few to work out. It's amazing how much things in the rest of your life improve when you're playing well. Unfortunately, he still makes the occasional mistake, like a couple of weeks ago when he put a headcover on Charlie Howell and tried to put him back in his golf bag.

Great Book!!! How do you write with your kids around, not to mention She Who Must Be Obeyed?

—Chris Ehlen, Maple Plain, MN

Thank you. Which book? The kids are in school and Anita loves it when I'm writing. It means two things: one, I'm home; and two, I'm not pestering her with weird requests that she put on some costume so we can play the aggressive cheerleader and the reluctant quarterback.

I enjoy your column and commentary—you have a great vocabulary and solid writing style. Having said that, I understand that you walked out of school at age 17, and your game benefited, I believe. My question is, did you ever go back and finish your education, and if so, where and when? If you quit school to better prepare for your golfing career, wouldn't it make sense to finish school to better prepare you for your current one?

—Derek, Charlotte, NC

Derek: What a great name. I always wanted to be named after something made with girders and I-beams and stuff. Did my dad put you up to this? No, I did NOT finish my formal education. You have a problem with that, huh? If I've done as well as I have without an education, how much better could I have done with one? Not much, I think. I'm not against education, I just knew what I wanted to do and did it. When I was 28, my Dad asked me if I was ever going to go back to school and get a degree. I said it would take five or six years and what the hell was the point of having a degree at that age? He said, "Well, how old will you be in five or six years if you don't get a degree?" The problem is, I'm not educated enough to understand what he meant.

Normally when the clubhead strikes the ball, where should my waist/ legs be? Facing the ball or already turning towards the target? What about my hands—in front or behind the ball?

—Mark, Marietta, GA

Good God, Mark, your swing must look like a strand of DNA! When the clubhead strikes the ball, it would be preferable if your waist and legs were still below your manly breasts, and at no time should your hands leave your wrists. However, your feet may occasionally disconnect from your ankles, but this is normal, and should be expected from time to time. It worries me that you don't seem to give a monkey's fart where your tongue is during this aberration. Where do you usually have it, molars, incisors, canine? Just have a lash at it, my boy, you're thinking way too much.

8.

Feherty's Mailbag

Online—Published: March 12, 2004

David, why is it that the second one guy starts wearing his shades upside down on the back of his head, so follow suit the next day?
— **Chris Grzesik, Wadhurst, United Kingdom**

Because they all got a call from their agents the night before who said, "Listen, you morons, Titleist isn't paying your useless ass $100,000 to be on your headwear just so you can cover up their name with a pair of dopey-looking Oakley reentry shields. Oakley, by the way, nimrod, isn't paying you s——t (and if they are, where's my 20 percent?). DON'T COVER UP THE LOGO, NUMB-NUTS!!!"

Why are all of our older heroes always wearing sweaters in pictures from their glory days? The trees are in bloom and it looks hot out. Global warming?
— **Rick Stuckey, Mt. Prospect, IL**

You own that Stuckybowl joint where they film *Ed*? I love that place. They're wearing sweaters because the shirt companies wouldn't pay them then and the sweaters guys would. What gets done, Rick, is what gets rewarded.

What is your best advice for the new-to-the-game player?
—Jeff Tessing, Deptford, N.J.

The next time you're in London, stop in at the Holland and Holland store in the Mayfair section of the city. Go straight to the counter and ask for Cavendish. Just as there will always be an England, there will always be a chap named Cavendish at Holland and Holland. Tell him you want an over/under with upgraded French black walnut burled wood and gold engraved side locks with a hunting scene. He will present you with a bill for about $55,000.00. Pay it without question. When you get the gun home, find a really ratty gun club. You know, the ones with the toothless, tattooed woman behind the counter who during breaks goes out and picks up the unbroken targets in the field? Then never go near a golf course again and we'll all be the better for it.

I use a set of cavity-back irons and sometimes I find it difficult to shape the ball. My question is, is it easier to shape shots using a blade iron rather than a cavity-back iron?
—Benny Lopez, Hammon, IN

Benny and the Jets: Why do you want to shape the ball? What's wrong with round?

I'm a 3-handicap. I have one problem of sliding my hips through the downswing instead of turning. Any drills to help me improve? Thanks.
—Trace Dandrea, Boise, ID

Trace: Is that a guy's name? Fly to Nashville, Tennessee. Rent a van. Drive to the Jack Daniel's Distillery in Lynchburg. Buy a barrel of their finest bourbon. (Don't get caught drinking any in Lynchburg, though, believe it or not, it's a dry county.) Drive all the way back to Boise. Invite all your friends over for a party. Drink the barrel dry. After it's empty, and the cops and the firemen have all left, take the top off the barrel. Go out back, climb in the barrel and start swinging, my man. Problemo solvedo!

I don't have a question to ask Uncle Dickie, just a few comments I would like to pass on. In my view, there is no one out there in the golf reporting field that can even come close to your refreshing outlook on life in general and golf in particular. I have read every one of your articles and even printed them for my golf-addicted friends so they can also split their sides laughing at your clever and entertaining witticisms. Your literary contributions to our sport are just what the doctor ordered. Keep up the good work! P.S. Hard as it may be, try and go easy on your cohort McCord. He's only trying to make ends meet.
—Paul Lanoue, Frankfurt, Germany

I love you, man, but McCord's a bedwetting cross-dresser. I'm sorry.

9.

Feherty's Mailbag

Online—Published: March 29, 2004

You obviously have a lot of respect for Arnold Palmer. And you were a colleague of Ken Venturi's at CBS. Given your insight on both men, what are your thoughts on the rules dispute between the two in the 1958 Masters and Mr. Venturi, including the incident in his new book? Thanks and keep up the great work.

—Tom Sarosky, York, PA

That's a tough one, because I love them both. Kenny's a crusty old codger who says exactly what he thinks and the King is, well, the King. It's one thing to tell the emperor he's got no clothes (or in this case green jacket); it's another thing altogether to accuse him of stealing the clothes he's not wearing. The thing is, I don't think Kenny needed to make an accusation to sell the book. I think people would have bought it anyway. I suspect he may have had some "help" in making the decision to put it in. I hope the whole thing blows over and is quickly forgotten.

My 10-year-old son, Andrew, and I love your Cobra commercials; however, he is driving me crazy by repeatedly reciting the one where you express disdain for the term "nice ball." Also, we can no longer say "nice ball" to each other in earnest because in light of your commercial it sounds like a put-down. So I have two questions. How can I get him to stop imitating you and are there any other golf terms you intend to target?

— Larry Levitt, Laguna Niguel, CA

Actually, I wanted to say "Nice balls," but they wouldn't let me. To get young Andrew to stop imitating me, I will send you a CD-ROM of my most recent colonoscopy. Make him watch it over and over until he realizes if he doesn't stop mimicking me, he may grow up to look just like it. I am currently evaluating new candidates for derision. They include: *center cut*, *down the fall line*, *golf swing*, *golf ball*, *golf game*, any description of a ball "chasing" somewhere and pretty much anything uttered by Johnny.

A few of us were recently discussing our dream foursome. Mine included Jack Nicklaus (because he is the best ever), Tiger Woods (in case I'm wrong about Jack), and David Feherty (because I'd like to beat one of them). Who is in your dream foursome?

— Colin King, Saskatchewan, Canada

Uh-huh, Collywobbles. It's definitely a dream if you think you can beat any of those three, including me. Just because I don't play anymore doesn't mean I'm not still majestic. I know there's not a lot to do in Saskatchewan (which, by the way, is Indian for "Don't put your tongue on the pump handle"), but you may want to lay off the pepperoni before bedtime. My dream foursome would be Richard P. Feynman, the Nobel Physicist who discovered quantum mechanics. There's some stuff I want to go over with him. Then there's Sir Herbert Turd-flurry, the inventor of modern underpants, and of course Rosie O'Donnell, who scares the living s——t out of me. Ideally, we'd go to the practice green, she'd hit a few putts, then I'd run away, skipping the golf altogether.

Just a comment on your article about Arnold Palmer. I have met and talked with Arnold Palmer only once, but like everyone else who has had the opportunity, I came away from the experience with the feeling that he was glad to meet me and he would be happy to talk golf as long as I wanted to. He is one of the real gentlemen I have met in my life (I'm 65) and, like you, I hope he continues to play and be a part of the game for a long, long time to come. Thanks for the monthly column and the on-course commentary.

—Lynn Baker, Bellingham, WA

That's the way Arnold treats everybody he meets. I once over-heard an idiot say, "There goes Arnie; a multimillionaire for hitting a stupid little ball around." The guy he was talking to, to his credit, said, "Arnold Palmer would be a multimillionaire regardless of what he did in life, you moron!" Couldn't have said it better myself. Thanks for the kind words; hard to believe they pay me for this.

I just got done reading your mailbag and it came to me why you're funny. You're the golf version of Don Rickles. Do you ever go to the local muni and insult people? Or do you only do that through your column?

—Kyle Stoltenberg, Sioux Falls, SD

Which muni will you be playing this week? If I'm around I'll stop by and hurl insults at you during your backswing. I love Sioux Falls, by the way, and anyone named Don, especially Don Cherry. I do a speech up there every August for the Make a Wish folks.

10.

Out in 45

Golf Magazine, *10565493*, April 2004, Vol. 46, Issue 4

I'm 45 myself, so I've been trying to figure out why the hell they'd be celebrating their 45th birthday at the cube farm where this magazine is made. Forty-five isn't 50 yet, hasn't been near 39 for too long, and is truly between the upper armpit and lower exit of existence. (I can't wait for the gala 46th. If these are major anniversaries, what will they do for the 50th, deck out the building in plaid polyester and stamp it with dimples?)

But duty calls once a month, so I delved through the grubby pages of time and came up with the first edition of *Golf Magazine*, dated April 1959. There was old Sammy Snead on the cover, slamming away in a pair of breast-high Sansabelts. And for the princely sum of 50 cents, you, the weekend golfer, could get inside President Dwight Eisenhower's game. Apparently Snead told Ike, "You're not getting your butt into it, Mr. President." That's a piece of advice that has been offered to several presidents since, from Kennedy to Clinton, albeit not from golfers.

The letters back then were from the same putt-struck addicts intent on improving their games, and the instruction department of the magazine is a monument to the teachers whose purpose in life was and always will be to screw with golfers' minds. Frankly, I'm surprised nobody has sued the magazine—or better yet, The Golf Channel—for emotional distress caused by exaggeration of the benefits of some new trick or gizmo. We're like the makers of SpongeBob SquarePants, who have tricked my youngest son, Rory, by wildly distorting the feasibility of living in a pineapple at the bottom of the sea. It might . . . just . . . work!

There's a lot to like in the 1959 version, like seeing Ben Hogan described as a "grim gypsy." But my favorite is a little half-page article called "How to Bet—a Glossary to Golf's Myriad Ways of Wagering." Great stuff! I mean, does anyone remember the bisque? It wasn't a lobster in your opponent's bag, but a shot given to a match-play opponent, to be used on any hole, provided it was declared before teeing off. Then there was the Pinehurst, a delightfully silly format in which partners had to play each other's tee shots, then select one ball with which to finish. I think they should use it next year when the U.S. Open is at Pinehurst. Let's see how the smarmy bastards who can hit those fairways do then!

There is only one logical explanation for this 45th-birthday frenzy: *Golf Magazine* is having a midlife crisis! Actually I'm quite relieved, as I was thinking it was just me. I hit the less-than-magical 45 last August 13, a birthday I share with two of my heroes, Ben Hogan and Annie Oakley, neither of whom (by bizarre coincidence) ever called Arnold Palmer by his first name either. Hogan hated anyone playing better than he did, and OK, Annie died in 1926. Still, when you factor in that I've never called Arnold anything but "Mr. Palmer," it is pretty spooky. Or it would be if you, too, were 45 years old, lost in a jungle of salt-and-pepper nose hair, battling love-handles and a bum-numbing addiction to Preparation H.

I wonder—should I have my love handles re-gripped? It's all the rage now, Buttox injections or whatever they call them.

I should probably start with my eyes. The bags under them have gotten so big they won't fit in the overhead compartment anymore; I have to check them at the gate.

Now that I think of it, the last few editors of the rag have been progressively younger and better looking (ha—they'll run that), and the whole damn outfit is in the middle of a make-over. This is bollocks! I remember when this publication was a great addition to the dumper. It was soft and strong, and yet so thoroughly absorbent. Now it's slick and shiny and liable to give you a nasty paper cut. What kind of journalism is that?

We may be out in 45 and halfway to 90, but I'm sticking to my guns on the old back page. With advances in medical science, 45 years from now they'll have done a Ted Williams on my head and I'll still be getting paid for churning out crap like this. I smell Pulitzer!

11.

Long Live the King

Golf Magazine, *10565493*, April 2004, Vol. 46, Issue 4

In 1955 most good, solid, buttoned-up Americans thought Elvis Presley was the devil in disguise, trying to capture the hearts and minds of their innocent children with his antics on stage, screen and radio. The golf course was the last place anyone looked for hell to be raised, so it must have been a shock to see Arnold Palmer for the first time, all 180 pounds of him with his 30-inch waist and bulging forearms, half James Dean, half Marlon Brando, staggering around on the follow-through like a drunk, his pants sliding down impossibly slim hips, tossing out his shirt front to reveal a hard, flat belly.

Arnie was a head-turner from the word go. Men thought he was disgraceful, women agreed, and neither could keep their eyes off him. There was something about him, some kind of animal musk that still drifts in the air around him today and has intoxicated millions. And better than that, the tractor boy could play.

Until Tiger Woods, no one had ever imposed his will on a golf ball like Arnold Palmer. His swing was always athletic and agricultural, an extraordinary, barely controlled spasm. It looks like it should be impossible to do once, never mind repeat. He plays the ball like it's a bonefish, rod tip up, his stare an unbreakable filament, daring the ball to miss the target, and if it does, he hunts it down and dares it again.

It wasn't always so. In the early years, if Arnie wasn't in contention for a title, he was liable to pick up his pill and head for the parking lot. If he couldn't win that week, he wanted to get ready for the next one. It was about winning and nothing else. His 62 Tour victories are remarkable enough, but he managed to retain his Average Joe persona through it all, and that may be something no one else but Byron Nelson can say. It's almost as unlikely as going through a legendary career without collecting an enemy on the way. If you hear someone say anything negative about Arnold, you are in the company of a major flamehole in severe danger of being struck by a bolt of lightning.

The times I got to play with Arnold are among my most treasured memories. I have few enough trinkets from my playing days, but there is one that will have to be hacked from my cold, dead Foot Joy glove with a rusty sand wedge. In the third round of the 1981 Canadian PGA Championship, guess who I got drawn with? That's right, ARNOLD F——ING PALMER! I know it's not normal to insert an action verb in the middle of a man's name, but there have been three players who inspired enough awe to warrant such an honor: Jack f——ing Nicklaus and now, of course, Tiger f——ing Woods, but ARNOLD F——ING PALMER was the first, and therefore most important.

Let me give you an illustration of how this works. Two players are discussing the coming day. One asks the other, "With whom," for he is a student of language, "are you playing?" His friend picks up the drawsheet, scans down to his name, and replies excitedly, "ARNOLD F——ING PALMER! Who've you got?"

His friend's eyes narrow slightly as he reaches his name on the list, and then his shoulders slump. "F——ing David Feherty," he sighs.

Same action verb, different position, different meaning altogether.

I remember standing on the first tee at Westmount Golf &
Country Club in Kitchener, stretching my hand toward his. I
almost wanted to stop it short and feel for eternity the sweet
agony of that anticipation, like those two naked guys on the
ceiling of the Sistine Chapel. His hand was big and rough and
warm, and when it closed around mine, he smiled his roguish
smile and said, "Hello, David, it's nice to meet you." It sent a
swarm of warm goose bumps racing through me, and I thought
goose bumps were supposed to be chilly. I got to keep my
scorecard from that day at the Canadian PGA, a one-under 71,
with Arnold Palmer's signature on it, and if there were a fire in
my house right now I would have a death grip on it as She Who
Must Be Obeyed carried me out the door.

The next day, Arnold made a point of strolling over to the
putting green, calling me by name, shaking my hand once
more and wishing me luck. There were thousands of people
there, and in that instant they all knew that I knew Arnold
Palmer and that Arnold Palmer knew me. I got the gift he gives
everyone he meets—his own importance (of which he is barely
aware) flowed out of his fingertips and into mine.

Professional golfers of every generation speak of Palmer
with an affection that is rooted in nothing other than gratitude.
To say he is the single most important person ever to play golf
is an understatement that will earn you a "DUH" from everyone but Arnold himself. From Arnold, it will get you a look that
says, "Don't be such a f——ing brownnose." But it's true. He
took a stuffy, upper-class, country club sport and turned it into
a game of sex appeal and excitement, risk and reward, triumph
and heartbreak, guts and "glory be, I think Arnie's going to go
for it!" There were other factors—Jack Nicklaus and Gary
Player and Frank Chirkinian and Mark McCormack—but it
was mostly Arnie, hard driving with the throttle wide open and
a cigarette so far into the corner of his mouth it was almost

hanging out of his ear. He grabbed the game by the collar. I don't want to go off on a Don Cheadle here, but Arnold took the name "Arnold" and made it cool. Hell, if he hadn't done that, Gary Coleman might be governor of California.

But I digress. My original brief for this piece was to describe what I thought Arnold Palmer has meant to golf and golfers everywhere. Thankfully the old adage "You don't know what you've got till it's gone" does not apply to us, not yet. But we have had to say goodbye to the King, at least in three of the majors. I have been an Arnold fan for as long as I've swung a club, but I didn't know how much I cared about him until the 1994 U.S. Open at Oakmont, where he missed the cut. As I watched him break down and wipe his face with a white towel, this cynical shot-jockey had a Titleist in his throat and casual water on his face. And then there was St. Andrews and his so-long on the Swilcan Bridge. I cared even more about that one, and there's that word again—*cared*. That's the key—sports heroes come and go, and the word *love* gets bandied about: I love that guy! But in this age of overpaid, undereducated, whining tosspots, how many do you actually care about?

I hope Arnold Palmer plays for as long as he damn well wants to, because as long as he does he will be signing his name on someone else's scorecard, and that golfer will have a treasure like mine. Everywhere he goes, Arnold sees people he has known for decades. With a wave here and a handshake there he is all things to all golfers, his special brand of pervasive love potion trailing deliciously behind him. He is the patron saint of the greatest game ever played, and even though he believes that walking is an integral part of that game, if it comes down to it, I think we should hoist him up and carry him around in one of those big-ass Pope chairs with the four handles. Damn right I'd bear that load, but I'd be a long way back in a line that would have at the front Tiger and Vijay and Ernie and Phil and Seve and on and on and on.

12.

Feherty's Mailbag

Online—Published: April 16, 2004

When Colin Montgomerie got heckled at the U.S. Open, everyone told him to quit whining about it and play golf. When Davis Love III gets heckled [at the Match Play Championship in February] while playing with Tiger, everyone is up in arms. Have golf fans become worse or is this a case of the personalities involved?

—Dave Hodgson, Vancouver,
British Columbia

No professional sport allows the fans to get as close to the players as golf does. The quid pro quo is that proximity comes with a price; in this case, courtesy. That's the nature of the sport. What happened to Monty at the Open was a disgrace, regardless of who the target was. It certainly doesn't help if the player reacts. The DL3 incident was a little different. The guy was playing head games with Davis. That can be even more disconcerting and distracting than some drunk just screaming at you. Davis has said he would handle it differently if he had it to do over again. I would have said nothing myself, but let me say this. That man would have had a visit from a large Sicilian man named Guido. In the future, the player will simply advise the rules official and let them handle it. The player will not be directly involved in a confrontation with the fan.

But that's one of the problems with golf; there's no defense on the field. Players should be allowed to interfere with one another's swing, and head butt stroppy fans. A perfectly executed, well-timed body block should be part of the strategy. Cross-checking should be encouraged. Now THAT would be fun to watch. John Daly taking out Corey Pavin. Yes!

I speak English, American English for this matter, and never had the opportunity to be in Ireland or whatever town you came from, so I'm not familiar with a lot of the slang and terms used in your columns and books and by some of your peers. Now that you are an assimilated Texan and since golf is another one of your homeland gifts to the world, I think it would be fair for you to write some sort of glossary of golf terms, specially for us with non-UK heritage, I promise to read again some of your gypsy terms plagued columns . . .

—Martin Lopez, Irvine, CA

Not a bad idea. Maybe I can compose an entire piece out of Anglo-Celtic slang terms and phrases, which would render it as incomprehensible as your last four words. Or then again, I could just take my own life.

I am in my 50s and playing worse than ever. I have this terrible habit of sliding forward through the downswing so that I am way ahead of the ball. Now, on some days I top it, some days hit it fat, and occasionally fan it. At one time, I was a 12 handicap. Now, I am only barely making slight contact with the ball. I cannot stop sliding. Other than quitting, how can I stop this bad habit?

—Bob Mathis, New Orleans

Are you any relation to Johnny? Man, that guy can sing; even if he is a little light on the loafers. Top, fat and fanny, eh? Sliding is okay in baseball and waterskiing, but bad for golfers. Try this: load an AK-47 with a full clip and set it up on a tripod. Release the safety, and set it on full automatic—we don't want any flinching here. After you have taken your stance, aim the weapon directly at your left gonad. Then run a strand of picture wire through the trigger and attach it to your belt so that when you move forward during your swing, the gun fires. I absolutely GUARANTEE you will never slide again, or at the very worst you'll only do it once. Hell, you said you're in your fifties. I mean, how much do you have to live for anyway?

Why are there no Europeans in the world top 10? Now that Padraig Harrington's hair matches a pop idol, his game has fallen away.
—David Collick, London

Dave, are you looking at the Sea World top 10? Check the world rankings, and bear in mind that Ernie Els, Mike Weir, Vijay Singh, Stuart Appleby, Retief Goosen and Charlize Theron are not American, therefore they must be European.

I have an autographed photo of you and me, taken at a company tournament. In these trying economic times, can you tell me what it's worth?
—Brad Jones, Lawrenceville, GA

It's obviously priceless. Send it to me, and I'll autograph it too.

I would like to comment on your style of writing. I've read all the columns on GOLFONLINE and find them entertaining, to say the least. What I find somewhat disturbing is that you seem to be getting meaner with your commentary. It doesn't appear as much "witty" as it does "mean," or at the very least, more cynical than in the past. Just

my observation. I do still enjoy you on television and hope that I am
wrong with the above.

—Ken Rimes, Savannah, GA

*You're right, I am getting meaner and more cynical, and occa-
sionally even mindlessly judgmental, you idiot, cracker son of a
bitch.*

Sorry, sorry, sorry, Kenny, that was just the Vicodin talking.
Bear in mind that I very seldom insult anyone but my friends.
It's kind of what I do. If I say something nice to you, you might
want to watch out, though. Also, I'm getting toward the end of
writing another book, which is making me suicidal. I always
hated homework.

13.

The Life and Crimes of Heavy D

Golf Magazine, *10565493, May 2004, Vol. 46, Issue 5*

This was a tough one to write. I was with John Daly for the last two rounds and the playoff hole at the Buick Invitational, and it was all I could do not to root for him on the air. Lucky my mike was closed when he hit that tournament-winning sand shot in the playoff—I was screaming, "GO ON, FAT BOY, GO ON!" I just love the guy, and if his galleries are anything to go by, I'm not alone. I suppose I could do the right thing and attempt some semblance of objectivity, but at the end of the day I'm a golf fan, and there aren't many of those who are unhappy to see the return of John Daly.

Golf has had a few greats, some of whom have been a little reality challenged or even totally f——ed up, but compared with John Belushi, sorry, John Daly (Freudian slip), they all look like choirboys. (With the possible exception of Tom Weisk——f.) But this is a love story, not a fearless exposé. That's right, JD's life is a soap opera, minus the bad plot, crap acting, great makeup and, of course, the suave, handsome, sophisticated hero.

The bottom line is that we luuuv this big boy like one of our own because that's what he is. You see, I believe every honest soul among us has a little Johnny inside, some nasty little character parasite that we struggle to suppress but that aches to take us over and expose us. Mine is an addiction to Bushmills, coupled with a pathological fear of Bill Murray. Heaven forbid anyone should discover our dark little weaknesses or hear our inner squeals for help. Johnny's flaw isn't so little, though, and not very well hidden. No, we're talking about a guy with a crack the size of the Grand Canyon. (Plus a smaller one that pops out every now and then as he bends to pick the ball out of the hole.) That big ol' crevice in JD's disordered personality is held together with gaffer's tape, chewing gum, quiet desperation, Diet Coke and nicotine, and it looks like it could burst at any time, exposing the hairy, scary black hole of the big lad's innermost nowhere. Sports fans are a little evil, you know—we watch because we want to see a crash, and we don't mind serious injury as long as there's a survivor to ogle afterward.

Call him what you will, but Johnny's one hell of a survivor.

I knew him when he weighed 160 pounds and his mullet was just a guppy. I was leading an event in Africa by a shot after three rounds and was introduced to him on the 1st tee. He hit it so far past me that day, he had to wave me up several times, and he wound up beating me by one stroke. Who knew this lunatic would win the PGA and the Open Championship? He has married himself out of a couple of fortunes, almost died of his enthusiasms and made an album for WalMart, and the only reason he's never tossed himself off a tall building is that with his record on personal decisions, he'd probably land on someone he loved.

Johnny hasn't won more because he has always had a habit of letting the crowd choose the club for him. And that would be the driver—people don't come to see Long John lay up, and he's never disappointed them. Whether he crashes in flames or lands perfectly, he's always giving value.

We're talking about a guy who won the Open Championship at St. Andrews, man! Same place our favorite big, fat sinner was seen at the 1993 Dunhill Cup, sitting on the steps of the Royal & Ancient clubhouse with tattered jeans hanging out of battered rain pants, chewing a burger right out of a McDonald's wrapper. The Claret Jug he won there in '95 has often been filled with beer, champagne and occasionally even claret, but I guarantee you only Daly would get ketchup on it.

And don't think John is just a champion for the common man. His win this year at Torrey Pines made him a hero and a symbol of hope for the millions of Americans who are held hostage by addiction or united by that lowest of common denominators—the horrifying disease of depression. Whether you live in a refrigerator carton under the interstate or you're the chairman of the greens committee, John Daly is an inspiration to you or someone close to you. He is to me. So let's bless his giant liver, his even bigger heart and his huge, fat ass while we're at it, for John Daly is a good man, a kind man and a brave man, and we are lucky to be seeing him do more than just survive on the PGA Tour.

14.

Feherty's Mailbag

Online—Published: May 14, 2004

David, what happened? Either CBS had you on Prozac or a 30-second delay this past Masters. It must have nearly killed you to have to be polite the whole time. Kudos to Mr. Phil—he came through in the clutch! PS: I'm planning a 25th wedding anniversary trip to Ireland/Northern Ireland this fall—get to play golf at least twice—recommendations?

—Hugh Quinn, Vestavia Hills, Alabama

The delay is because everything I say is a third or fourth option. It takes me a while to filter out the stuff that won't work.

Play Royal County Down, Royal Portrush (and don't forget the little course there, the Valley), the Ava course at Clandeboye and Portstewart, Baltray on the way down south and then renew your vows at Dirty Nellie's near Bunratty Castle.

Since the Masters ended, I've been constantly searching for news on the Sergio Garcia "attitude" to interviewers. I haven't found a single comment. I don't know if it's a matter of no one in the media wanting to explore it or what. What are your views regarding what's going on with Sergio's attitude? He seemed to indicate it's a "Tiger gets all the press" thing, but I can't imagine it's that simple.

—Ric Holland, Loganville, GA

You don't own that tunnel in New York, do you? Man, that's got to be a money-maker for you.

Isn't it funny how when players puke in their shoes and play like 10 handicappers, they don't want to talk to anybody? Then when things turn around and they shoot lights out, "the press guys are a bunch of derelicts who only want to cover the leaders and no one cared when I was shooting 11 over and to hell with you bastards and I don't have to talk to you 'cause you're not the boss of me and anyway, I don't like you and I'm going to my room now and never, ever like have to talk to you like EVER again and I'm gonna hold my breath 'till I burst. That'll teach you, you geeks! I HATE TIGER! I HATE HIM, I HATE HIM!"

Other than that, I think Sergio behaved in a very mature manner.

David, my friends and I were discussing Phil Mickelson's Masters win and have reached a disagreement we were hoping you could settle. Just prior to Phil's winning putt, DiMarco had to putt along the same line as Phil. When DiMarco putted his ball, Phil quickly ran behind DiMarco to watch how his putt reacted. Though legal, I found the action very unprofessional and ungentlemanlike and never have witnessed this action prior to this (not even playing with hackers on the weekend). My friends disagree and state, "Anything to win." What do you think?

—Robert Genetelli, Wantage, NJ

Come on now, Bobby, how many guys called you "Genetalia" in high school?

Well, let's think about this . . . I'm the best player never to win a major . . . all I have to do is make this putt . . . the damn Masters, for God's sake . . . finally, a MAJOR . . . after all this time . . . Mr. Palmer's last Masters . . . everybody's pulling for me . . . should I look at this putt to see what it does??? Noooooo, that would be rude. People will think me impolite, for God's sake! What would Emily Post say? The boys at La Jolla Country Club will be appalled. OR . . . I could lose this thing. Yeah, I'm checking it out!

Phil's actions were not only legal, they were as professional as it gets.

I've watched Masters tournaments on television for about 45 years. Your work on Sunday was by far your best effort ever. It was refreshing to witness you being humble, appreciative of great golf, and not continuously trying hard to find something funny to say. Great job!
— Frank Watson, Spartanburg, SC

You're no relation to Tom, are you? If you remember, it was his letter about McCord that got him (McCord, that is) the boot from Augusta. While I appreciate you saying those nice things, I never try hard to find something funny to say. I just say what I think and if it comes off sounding funny, well, okay.

15

Side Spin Phil!

Golf Magazine, *10565493, June 2004, Vol. 46, Issue 6*

I don't want to come off as a genius here, but I did predict this one. In a CBS promo shot way before The Masters—you've seen it by now—I prayed for Phil Mickelson to win a major. At the end you saw that my jammies and sheets were festooned with Phil faces. Ha ha, that's a wrap, end of script. But I didn't like it.

"Ye faithless Philistines," said I. "Phil will win!" Now, others may tell you I actually said, "might maybe just possibly" instead of "will." The point is, I made them shoot an alternate ending, thanking the golf gods for a Mickelson victory.

I almost lost faith on Sunday. It looked like the usual Sunday afternoon at The Masters: The leaders went out, and Phil started knocking nails into his own coffin with a big left-handed hammer. He wasn't the only one on the funeral march, either. Until Ernie Els's eagle on 8, the whole show was looking like a train wreck. And who should emerge but Mr. 0-for-46-in-the-Majors?

I can't remember a major in which a leader faltered so badly, then regained his momentum. That takes some serious subcutaneous heart, but Phil's demeanor was positively beatific all day. Even when he flubbed his second bunker shot of the day, at the 5th, there was no dismay. Rather, there was a centered, almost blissed-out look about the big man, and finally, when Chris DiMarco's bunker shot trickled over his marker and came to rest about an inch behind it on the 18th green, giving Mickelson a perfect read, you just felt it was Phil's day.

The atmosphere over the last few holes was crackling like the top of the mast above Frankenstein's lab. Phil didn't blink, not even when he stared at the scoreboard after Ernie's eagle at 13. There was a roar, then a number changed on a scoreboard, and then another roar. Again and again it happened. After Phil went through the 15th hole I stayed in my tower there, riveted to the monitor. Fans all over the golf course were gathering beneath camera towers, waiting for news, wanting the roars and cheers they were hearing translated into whos and hows. Our cameramen turned their cameras around so the fans below could watch the action on tiny 6-by-4-inch black-and-white viewfinders. Augusta National had never seen anything like it. Martha Burk could have run naked down Washington Road and people would have paid her even less attention than they did last year. This was about Phil.

It was Guinness-ad brilliant, that's how good it was. In the week of Arnold Palmer's 50th and last Masters, it was exit one people's champion and enter the next, landing flat on his big, awkward feet on the greatest stage in golf. Phil doesn't hitch his pants as much as Arnie did, but his connection with fans is the same. His win was one of the biggest sports moments of the new century, maybe the biggest, and it laid to rest the notion that golf can't generate a buzz without Tiger Woods. If Tiger is the new Jack Nicklaus, Phil's the modern Arnie.

I always figured he was going to win a major no matter what. As well as he played in them—three straight thirds at Augusta—at the very least someone was bound to brain-fart the lead away and he'd be there to catch it. But nobody fainted and handed him this one. When it mattered most Phil beat Els, a great front-runner at the peak of his game, and he did it with his head and his heart. His win was golf's best clutch performance since Bobby Jones won the 1930 U.S. Amateur at Merion to complete the Grand Slam. Sure, there was Nicklaus at Augusta in '86, but Jack wasn't the "Best Player Never to Have Won a Major."

It's fitting that Arnold's last major was Phil's first win. They both play the way most people would like to: with bollocks-to-it-I'm-only-here-once abandon. This time it was all swash and no buckle for Phil. With King Kong finally off his back, he might really go deep now. Hogan was 34 when he won his first major, and he went on to win eight more. Phil turns 34 on June 16. If he wins a slew of majors, there'll be roars of joy all over the place.

Fans may look at Tiger with awe, but they look at Phil with love. Because it's just golf after all, and the truth of it is we all believe we can pull off that crazy shot or stare down the winning putt and knock it in. Like Phil Mickelson, we might fall short 46 times in a row, but we only need to get it right once to prove that sometimes, just when we need it most, the golf gods hear our prayers.

16

Feherty's Mailbag

Online—Published: June 4, 2004

David, do you and Gary McCord ever play against each other and who often wins? (Note: I hesitated before typing the "who wins" part because I can guess the answer.)

—Kevin, Atlanta, GA

We try desperately to avoid playing on the same planet together, let alone on the same golf course. Actually, no, we don't play together at all if we can avoid it. I can't stand to see him mincing around, listen to him sigh and cluck when he misses his 45th putt of the day, constantly yakking on the cell phone to one of those Hollyweird producers about some hair-brained, stupid, half-baked golf sitcom, while all the while waving at a "so 5 minutes ago" celebrity while simultaneously muttering under his breath what a loser the guy is. This is not my idea of fun golf.

And I have never lost to him.

I love your online golf instruction section on the web site. Good stuff and funny. So I have to ask . . . When are you going to do a golf instruction book or maybe a video? Golf the Feherty way.

—Vern Suesse, Phoenix, AZ

HEY, VERN . . . Did you write that "Cat in the Hat" thing? My kids love that stuff. Green eggs and ham and all that. Brilliant. I've just finished a book on the history of the Ryder Cup and I'm not writing any more for a while, especially not on golf. I hate golf. I've used up my store of words and I have to let my head refill before I can go back for more.

What are your thoughts about the Battle at Big Horn match this summer between Tiger/Kuehne and Mick/Daly? I think the Mick/Daly team is the most interesting. On one side, you have Phil, who seems more like a wine and cheese guy. On the other, you have John, who is more of a beer and cheeze-whiz type guy. How's that going to play out? From watching past Battle events with Mick, he likes to talk quite a bit with his partner on the greens. I even sensed some tension in this area when he teamed with Sergio.
— David Castle, Garland, TX

These contrived matches bore me to tears. I'd rather watch George Carlin and Steven Wright go at it in a comedy laugh-off for the right to force Barbra Streisand to write a check to The Committee to Re-elect George Bush.

I was wondering how much money Nike paid you for your brilliant idea featuring Tiger and Frank. Just as you said, Nike should feature a commercial where Tiger puts a larger driver into Frank, and what do you know, the folks down at Swoosh central LISTENED TO YOU. Hope you are getting a little bit of that cash.
— Ryan O'Neil

You're absolutely right, I wrote that commercial months ago, but I'm sorry, I can't discuss my arrangements with Nike, with whom I have no association. I'm a Cobra ho. But let's just say, if I don't get a check, like tomorrow, a certain Mr. Knight will be hearing from my attack attorney, Turdley McGoldstein.

My sales staff for Christmas chipped in and purchased for me the PC version of EA Sports "Tiger Woods 2004." At my age (48) and being video game challenged, I must say it is quite fun to look at the virtual remakes of those famous courses loaded into the software, even if I still cannot shoot a decent score. To my surprise the commentary provided by you and Gary McCord is very humorous and quite entertaining, it is really like you are commenting on my horrific shots. That time in the studio must have been a hoot. Have you played or listened to it yourself? Thanks for your wit and humor added to a video game.

—John Cole, Fairfield, OH

Come now, you're smoking me, right? You can't really be a sales mangler, can you? I mean you've just put 200 words together without making a sentence. You can't possibly think McCord actually had anything to do with creating that drivel, can you? Look John, a 48-year-old man should not be playing golf video games all day. Has it occurred to you that your sales staff might be taking advantage of you? I guess it's true, when a salesman becomes ineffective in the field, they make him the "VP of Sales." I'm thinking they're all in a bar at this very moment, laughing their collective asses off that they got you a video game and you've forgotten completely to ask them for their numbers this week. And yes, I've played it—but not very often. I can't take the commentary.

17.

Feherty's Mailbag

Online—Published: June 22, 2004

You are so young and still very talented. Why did you stop competing?
I remember the '91 Ryder Cup matches. You were unstoppable.

—Tobin Bogard, Newport Beach, Calif.

A perceptive person you are Tobin, but you left out fat, and yet strangely attractive. And I was un*bearable*, not unstoppable. Sam Torrance, Payne Stewart and an inordinate fear of letting my side down propelled me through the '91 Ryder Cup. That experience was as close as you can come to the electric chair without actually frying. Contrary to popular opinion, not all the Irish are thick. I knew I could never be number one at playing, but talking? Now that's a pig with a different snout.

Hey David, love your columns and wit on the TV broadcasts. You and McCord keep things in perspective. Can you give us an update on David Duval? Is this a clear case of how mental the game of golf is? I think that, in his short career, he has been very good for golf and is a great talent.

—Dion Hannum, Alhambra, Calif.

David was suffering from vertigo problems the last few years, and balance may be the single most important element in a successful golf swing. Without gallons of it, you simply can't make proper contact. For proof, before you go out to play next time, chug down about a quart of Bushmills, and then take a lash at it. I have tried this many times and I know what I'm talking about. David's very funny, quirky, and clever, and I don't think his problems are as mental as they are physical. It would be great to see him back on tour and playing well, but if it doesn't happen, he's still an Open Champion to me.

Would you ever consider coming back to the UK and working for the BBC? You seem like the natural successor to Peter Allis, talking about anything but golf at times but in a very entertaining way.

—Lars Salmon, London

Good God, man. Is Peter ill? I'd be more suited to take Prince Charles's place, don't you think, old fruit? Besides, I don't think I could work for anyone who let John Cleese get away.

Anyway, they want me to work but they don't want to pay, and I'm kind of old-fashioned when it comes to that.

My father is a big golf fan and loves to play the game. We used to play every weekend until he was diagnosed with cancer and had to go through treatment. Could you please send him something to cheer him up? Thank you very much.

—Andy, Atlanta

Certainly I will. I'll send him something I know will cheer him up. *You. You* are the reason he played every weekend with you. Your dad knows the value of time now, and every minute he spends with you will be precious, whether it's on or off the golf course. Make him promise to play again as soon as he can, and hold the old fart to it. Write to me and let me know when you play your next round, and I'll join you if I can. Good luck.

By the way, I once sent McCord a fart in a ziplock bag. If your father would like one, it would be my pleasure.

My question may be a little odd, but here goes. Have you, or any tour pros that you may know, ever attended a Grateful Dead concert or listened to their music while out on Tour? I guess my question is this—is there such a thing as a PGA Tour pro who's a Deadhead? I do know Michael Allen, and I'm pretty sure that he grew up on Jerry Garcia.
—Gary Rotter, Scottsdale, Ariz.

The only tour Deadhead I know for sure is Fluff Cowan, Jim Furyk's caddie. I'm sure there were other players who were familiar with the band, like Peter Jacobsen for example, but I don't know if he qualifies as a true Deadhead in the purest sense because he remembers part of the seventies. But Fluff definitely cried when Jerry assumed room temperature.

I've been following golf coverage for a couple of years now and I really like what you do on the CBS team. You and McCord are the best ever man!!! Here's my question. Who are you a bigger fan of, Tiger or Phil?
—Sergio Montiel, New York, N.Y.

I can't decide whether I prefer Tiger or Phil, or for that matter Ernie. I like 'em all for different reasons. Tiger's got intensity, drive, intelligence and extremely rare focusing power. Phil's personable, self-effacing, possesses uncanny skill with a wedge, likes to gamble and will stand there for two hours and sign autographs until the very last kid leaves. Ernie is a big friendly giant, and if he ever gave a rat's ass, he could probably beat the other two's best ball. Maybe we could combine them and call it

Tigernie MickELSon. Those three would be a fine pair, if ever I saw one.

Do you think that "distance finders" should be allowed in competition? As strokesavers and advice from caddies are allowed.
—Gordon, Cumbernauld

Where the hell is Cumbernauld? I think I may have exposed myself there once after a tournament.

I think absolutely *anything* that helps a person score better should be allowed. You should be able to fire flaming arrows into the back of your opponent, use a dwarf as a sand wedge, check with the blimpcam to ascertain where your errant shot may have gone, have séances in the locker room and use naked exotic dancers as caddies. It's all about ratings for me now.

Maybe I was busy or something but I totally missed the R&A adopting the USGA ball size. Was the smaller ball better in windy conditions? And with tournament golf bags being bigger than my Aunt Wanda how many clubs does a professional travel with? What other stuff is in the bag? Thanks for all the laughs. I have reoccurring nightmares of McCord in a rubber teddy. Please suggest a cure.
—Harry Heilmann, Silver Plume, Colo.

The small ball was longer and easier to hit into the wind and crosswind, but it was tougher to fidget with around the green. Personally, I thought the British changed because the bigger ball was more difficult for English setters to swallow and they were eating them by the gross. They proved to be difficult to, um, let's say, pass. Vets all over the place had to go in and do something like a Dunlop Cesarean section.

Pros play with 14 clubs in accordance with the rules. They

don't travel with many more, although they may have an extra putter, wedge or driver if they're experimenting with something. All of the club manufacturers dispatch a mobile club repair facility to virtually every tournament in the country. So if the pro needs something repaired or replaced or wants to try something new, they are right there to accommodate them. The caddie is hauling around 40 to 50 pounds every day as it is, so they don't take a lot of extra stuff. Generally they have the same stuff you carry around in yours: extra gloves, balls, Preparation H, tees, ball markers, narcotics and whiskey.

The only cure for recurring dreams of McCord in a rubber teddy is to imagine him without the teddy and standing in front of you with nothing on but a red silk, high-cut thong bikini with the "Magnum Pouch." I guarantee you will wake up screaming every time, but you *will* wake up.

18.

I Swooned at Troon

Golf Magazine, *10565493*, *July 2004, Vol. 46, Issue 7*

Ah, the Open Championship is back in bonnie Scotland. The name of the game, where the skirl of the pipes and the sweet bleat of a nice wee sheep can put a tilt in yer daddy's kilt. Lovely biscuits! Royal Troon was the site of my first and best chance to win the oldest major of them all, and I couldn't have choked harder if I'd been swallowing Donald Trump's hair.

The night before, I had seen my name spelled incorrectly on the giant, piddle-yellow scoreboard at the 18th—me, within striking distance of the lead!—and the shock had settled in for the evening. Believe me, sports fans, I knew I wasn't good enough to win a major. So I had no choice. I had to avoid accidentally getting so close that I'd have to bugger something up spectacularly toward the end and look like a total Van de Velde.

I was a normal tour player, not one of those freaks who live on adrenaline, hammering in three-footers for par all day like they're as relevant as Ricky Martin's girlfriend. Putts that mattered terrified me. On every one, I was so clenched you could have held me by the ankles and used the cheeks of my ass to cut the wires on the Golden Gate Bridge. And so my wins were in the minors, and after each one I would go deep the other way. A Feherty victory was always followed by months of anti-climactic, post-orgasmic mediocrity. Until I needed money again. If my career was a song it would be Tom Waits's "Emotional Weather Report": "High tonight, / Low tomorrow, / and precipitation is expected."

Broke, I would panic and set about eating All-Bran, practicing, running and as a last resort begging the Almighty for forgiveness. (Funny enough, that last trick always worked.)

So there I was at Troon in '89, drawn with Mark Calcavecchia in the last round, and as luck would have it, the idiot's zipper was at half-mast on the 1st tee. As usual, he looked like a human laundry basket. What chance had an ugly American here, at this sacred golfing mecca nestled between the edge of runway zero-niner at the Prestwick airport and a trailer park full of bluish-white people who eat their young? (Why are most of Britain and Ireland's great courses bordered by bluish-white-trash trailer camps?)

I, on the other hand, was magnificent—slim, tanned, tailored and, with four large brandies cunningly concealed in two cups of coffee at lunch, hardly even shaking. I was ready to instigate my cunning plan: I reckoned I would stay in contention until we reached the Postage Stamp, where Sarazen made 13 back in 1426, or Weiskopf went elk-hunting or something, and where I could feasibly take a large number and still look windswept and utterly heroic as I limped heartbroken into the canyon of the last hole. "Had it not been for the dreaded 8th hole," Peter Alliss would say between sips of Bollinger, "the bold Ulsterman might have been Open champion."

Which, as Peter knows better than most, would have been bollocks. Truth is, I thought I wanted to win the Open in '89 and again in '94, but when it came down to it (just like Jean Van de Velde) I didn't want the responsibility. There must have been a pivotal putt or shot, but I don't remember missing it. I do know I wasn't brave or dumb enough to stay in contention and then flop at the 18th. That could ruin a man for life.

Open champions are men like Greg Norman, Nick Price, Ernie Els and Calcavecchia, who played the last six holes that day like a man possessed by the opposite of whatever it was that had me by the nads. He hit a driver from the bony fairway of the par-5 16th to the heart of the green, a shot like nothing I'd ever seen. He hit an 8-iron from the rough at the last that landed by the flagstick like a sack of spuds, making the old farts in the bay window spill their gins and tonics and start squealing about square grooves. He knocked in the putt for three, then went out and won a playoff with Norman and Wayne Grady. I had no business being near that.

If my career were a poem, I'd want it to be Seamus Heaney's "Digging." Heaney told of how his father and grandfather dug potatoes from the ground. "I've no spade to follow men like them," he wrote. "Between my finger and my thumb / The squat pen rests. / I'll dig with it."

I've no clubs to swing with men like the Open champions, but I have these words. So I'll swing away with them and be happy.

19

Naked Came the Dangler

Golf Magazine, *10565493*, August 2004, Vol. 46, Issue 8

I've suspected it for decades, but now it's official. The end of the world is upon us. The legendary Portmarnock Golf Club in Dublin, home of the Irish Open and probably the best course in Ireland, has been sued for discrimination against females, and found guilty. Will the club be fined or closed? Oh no, dear readers, this is much more bloody serious. Believe it or not, a judge (a chick, no less) has ordered that the clubhouse bar be closed for one week.

A whole week! Let me remind you, this is Ireland we're talking about, not Utah. I could understand a symbolic minute of abstinence, but a whole week of dryness at an Irish golf club? It could cause another civil war.

I might have been in this legal wrangle myself, as a Portmarnock member, if not for an unfortunate misunderstanding in the locker room at the Irish Open in 1986, when I was accused by the then-oldest member of actually being a woman. The myopic old fart had a conniption when he saw me mincing toward him, love handles akimbo. "Young lady!" he screamed. "Put your drawers on immediately!"

That was the last time I failed to follow the unwritten men's-locker-room code, which should it ever show up in print, perish the thought, would go something like this:

A gentleman member should never appear naked until such time as he has rendered himself—by warm soaping or other privately conceived means—recognizable as a male of the species.

I suppose it's acceptable to wander around the locker room boys-out, but I find it a little weird. Do the ladies act that way over on their side of the clubhouse? Dear God, I hope I never find out.

But back to the judge's ruling, a heinous act that strikes at the very heart of the nation. In all seriousness, I believe that all-male clubs provide an essential service. To women. The point is this: Elderly white men cherish every opportunity to mill around naked, farting bitter little clouds of cheap talcum powder and leaving half-squeezed tubes of Vitalis in the sinks, even though most of their hair grows from the neck down. But their wives won't allow it. She Who Must Be Obeyed certainly won't have such behavior in her house and does not want to hear locker-room talk, which usually centers on market fluctuations or how the latest blonde Fox News anchor is brilliant compared to that Canadian pinko Peter Jennings.

And so we men have no choice: We must gather naked at golf clubs.

Still, since the Portmarnock incident these sad little men-only sanctums have been emotional minefields to me. I can barely stand to see myself naked. The other day I was standing fully clothed by a wash basin when I was joined by a horribly sprightly 87-year-old nudist who took up a wide stance at the sink next to me and began to hum while brushing his teeth. (I know you're not supposed to look, but he took his teeth out to do it.) It was then that I let down my guard and looked lower, and noted that gravity is a cruel master indeed. Leafing through the naked-elderly-person-at-next-washtub protocol manual in my mind, I found no entry under "Avoiding Octogenarian Pendulum." Then I realized that its owner had put his teeth back in and was looking at me.

"What are you staring at, sonny?"

It was hard to say, really. It was like two Titleists on a string hanging from a mushroom in a chickadee nest. And there I was, busted in a bathroom, way too interested in another man's wobblies.

I apologized and beat a hasty retreat to my rental car, where I turned on the AC and the radio, assumed a fetal position and sucked my thumb for the first time since my 19th birthday. The next song up was the Village People's "YMCA," and I haven't been the same since.

I'm no barrister, but I have a solution to the Portmarnock problem. Let the women in, I say. Let them gaze upon the cottage cheese of our inner thighs, sit upon our cold, wet porcelain and wander around naked. Whereupon Judge Mary Collins can have mercy and reopen the bar. Because you know the photos will make the Internet, and then we'll all need a stiff drink.

20.

Feherty's Mailbag

Online—Published: August 5, 2004

I'm one pissed off Canadian golf fan, and I need some answers from the oracle of golf. But since Gary McCord doesn't have a column like this, I'll just ask you. Just kidding, you da man! I don't know if you caught the TSN.ca's interview with Canadian Mike Weir after the final round of the U.S. Open. I'd like your honest opinion of a shamefully bizarre tactic employed by the USGA during the final round. Weir commented on how the greens on the back nine were being watered every other group. So when Weir played certain holes, the greens were harder than when the next group played them after an immediate watering. This is absurdly unfair. I mean, get real. How can that occur in an Open? I wonder what Weir's playing partner, American Jeff Maggert, thought of the whole thing, and I also wonder if they were watered for Phil Mickelson and not others, say Goosen and Els. I'm really hoping you can use your access to information to find out which holes were watered, why and for whom?

—Fred, Great White North

I'd rather stick my ass in a wood-chipper than waste my time trying to find out which greens were watered, but I know they weren't watered for anyone in particular. Here's what happened:

After the second day, the lead was at 6 under, and the USGA panicked at the thought of the winning score getting close to, or even surpassing 10 under. So they stopped watering and put the flags away. Then the wind blew a bit, the whole place got harder than Martha Burk's heart, and turned into putt-putt. All they needed was the windmill. So they panicked again, sent the grunts out to water during play, and turned the whole thing into a Chinese fire drill. Here's the acid test. On any given hole, take any great shot from any great player. Then, take a golf ball, shove it up your ass, and blow it in the same general direction. If both balls end up in the same place, then somebody has lost control of the condition of this golf course. It was a great shame to see what happened to Shinnecock, but to be fair, they almost got it right. But they didn't.

Re the U.S. Open, any word on how the members of Shinnecock have reacted to the USGA killing their golf course? One would expect that the attack attorneys have already been retained.

—Don Lewthwaite

Thankfully, the golf course was not killed, just severely wounded. Word has it that it will have completely recovered by May of 2006, by which time 80 percent of the present membership is expected to have assumed room temperature anyway.

While I have always liked your commentary on the course, I have been really impressed with your knowledge of the trees. Instead of saying, "he has to get over that big tree on the corner," you'll actually identify exactly what kind of tree it is. Where did you learn that?

—Tom Timmons, Woodland, Wash.

When I was playing, I spent most of my time in the woods. I adore trees. They're like relatives to me (except trees are smart and I like them).

What is this shaved eyebrow and ham sandwich deal you talk about in your commercial? My husband and I are intrigued.
                              —Helen Michlik, St. Catharines, Ontario, Canada

Actually, it was a shaved ham sandwich and a highball. Your husband and you are deaf.

Which golf courses have you designed besides National in Turkey?
                              —Martti Ratia, Jyvaskyla, Finland

Is Jyvaskyla anywhere near Pjjtsnbbust? I had a coffee enema from a holistic Israeli dentist there once . . .

Anyway, I helped with the layout for a course near Aldergrove airport in Belfast, the name of which I can't remember, I did the south course in Pukalot, Trashcanistan; the Resort Course at the Ritz Fartlington Mogadishu, and the Naval Officers Course on the flatulent side of Viequez which the navy now uses for target practice.

Now that Phil Mickelson has won his major, whose turn is it in the barrel?
                              —George Burger, New Jersey

Cheese,

Either Richard Simmons, Chad Campbell, or Davis Love the Fourth.

Four of us are playing golf in Ireland in August. Since we're closer to as old as God's dog than we may care to admit, we regularly visit trees along the fairway, as per the U.S. custom of purging last night's recreational beverages and today's coffee. Is such conduct acceptable on Irish courses? I don't mind being the "ugly American," and surely, wherever we are, we've been thrown out of worse. But I'd be loath to get the gate for avoidable stupidity; particularly if I happened to have parred a few consecutive holes.

—Steve S.

You and your pals could be in deep trouble. Where you're going to play, there are no trees. Hang it out wherever you want, but first check the area for sheep. Some of them can be very aggressive.

21

Feherty's Mailbag

Online—Published: August 19, 2004

You close your book, "Somewhere in Ireland, a Village is Missing an Idiot," with a small plug about the charity contributions of the PGA Tour. I've always been a bit impressed with the charity aspect of various Tour events. I'm just a little suspicious though that it's more hype than substance. I know each event is different, but does the charity money tend to come from gate receipts, sponsors, or vendors? The Tour isn't going broke, and the purses are huge these days. Have the charities proportionally benefited as well?

—Kevin O'Connell, Orlando, Fla.

Why is it the Irish are always the skeptics?

Interesting question, you vacuous meathead. OK, this is Professional Golf 101, Professor Feherty presiding. This is a pass/fail course for absolutely no credit. No payments, no interest, ever.

First, the PGA Tour sells the rights for golf broadcasting to the networks. The money they get is used to supplement the purse of an event. The Tour gives the local host organization (always a 501(C) 3 charity), 62 percent of the purse number. The host organization supplies the rest of the purse, the remaining

38 percent. Since the host organization is a charity and, alas, has no money, they call upon the title sponsor for help. The title sponsor then secures the naming rights which come with certain assets: pro-am spots, food and beverage, tickets and the like. That number, let's say it's $3 million, is used to help defray the cost of the purse. That's how an event becomes known as the Slightly Open. The host organization then operates the event. It costs money to prepare the location for a PGA Tour event. The host group sells as many sponsor positions as possible to offset the cost of putting on the tournament. They are hopeful that the revenue raised through ticket sales, sponsorships, program advertising and all other revenue streams exceeds the expenses incurred. The difference goes right to the charitable bottom line.

The claims you see on the broadcast are really true, and in fact, in some cases, are actually less than what the group contributes all year on an aggregate basis. Hey, let's not get crazy here. The PGA Tour and the players make their cut, but what they say about charity is true.

First of all, I would like to say thank you for the countless laughs. I recently read your book "Somewhere in Ireland, a Village is Missing an Idiot," and I have to say that although many may disregard your insight for the game, I think you are a well-spoken man with great opinions. What is it like to be able to see all of the greatest courses, and can you recommend any courses to absolutely avoid?
—Cody Powers, Gallatin, Tenn.

Anyone who questions my insight into the game is someone to be avoided at all costs. It is obvious to even the most casual observer that my studied, well-formulated and keenly presented opinions are irrefutable and carry the weight of a Papal Bull, which, as we all know, cannot be questioned by secular authority, including Tim Finchem, David Fay or Dick Cheney.

My list of courses to avoid:

1. Any course in North America that names its holes. (And don't worry about Augusta, you ain't playing there anyway.)
2. Courses anywhere that contain any reference to devil worship in their name, i.e., Devil's Ridge, Beelzebub's Butt, Mephastrophie's Meadows, etc.
3. Anything designed by Arthur Hills. Eva and Adolph would have committed suicide three months earlier had they been in one of his bunkers.

I love reading your columns and your commentary on TV. When you are not on TV, the coverage is very boring. My question is this: when will TV stop calling fairway woods metals? Nobody that plays the game calls them metals. Just a simple thing, but I was interested in your comments. I'm sure you could write a column about it and other language unique to golf.

—Bob Swanson, Danville, Calif.

Bob, you're quite right. Only an idiot would call a wood a "metal," no matter what it's made of. It just doesn't sound right. Those who feel our equipment description should be metallurgically accurate have my blessing to start calling irons "steels."

Let's think about this . . . College baseball . . . "Strike Three!! He never took the aluminum off his shoulder."

I laughed out loud reading about the gut-wrenching, butt cheek-clenching fear that, even for a professional athlete, can be fostered by the belief that somehow "I don't belong here" or "I'm not good enough to be The Open champion." Do you think that things might have been different for you had you worked with a sports psychologist who could have helped you with the tornado watches issued on Sundays for the areas including the western region of your mental

health and the northern portion of your ability to deal rationally with
your disconcerted precarious emotional situation? What's your
opinion of tour players using shrinks?

—David, Richmond, Va.

I have no problem with those guys using shrinks. There are
some seriously deranged people out there, and a lot of them
need those mental colonoscopies. Mac O'Grady was on the
hairy edge of "The Twilight Zone" for a number of years.
Remember what he said, and I'm paraphrasing here, "Wish I
was a Kellogg's Corn Flake, floatin' in my bowl takin' movies.
Relaxin' a while, living in style, talking to a raisin who occasionally plays LA. Casually glancin' at his toupee. Wish I was
an English muffin, 'bout to make the most out of a toaster. I'd
ease myself down, coming up brown. I prefer boysenberry
more than any ordinary jam." (Apologies to Paul Simon.)

If I had worked with a sports psychologist the poor devil
would be making wallets in Switzerland right now.

Do you prefer Guinness or Murphys?

—Jim Lyons

Either one's nothing but a beer sandwich. If someone has
made the decision to throw a pint in my face, I prefer Murphy's. If they're gonna pour it down my throat, it'll have to be
Guinness for sure, and it tastes like an angel's cryin' on your
tongue.

Congratulations on the return to pure, self-effacing, non-abusive (with
the exception of McCord), uproarious humor. Gone are the mean-
spirited vitriolic attacks (again, with the exception of McCord). The
June 22 mailbag was a return to the old Feherty-style magic. Now, if
we can just get Tiger to set aside his ego and call 1-800-BUTCHIE, the

world can get back to normal. Hell, it may even bring peace in the Middle East.

—Mark Limbaugh, Columbia, S.C.

Mark, any relation to Rush? Love that guy.

I've never been vitriolic or mean-spirited in my life you panty-waisted, bulbous-nosed, gerbil-jamming, Depends-wearing idiot. Oh, oh, sorry, man. Temporary regression.

Hey, I love you, man. You're the best. But it would take a lot more than a Butch and Tiger reunion to resolve the Middle East problems. It would have to be something really important, like Dottie Pepper reversing her decision to retire.

Enjoy your schtick, and you do have a talent.

re: Poet Heaney. Thanks for sharing: "I've no spade to follow men like them," he wrote. "Between my finger and my thumb

The squat pen rests.

I'll dig with it."

Though my last name of Feher is similar to yours, I suspect we're not related as my pen is not so "squat." I do enjoy the digging nonetheless.

But the real reason I'm writing is to share a favorite quote from Red Smith, another talented sports writer: "Writing is easy. You just sit down at the typewriter and open a vein." I doubt most readers realize the work you must put in to seem so casually irreverent. Thanks for the effort.

—Albert Feher

A kindred spirit; rare indeed. There is nothing casual about my reverence as you have discerned, you clever boots, you. On the other hand, do not ascribe too large a dollop of earnestness where no evidence of such was intended nor existed. My struggle lies in the application of the tourniquet to stench the flow, not with its initiation. Or in other words, I'm full of it.

22.

Soap Inside the Ropes

Golf Magazine, *10565493, September 2004, Vol. 46, Issue 9*

Butch knew it was over when the damned headcover bit him. He tried to interlock his gloved fingers around its striped neck, but he had to give up. The padding in his glove wouldn't let him do anything with his hands but grip a golf club perfectly.

"Damn it!" he sobbed. "Damn it! Damn it!" His relationship with Tiger was over, but why? For the love of God, it was obvious they were meant for each other. They had been a perfect match, hole mates. Then Tiger had said, in that flat voice of his, "Sorry, Butchie. It's not you, it's me."

Butch knew there was another guru. He could see it in Tiger's eyes, in his narrower stance. For years, Butch had filled that crucial gap between Steve Williams and the best camera angle on Tiger, so that no player, coach or network could spot the secret move Tiger called "Big Pussy." Butch went to yoga classes until he was flexible enough to assume the "Leadbetter" position. It wasn't easy for a man of 5-foot-6 to get his feet so far apart, but he did it, and now, with his massive trousers and specially weighted underpants, he had the networks' low-angle cameras blocked. He could say good and nice as well as any coach who had ever lived, but it was all for naught. Tiger (or the mastermind behind Tiger) had canned him. Well, to hell with Tiger Woods and that overpaid skycap Williams. To hell with them all! He'd always have Adam . . .

In an underground laboratory in Oregon, Phil Knight looked over Professor David Duval's shoulder as the professor opened a flap of skin behind the android's knee. No one at Georgia Tech had looked twice at Duval, a nerdy, introverted bioengineering student, especially after his early experiment, Charlie Rymer, had gone so horribly awry.

With a pair of tweezers, Duval loosened a chip and held it up to the light. "I'm close," he said softly, cocking his head to one side, peering at the tiny sliver of silicon.

Knight frowned. "Uh, like where have I heard that before?" he said sarcastically. "You need to be more than close. Kostis is close, too. Next thing we know that evil bastard will have his massive Greek thumbprints all over his super-slo-mo shots and the game will be up. How will the Swoosh look if people find out that to Just Do It, Tiger needs eight D batteries shoved up him?"

"Listen," Duval said. "If you think I faked the death of my own career so I could sing backup vocals in Daly's trailer or hang out with Frank Lickliter, throwing knives at a cardboard cutout of Michael Moore, you've lost your mind. I'm on this, OK? Just make sure his damned shoes fit this time, and maybe we can stop his knee from exploding after 500 swings."

Knight smiled. "You know, it's ironic, Duval," he said. "For a while there, everybody thought you were the robot."

Meanwhile, back at Tour HQ, Vijay Singh was digging a hole in a bunker, cursing on every follow-through. He'd been so close to catching Tiger. Soooo close, and then that grinning, subcutaneous second-place suck-up Mickelson suddenly figures out how to swallow and now the whole shooting match is up in the air. Then there's Els and Goosen, two stiffs hitting a few balls between cases of beer. It wasn't right! Singh dropped his sand wedge and stamped up to the fitness trailer.

———

Later, in the trailer, Vijay, Phil, Ernie and Retief are playing poker on Tim Herron, who has passed out on a massage table. They are surrounded by beer bottles and mountains of Cialis packets.

Retief: "Man, maybe we shouldn't have told him they were sugar-free."

Ernie (poking Lumpy in the chest: "Ach, hey, he's as firm as he's ever been."

Retief: "Maybe we should try the defibrillator on him."

Ernie: "Ja man, it worked for you."

Phil (tossing cash onto Lumpy): "I'll raise you 50 grand."

Vijay: "Do you have a gambling problem or something?"

Suddenly the door bursts open. In strides Professor Duval, followed by a tall, shadowy figure dressed in red and black.

Duval: "Gentlemen, meet the new, improved . . . Tiger!"

Vijay, Phil, Ernie and Retief: "No!"

Duval: "Hahahaha!"

Tigerbot: "I'm back, and I've brought . . . a friend."

He reaches out and clasps hands with the professor's latest creation: a tall, slim she-bot. Yes, it's the Wiebot.

Vijay, Phil, Ernie, Retief and Lumpy: "Noo-oo-ooo!"

WILL TIGERBOT DESTROY PAR? IS LUMPY CARRYING ERNIE'S BABY? CAN THE WIEBOT DEFEAT ANNIKABOT? DON'T MISS THE NEXT EPISODE OF *AS THE WORLD SPINS SIDEWAYS*. (Or, *The Old and the Pointless*)

Golf: the ultimate daytime drama.

23.

The Alternative Ending

Online—Published: September 1, 2004

Just like the latest DVDs, David Feherty's shocking cliffhanger of a September "Sidespin" column could spin off several endings. Here's one—from the late-night musings of FrankenFeherty himself.

There they stood; straight as ramrods, eyes focused, abs twitching, The Stepford Golfers. Tiger went to the stair climber, Annika to the military press and Sergio to the fridge for a Michelob Ultra. The tension grew thicker than Lumpy's midriff.

Sergio: "Can anybody get in this game or do I have to piss and moan about being mistreated?"

Vijay: "Depends; are you going to blame your caddy if you lose? Hey, Annika, how about fixing me a ham sandwich and opening a beer for me? And as long as you're up, see if you can find the England–Fiji cricket match on the satellite dish."

Annika: "Hey Vij, how 'bout you spend a few bucks and get rid of that big toe on your forehead?"

Phil: "Hey, anybody seen my green jacket? I had it when I came in."

Something begins to stir under Herron's stomach. The movement travels under his skin toward his throat and as his mouth opens, a slime-covered, sharp-toothed miniature Steve Williams emerges, hissing and spitting phlegm all over the trailer. The alien serpent-caddy begins attacking everyone in sight.

Just when it looks as though all is lost, Butch Harmon bursts through the door. He has a Winn-gripped Medicus perfectly gripped in his pudgy little hands and he swings with deadly accuracy at the Williams thing. A sickening thud, followed by another and yet another. Oh, the humanity! God, his grip is perfect with those gloves! The Williams thing now lying on the floor, oozing Fosters, making one last weak attempt at confiscating Ernie's camera, then collapsing, spent and lifeless.

Tiger and Butch exchange meaningful gazes, held just a hair too long. Woods even allows a small, toothy grin then quickly averts his eyes as Butch is obviously welling up. The two embrace and shouts of "Huzzah!" resound from the entire group. Retief and Ernie sit back down to finish lunch, so overcome with emotion they both forgot the mayo on their sandwich. Phil locates his jacket, Vijay is on the phone, discussing options with his orthodontist about his overbite, Annika is weighing offers to enter the men's final at Wimbledon, and Tiger and Butch are planning a cruise to the Balkans.

24.

Feherty's Mailbag

Online—Published: September 2, 2004

Hey Dave, a "toast" to you on your 46th birthday (August 13):

From a wee Irish lad, a strange man he became,
First a fine golfer, now calling the game
At CBS Sports and EA Sports too
The bigshots are nervous, oh what will he do?
Will he blurt out an insult, tell an off-color joke?
Will he mention his "willy"? Of farts he once spoke
Thank God for the "kill switch" and 6-second delay
For they haven't an inkling what David might say

He's cunningly witty and funny as hell
But obsessed with ham sandwiches, seems troubled as well
He's sporting a goatee, still clinging to youth?
Don't worry old boy, 'bout getting "long in the tooth"
Sure, you may become saggy, get wrinkled old prunes,
Lose your mind and be constantly humming show tunes
But fear not, for as long as you're sexy and silly

There are hundreds of ladies who'd love to "free willy"
Happy Birthday, David!

—Debbie Young, Toronto, Canada

Hey, that was really very good! How many Debbie Youngs are there in Toronto, because She Who Must Be Obeyed wants to know how much ammo to bring?

I wish I had a witty question to ask, but I don't. Just wanted to say that I had the opportunity to meet you at the recent "My Queer" Dino Ciccirelli charity scramble, and it was a pleasure. Hey, I just thought of a question. Will you be doing a book tour now that your new (heavy) book on the Ryder Cup is out? Good luck with sales on that one. I'm sure I will be seeing it at the top of the bestseller list soon.

—Rebecca Brydges

I will not be doing a book tour, largely because as you point out, the damn book is too heavy. Should it ever get near the top, the bestseller list would probably collapse under the weight.

But let me ask you something. When you met me, did my rear appear big in the slacks I had on that day? How did my chins look? Did you like my new beard? Some people there criticized me for being too self-absorbed that day. Can you believe that?

Hope you like the book, but as I said, I won't be going on one of those book tours. I tried that before and the only thing worse than having to answer inane questions from radio talk show hosts that don't know a thing about golf and didn't read the book is having to sit in Barnes and Noble for four hours, sober, while three drunks who just stumbled out of the bar next door want to know if that was REALLY Tiger Woods' girlfriend on the Internet.

I was watching The Golf Channel the other day, and they showed the highlights from the 1991 Ryder Cup. You actually won a couple matches, eh? You looked young, fit and like you knew what you were doing on the golf course. My god, man, what the hell happened?
—Zack Stevens, Shrewsbury, Mass.

That wasn't me. The Golf Channel knew this all along. They called me for a comment on what appeared to be some kind of cloning experiment that went horribly wrong. I tried to explain that it was a different David Feherty, but they were having none of it. I'm in the process now of suing The Golf Channel for slander, libel, misrepresentation, rape, sodomy, beastiality, malfeasance, character assassination and intestinal gas. Oh, don't you worry, they're gonna pay, all right. When I'm through with them, they'll wish they never HEARD of David Feherty.

Hey David, we met at Colonial. I was in a yellow hat, shirt, and navy slacks. Some friends of mine were wondering after everyone involved gets their cut (taxes, caddie, etc.) how much of the $1.2 million does Todd Hamilton put in his bank account for winning the Open Championship? Keep up the great work.
—Wes Parham, Fort Worth, Texas

Thanks Wes, I remember running away from you. Ten percent of Todd's loot goes to his drunken bagman, about 40 percent goes to his evil agent, and the rest goes to his wife. Just like the rest of us, he gets bugger all.

At the U.S. Open at Shinnecock Hills, I noticed that players in several of the early groups on the weekend were not marking their balls before their playing partners played (from off the green). On Sunday at the sixth green, Tim Petrovic hit a shot from the greenside bunker to

within 2–3 feet and made no move to mark the ball. Spike McRoy was
about to putt from off the green when the USGA official came over and
said something to him. At that point, McRoy said to Petrovic, "Go
ahead. You'll have to mark it." Was there some sort of organized
protest going on? What's the scoop?

—Nick Helm, Plano, Texas

The U.S. Open was clearly an organized protest. Against the
game of golf.

My buds and I just finished playing 70 holes of golf in one day. We
played the TPC at Deer Run. I was wondering, what is the most golf
you have ever played in a day?

—Jeff Panozzo

You idiot, you have no life. Who in their right mind would play
70 holes in a day when they could spend the time eating, drinking, sleeping and breaking wind?

I haven't played more than 9 since 1996.

Your "I swooned at Troon" article (July 2004 issue of GOLF MAGAZINE)
is perhaps one the most insightful I have ever read. It works on so
many levels: humility, humor, insight, anthropological, psychological,
sociological, entomological, herpetological . . . all right, the last two
don't count, and I'm exerting too much effort, but let me end by
saying, my man, you're not half bad.

—Ed

Whoaaaa, hold on now there, podner. Way too many logicals in
there. I'm not smart enough to figure out that many angles
simultaneously or even at the same time. Appreciate the credit,
though. I'll keep writing as long as you keep reading. Thanks.

25

Feherty's Mailbag

Online—Published: September 16, 2004

Have you ever taught She Who Must Be Obeyed how to play golf? Do you play (golf that is) together? Your thoughts on the subject in general.
—Vladimir

Vlad. Have you lost your mind? No man should teach his wife to play, you cretin, and the reason is obvious. She might like it! Obviously, you're Russian, and it is questions like this that point out some of the disadvantages of freedom of the press. If the KGB were still a force, you would be clapped in irons and have electrodes attached to your testicles running to a car battery that would be switched on periodically until you promised to never bring up the subject again.

The other day at work I was bored so I rifled through a stack of magazines in the corner. I read an article in GOLF MAGAZINE that you had written about women athletes (Sept. 2002). The last few paragraphs made me well up; I myself was in your place not too long ago. My question is how is Erin and is she playing golf? Good day!
—C.M. Bond

Hey, what the hell were you doing in my place? Where was I, on the road somewhere? You bastard. Oh, I see what you mean. Sorry, C.M.

Erin is lovely, thank you. She isn't playing golf yet, but I will surely expose her to it as she becomes more able to handle the physical aspects of it. I don't really much care what sport she chooses to play, as long as she has fun and approaches whatever she decides with enthusiasm and commitment.

My cousin Douglas Rea grew up playing golf in Bangor, Northern Ireland. Any chance you knew him? He's about 5 years your senior.

—Brian Keith

I do know Dougie Rea and next time you see him tell him I'm still waiting for the money he owes me for taking his astonishingly homely sister to the dance at the Convent of the Mothers of Perpetual Pain. Better yet, I'm going to be in Bangor this month for an AT&T gig. Send me his address. I'll send a couple of my buddies from the RUC around to collect. By the way, he was a hell of a rugby player.

Hi David. About two years ago you actually phoned me to answer a question I had asked. I ended up sending you a green Canadian Coast Guard shirt. Just a couple of weeks ago you MC'ed Mike Weir's charity tournament in Sarnia. I was standing right beside you but didn't have the balls to say "Hi" because I was helping a journalist friend of mine and didn't think it would be professional. Anyway, next time you're in Sarnia I'd like to smoke a nicely aged Cuban and perhaps have a little nip at the course with you. I'll be the press guy watching the pros' golf swing instead of taking shots!

Hope to see you next year.

—Steve Klamer

Weir's gig is one of my favorites. No one considers it professional to say hello to me. I prefer amateurs anyway; they're less pretentious. And just for the record, I don't think you should be smoking "nicely aged Cubans," my friend. I mean how would you like it if Castro fired up one of our senior citizens? And if we're gonna have a nip or two, let's do it in a nice pub. The only time I set foot on an actual course these days is when CBS is paying me.

At which hole should you aim if you are so hung over that you see two or more of them?

—Dan Bergthold, St. Paul, Minnesota

If there are two, aim at the one in the middle. For more than two, just pick the closest. We are talking golf, here, Dan? Aren't we?

I have been a big fan for years and really enjoy your columns. How long, on average, does it take you to come up with answers to these questions? Do you just rattle them off or need hours to make them sound funny? I know this is not golf related, but it gives you a chance to talk about yourself.

—Geoff Povinelli, Magnolia, Texas

Fortunately the only people who write to me are complete idiots. This makes it very simple to answer their questions. In fact, sometimes I just ignore them and write something completely irrelevant. (Rather like this.)

Hey, on the other hand, what do you mean, "funny"? I'll have you know I don't think there is anything funny at all about my responses. And I don't need to spend time talking about myself. That's what I pay my friends to do. Sorry, I'm being harsh. Thanks for your support.

You are the most insane of all golf writers and I love reading your pieces. If they ever fire you, I would have to stop reading the magazine for at least a week.

My question (or plea) would be to get your support for an official designation for Duffer's Rules. Duffer's Rules are based on the observation that they are out there and probably won't go away, so we need to ensure they play fast and get off the course. The basic ideas behind Duffer's Rules is ensure fast play and improve their enjoyment of the game.

1. A Duffer always plays best ball with another of the foursome (preferably not another duffer).
2. A Duffer can always improve their lie (even to the point of a forward carry).
3. Lost balls, out-of-bounds, water hazards are given a free drop in the fairway.
4. Eight shots is the maximum score, and Duffers are required to pick up their ball after shooting an 8.
5. Asking for advice is encouraged as long as it is quick and acted upon quickly.
6. When a Duffer plays quickly, he is awarded by subtracting a few shots. (Something like speed golf.) This would definitely encourage fast play.

The rules are more extensive, but this gives you the gist of the idea. Only you have the reputation to submit this idea and not be laughed off the magazine. Please help me distribute these rules and get those duffers moving along.

—Matt Little, Bear, Delaware

Matt Little Bear: Is that a full-blooded Indian name? If they ever fire me from GOLF MAGAZINE, I'll sue them—for a broken heart. I love those guys and nobody else has the salt to hire me. But they better come up with some serious chalupa this time around. The crooks I play with have already adopted those rules and some others I can't talk about.

Recently, I reached into my basket—by the john, of course—and found a December 2003 GOLF MAGAZINE issue. I read your "That Dog Will Hunt" SideSpin story and almost broke the john laughing when I read the part about the Chap Stick in the chamber.

The reason I laughed so hard was that about 50 years ago (yes, 50!) a friend of mine (Butch Jaworski) and I were hunting rabbits (or whatever popped up). Butch had a single shot 410 and had a head cold, and I had a JC Higgins bolt action 16 ga. (Nothing but the best!)

Well, a pheasant popped up. Butch took a shot, and of course, he missed. He quickly reached into his pocket for another shell and reloaded and all we heard was a "click." We both looked down at his 410, which was pointed downward, and out of the end of the barrel came sliding out his Chap Stick. I told him that, at least now, the pheasant could breathe OK and then ran like hell.

This is a true story. But what the hell, we had fun anyways. In fact we have (or at least, I have anyways) more fun retelling this story than we had when we were hunting.

Keep up those Sidespin stories. I love 'em!

—Bill Balyszak, Auburn, New York

Lovely story Billy. But why did you run? Were you afraid he was going to moisturize you?

26.

Save the Zebras!

Golf Magazine, *10565493, October 2004, Vol. 46, Issue 10*

As I write, the held staff of the PGA Tour is locked in a bitter battle with the Tour Policy Board over wages and conditions. Hey, search my shorts, but I can't figure out why. Maybe the players think tournaments run automatically. But the last time I checked, the 30 or so members of the field staff were out there before the first crow's fart, making sure we all get to see the astonishing conjuring trick that is an average Tour event. Field staffers handle temporary construction, security, sponsors, marshals and volunteers. They administer the Rules of Golf, coordinate with TV tyrants, take blame for the weather, monitor pace of play and course set-up and make sure the players-only potties have paper. And they are getting royally hosed in this labor dispute.

OK, I didn't actually check on them. That would force me to get out of bed as early as they do, which with my lifestyle would give me . . . let's see . . . about four minutes of sleep.

Professional golf is unique in many ways, but no more so than in the way the Rules are applied. In most sports, the refs are there to penalize, but in golf they operate on both sides of the ball. If a pro official sees a Rule about to be broken, it's his or her duty to run in and stop the proceedings before the infraction takes place. John Brendle did just that at Harbour Town this year, when he noticed Ted Purdy taking a free drop a little below shoulder height. Imagine that in boxing: If a ref saw a low blow coming, he'd be obliged to place his personal wobblies between one fighter's fist and the other's groin. In the immortal words of Sir Patrick Summerall, "Mmm . . . that's not good."

The Rules of Golf are complicated and occasionally daft, so I always feel for the poor zebra under the glare of the cameras, giving a ruling on a life-or-death penalty drop. I remember a European official by the name of George O'Grady, now a Euro Tour executive, who, whenever he had to give a player bad news, wore a look that suggested he was giving birth to a spiral-bound version of the King James Bible. George, like almost every professional official I've known, understood the game, genuinely liked the players and, most important, gave them the benefit of the doubt if he could. This principle is absolutely necessary for dealing with people who play golf for a living, and it's where Tour officials differ from those of the R&A and USGA. Giving rulings to pro golfers is no hobby to Slugger White, George Boutell, Dillard Pruitt and the rest of our PGA Tour officials.

Think about it: Pretty much every recent bad decision (and I say bad, not incorrect, for there is a difference), whether on course set-up or Rules, has been at the British or U.S. Open, where the R&A and USGA rule. Both events do use some officials from the professional tours, and when a pro asks for a ruling, believe me, he prays that he gets one of them.

You want amateur-hour horror stories? Monty got violated when Ernie Els got a break at Congressional. David Frost got cornholed at Carnoustie, and don't get me started on poor Mark Roe, who got sausaged at Sandwich in the 2003 British Open, when he and Jesper Parnevik neglected to exchange scorecards on the first tee. The scores were right, the names were wrong, and though the R&A had the leeway within its own rules to waive a penalty, it did not. The spirit of the game should never be so mean. And get this: Roe shot 73 in qualifying for this year's British Open, then gave his card to an R&A official, who told him no, no, it was 74. The adamant official, however, HAD ADDED UP THE NUMBERS INCORRECTLY! "It's incredible," said Roe. "All the R&A has to do is employ the people who do the scoring every week for the European Tour. But they won't do it." What a debacle!

Baseball, the only game whose rules come close to golf's in silliness, starts its umps at $85,000 per annum, and a 26-year veteran can make $340,000. If Tour officials had a similar deal, Wade Caygill, who is 106 years old and has 85 years' experience, would make something like $4,892,369 a year, which is what he deserves. But a PGA Tour official starts at $63,000, a 26-year veteran makes $189,000, and now they're being asked to fly on the lowest possible, non-upgradable, non-refundable fare! I'm sorry, but this utterly blows cheese.

To add insult to penury, the Tour won't let the field staff even speak to the players about this dispute, so most of them don't even know it's going on. That's why I'm writing this and leaving copies in all the clubhouse cans.

So enough already, boys! Pull your trousers up from around your ankles and march to your nearest Policy Board member. Tell him to cut your zebras some slack. What they ask is a lot less than they deserve, and it would cost the Tour less than Vijay's range tab.

27

Feherty's Mailbag

Online—Published: October 13, 2004

After seeing the USA get thrashed by the Euros in the Ryder Cup, I've had a dozen arguments about what went wrong. The most brilliant observation I've heard so far has been "we just got outplayed." Duh. The real questions are: "why?", "who can we blame?", and "how can we avoid getting walloped the next time?" If you'll answer the first two, I'll handle the last one. Here's my suggestion: we appoint a European to captain our squad. How about Nick Faldo? He seems mysteriously despised by the Euros, even though he's the best European player in the last 50 years. Think the PGA of America would go for that?

—Mark Limbaugh, Columbia, South Carolina

Uh, no I don't.

The reason the Europeans didn't like Nick was because he kept beating the crap out of them. He's stopped doing that now, so everybody's over it. He's our boy. The reason the Americans were outplayed was they were tighter than a crab's ass going up a hill. They looked like they were going to the gas chamber instead of playing a golf match. The Europeans practiced as a team, traveled as a team, dined as a team and putted like they were members. The U.S. team did everything but the latter, but the real reason that they are getting beaten so frequently is that the U.S. golf public and the media over here refuses to let them feel like the underdogs. In what other sporting event could a team lose 7 out of 10 and still be strong favorites the next time? The underdogs have a tremendous advantage in the Ryder Cup because so little is expected of them. It's time to put away the pride and admit that the Europeans are better in this event.

Do I have to ask if you enjoyed the Ryder Cup? I enjoyed it very much, especially since I had your new book as a companion reading piece. There were a few boring bits during the Ryder Cup where I could enjoy your perspective and witty captions. Do you think you would ever be asked to be the captain of the European team?

— Rebecca Brydges

Not if every European golf professional in the world over the age of reason were suddenly wiped out by a vicious pox. Not if I were the only living European left on earth after a nuclear holocaust launched by the remnants of the Taliban decimated the European PGA. Osama Bin Laden and Josef Mengele would get the nod before yours truly.

Other than that, I think the odds are pretty good.

I know you work at CBS and Johnny and his cronies are at NBC, but could you give him a call and tell him that we are "Europeans" NOT "Euros"! Euros is a currency. Tell Johnny he should therefore be calling the American side in the Ryder Cup the "Dollars."

— Paul Kelly, displaced European,
Victoria B.C., Canada

You are quite right, and EURO is a rotten name for a currency too. I like it though. We could start calling the individual team members by their respective currencies. Sergio and Ollie would be the Pesetas, Levet would be the Franc, Monty the Pound, etc. My favorite would be Bernhard the Mark. Great idea. I'll call Johnny straight away. Incidentally, I'm sorry you're displaced. Must be rough.

My question is about the 2006 Ryder Cup captaincy campaign. How is the captain picked? Do you have an opinion about who would be the best candidate? Apart from Sam Torrance, do you have a favorite past captain and why? Does the captain have any "intimidation factor" for the other team?

—Serge Alain, Jonquire, Quebec

The PGA of America and the European Tour have similar processes for picking the captain, and they both involve a consensus approach from a small committee made up of the officers of the respective organizations. I don't think the opposing team gives a fig who the other captain is, and no one on either side is intimidated by him.

My favorite captain, other than Sam, was Seve. He was a master at motivation and gamesmanship and absolutely lived to beat the Americans. He was probably the most intense/insane competitor I've ever met.

During the Ryder Cup Matches it was said that Bernhard Langer gave his team $45,000 Rolex watches. They said Hal Sutton had gifts as well for his team, but had not given them out yet. I never heard anything more about these gifts. Did he return them? Or did he in fact pass them out? I asked our sports writer here in Charlotte, and he had heard nothing either. So I figured if anybody would know it would be the great swami David Feherty.

—Fred Smith, Charlotte, North Carolina

Hal gave them all Bose Noise Canceling Headsets so they wouldn't have to listen to all the criticism from the press and the fans.

Since the Europeans kicked our butt and they were the party of the crowd, which of the American players do you feel, if any, would qualify for the next Ryder Cup based on their ability to party?

—Mike W., Nashville, Tennessee

Chris DiMarco, John Daly, Jeff Sluman, Neal Lancaster, Amy Mickelson, the bartender from Dick O'Dowd's Irish tavern in Birmingham, Michigan, Courtney Love, Rodney Dangerfield, posthumously, and of course, Marion Barry, the former mayor of Washington D.C.

I am a 17-year-old on our high school golf team and am struggling to break 80. I was wondering what your advice would be? I would like to know what you think about practice habits. Thank you very much. I read everything you have done.

—David Bennett, Richfield, Utah

Well, on the tour, we've got everything from Vijay, whose practice time far exceeds his actual playing time, to Carlos Franco, who thinks practicing is what lawyers and doctors do, so I'm not sure what to tell you about practice. I know something about struggling, though, and that may be the answer; stop struggling and have some fun. You're 17 for God's sake, enjoy the game, but don't make a religion out of it. If you're any good and you're planning on making your living at golf, fine, work your butt off. Otherwise, try hard to play your best and accept the results, but HAVE FUN. There's plenty of time to be miserable after you get married.

28.

Feherty's Mailbag

Online—Published: October 27, 2004

Out of all the CBS golf announcers and analysts who is the worst golfer?

—Kevin Holder, Riverdale, Georgia

McCord's so bad at everything it's hard not to pick him for worst golfer. He's certainly the worst dresser (he rendered Mr. Blackwell speechless), has the worst hand-eye coordination (he has to be vacuumed after he eats), the worst drunk (picture Benny Hinn singing "Feelings" after several bottles of communion wine), and the worst name-dropper EVER, (say, isn't that Bob Redford over there?). But hey, like I said at least he dresses badly. But on the golf side, he's actually our best player. If it weren't for Nantz, I'd be the worst.

I look forward to everything you write. I have two questions. First, my local library doesn't have a copy of your book. Could you look into that? Second, I was playing behind McCord in Vail, Colorado, a few years ago. He and his partner hit big drives down the middle of the first fairway (obviously a downhill shot) and raced to their balls. While we waited for them to clear they pulled a 180, went flying past us and the starter and shouted they had forgotten the "gun for the gophers." Is this a McCord for "we left the bottle in the car"? Thanks for making it fun.

—John Speranza, Colorado

My publisher will hear of this travesty. In the meantime, come on, cough up the dough, tightwad. Buy the book! It'll last you a lifetime.

McCord and his "partner" (and we all know what the definition of "partner" is these days, don't we?) may have decided to go back to Gary's place rather than finish the round, but it seems more likely they were going gopher fishing, a pastime that requires a fishing rod, a shotgun, and two congenital idiots. The fisherman makes a slip noose in his line which he carefully lays around the chosen gopher hole. Then they wait for the gopher to pop up for a look at what's going on, at which point the fisherman yanks the course-mangling little bastard out and the shooter does his best to pick the little bugger off. It's not as easy as it sounds, as gophers have a nasty tendency to run straight at the guy with the fishing rod. Best to wear orange if you don't have the shotgun.

I never did see the late Moe Norman in person, but I knew of him and heard many stories. Did you ever meet him or see him in action? If you did, could you share a story or two? Thanks.

—Barrie Barrington

Sorry, didn't know the guy other than by reputation, but I did meet him once at the Canadian PGA Championship. His wheel was spinning, but his hamster was gone. The really remarkable thing about him was the fact he could hit the ball at all with that god-awful method. If a real coach had gotten a hold of him, he might have been a world-beater.

I just wanna say I originally disliked you. But after hearing you talk about Payne Stewart during your "lessons from the pros" on The Golf Channel, I saw you in a new light I was refusing to see you in before. You are a genuine person who's got a lot of class. Well, OK, no class, but you're pretty damn cool. Do you have any other good stories about Payne Stewart besides the one from the '91 Ryder Cup? Thanks, and oh, by the way, "Somewhere in Ireland . . ." is fricking hilarious!
—Andrew, Toronto, Ontario

I have to admit, after reading your first sentence, I wasn't warming up to you much either. Payne glued my hotel room door shut once, and when I finally got it open, there was a groundhog under my bed, wearing a pair of my Y-fronts. I loved the bastard more than you could imagine.

I've imagined you and Lee Trevino in the booth together. Have you? Will you? I think the sky's the limit! Could you two inciteful, glib, energetic and extemporaneously humourous icons share center stage effectively?
—Robert L. Robinson, Bountiful, Utah

I can't think of the word "bountiful" without thinking of breasts. I don't know why, I just can't. I could never live there.

First off, I don't like the booth. I like walking the course and being down on the ground with the players. I don't think Lee would like that so much and besides, having two analysts together probably wouldn't work so well. We'd be arguing over which way the putt breaks all the time. I love Lee, though. Second to last of the great shotmakers. (There was that Tiger guy.)

But what Lee could do with a wedge was nothing short of Homeric.

As a 48-year-old golfer is it considered "girlie" to use hybrids, hacksticks, and fairway woods all the way up to a 7-iron? I carry no irons below the 7.

—Jim Logemann, Phoenix, Arizona

What the hell is a hackstick? There are a lot of things considered "girlie" in golf: pink tees, playing from the reds, culottes, Capri pants, NEVER giving a putt, arguing over rules you don't know, not watching your ball after you hit it, keeping score with the aid of a string of beads hanging from your bag, tassels on your shoes, little fuzzy balls that hang off the heels of your socks, Sesame Street character head covers, paisley bags and making little snowmen on the scorecard when you take an eight. But playing with the all-wood concept is fine. Kick some ass with your 11-wood, pal. Most of us would be better players if we had enough balls to be a little more girlie.

29.

Langer Management

Golf Magazine, *10565493*, *November 2004, Vol. 46, Issue 11*

By the time this rag hits the shelves we'll have swallowed all the Ryder Cup analysis we can stomach, so I'm not going there. This is not a postmortem, it's an admission of misdiagnosis. My bad—I thought we were going to lose.

That dog-and-pony show of an opening ceremony should have been a dead giveaway that something strange was about to happen. I can understand seeing Pistons coach Larry Brown and Red Wings captain Steve Yzerman up there—this was suburban Detroit—but Kathy Ireland? Donald Trump and Amelia Earhart? (OK, maybe it was The Donald and actress Angie Everhart, not aviatrix Amelia.) I loved hearing the national anthems, though the American one was a dog's-breakfast rendition, all frilly, trilly and gospelized to the point of destruction, mercifully drowned out by the jet-fighter flyover. Another high point was the horrified look on Chaka Khan's face when 40,000 white golf fans tried to dance as she sang Marvin Gaye's "What's Going On." What had been going on with Chaka? She looked like she'd swallowed one of the Budweiser Clydesdales.

And then there were the captains, Governor Arnold Schwarze-langer and Sheriff Hal Stetson.

I played with Bernhard Langer for the best part of 20 years, and I can honestly say that up until this Ryder Cup I really had no idea what kind of guy he was, other than a Bible-thumper and a very good skier, two qualities I felt would give him a better chance of surviving an avalanche than a Ryder Cup. Langer's choice of Anders Forsbrand, another Scripture quoter, to be his ass't-cap was a stunner as well, at least to me and some of the sinners who were trying to make the team. In my mind's bleary eye, I foresaw a stereotypical European fracas: The Germans would bugger up the battle plan, the British would ask the Americans for help, the Irish would get hammered and forget why they were fighting, the Spaniards would fall asleep after lunch and the French would surrender.

But my worries were unfounded. My native Europe held together for once, behind Captain Langer.

I'm happy to say I got to know a little more about Bernhard. He turns out to be both very cool and very warm. In all the years I had known him, I'd only noticed the first part of that equation. At Oakland Hills he did exactly what was needed: He got the hell out of the way and let the boys play. Sheriff Hal? I don't think he did a whole lot wrong. There was no air of mystery to him: His players knew from the git-go that they might not get to partner up with their best chums. They were supposed to be able to get up for this event; they just didn't. Tiger Woods and Phil Mickelson proved that they put their pants on one leg at a time, and at Oakland Hills they appeared to be trying to get into the same pair. I admired Hal's sense of theater in pairing them up and was among those who thought it a good idea at the time.

Until I saw the look on Tiger's face as the pairings were announced. On Tiger's face, a broad smile with no teeth is not a smile.

But to be fair, history tells us that no matter what your world ranking, anyone who gets drawn against Colin Montgomerie in the Ryder Cup is liable to get his buttocks served to him on a plate. Say what you like about Monty, this thingy is his deal. He's a perfect example of why the European team always over-achieves. In Europe, a player is judged not just by his wins, major or otherwise, but by his Ryder Cup record. Monty may not have won a major, but even if he never does, his play in golf's greatest stress test will mark his place as one of the finest players in history. In closing, let me note that the Ryder Cup was exciting enough, but my favorite part was the announcing crew's heroic struggle to find exciting, innovative ways to agree with Johnny Miller.

"Once again John, I concur."—Gary Koch

"Yup, Johnny—right on the money."—Bob Murphy

"You're not wrong, Johnny."—Mark Rolfing

"Why the hell am I here?"—Roger Maltbie

Oh, and one other thing: The Europeans have always had the advantage of being regarded as Ryder Cup underdogs. How many times do the Americans have to lose before they get a wee turn at that?

30

Feherty's Mailbag

Online—Published: November 17, 2004

I have enjoyed your column for years and have read all of your books. My question to you is, what is a besotted Irishman doing in Texas of all places? The climate is incredibly boring, and I know that one day you will let us in on what you really think of native Texans and your adopted state. Although I would suggest not letting us in on it until after you move far away—Texans are, as you know, notoriously short-tempered about insults to their state and/or persons. I'm sure you don't miss the food from the "Olde Sod," but the beer must drive you mad (as if you needed encouragement). I suppose the whiskey travels well, as confirmed by your mad monthly rants in these and other pages. Keep up the lunacy, as golf would be entirely too serious without you making light of our madness for the game!

—Jack Wolf, Pittsburgh, Pennsylvania

Wolf Man Jack:

Thought you were dead, man. Good to have you back.

I like Texas. I like Dallas. I like America and I'm proud to say I received my permanent residency card recently. Soon I will apply for the Texas green card as well, although I hear they're much more difficult to get if you don't own a pickup. I've even become accustomed to cold beer, and Irish whiskey is fairly easy to find if you look for it. All in all, I made a pretty fair trade. Ireland's my home and I will always be Irish, but I've made a nice life for myself here and I reckon I'll be stayin' fer a spell, podner.

Your bio says you live in Irving, Texas. This makes little sense, based on my own experience in Irving. I flew into Dallas–Fort Worth Airport for a conference in Dallas, but, since I registered late, the only place to stay was the Days Inn in Irving, half a mile from Texas Stadium, the one with the hole in the top for God to watch his Cowboys. It had been a long trip, culminating in having a native Texan, still working on freeway driving, take us from the airport to the inn. Tired, hungry and THIRSTY, I stumbled down to the diner. The first thing I asked the cute little Texas thing waiting tables was "what's on tap?" To which she answered, "We don't serve beer. Irving is DRY." Ignoring the contradiction of having a football stadium in a dry town, what is an Irishman doing in a dry town like Irving? Or have they entered the late 20th century?

— Mike McKeown

I don't live in Irving; I live in Dallas. Dallas is wet, very wet. Since I am aware Irving is dry, I have never even stopped for a red light there. The Irving police have a permanent warrant out for my arrest. For my part, I've begun a class action lawsuit on behalf of the residents of Irving as well as anyone who has had to pass through it citing cruel and unusual punishment. I'll keep you posted; you may be entitled to some compensation.

I have just spent many months in Colombia building a power plant. Before I left, a friend bequeathed his copy of "A Nasty Bit of Rough" and I purchased "Somewhere in Ireland . . .". Both were great reads and supplied badly needed humor in the middle of nowhere.

Any chance we'll get some more stories of the European Tour as those stories in the second book were wonderful. Or do we need to let a few die off so as not to embarrass?

Keep up the good work. The game of golf needs you with these walking stiffs populating so much of the game these days.

—Terry Kanaley

Welcome back and glad I could help. I designed a course down in Medellín, Colombia, a few years back for Pablo Escobar. He named it "Nostrils" Golf Club and Spa. It was only two holes, though. Apparently, he had attention span issues. He paid me $100,000 in $50 bills all rolled up like toilet paper. Took me forever to count the whole thing. Go to your book store immediately and buy my new book about the history of the Ryder Cup.

During a rather unenjoyable round recently I hit a shot into a swampy hazzard. I found my ball in the tall grass (is there any other kind?) resting upon a second golf ball, apparently hit by another unlucky soul. My question is this: Can I move the second ball so I can hit my shot without penalty? Also, what is the weirdest lie you've ever had in competition?

—David Chorzempa, Riverside, Illinois

Dave, I doubt that you spelled your surname correctly. There is no penalty for hitting the wrong ball in a hazard, so my advice to you is to take your best swing at them both and play the one that finishes closest to the hole. Walk quickly and carry a clipboard, and no one will ask any questions. The weirdest lie I heard in competition was when McCord told me he was having fun on the Champions Tour.

31.

Practice Blows

Golf Magazine, 10565493, December 2004, Vol. 46, Issue 12

I vaguely remember the range. In my brief prime, if a player spent three hours on the range after his round, maybe 30 minutes would be spent hitting balls. The rest was frittered away playing grab-ass, telling jokes, releasing stunt flatulence, fiddling with new clubs, watching other players hit balls and generally trying to find any excuse not to hit any yourself. Players would covey up behind anyone who was actually trying to work, either to poke fun at him or to toss in their two cents' worth of genius.

Nowadays, the range is a row of much grimmer professional athletes, plus superstar coaches who pinch off mean little loaves of inaudible encoded information for their protégés. Not that there's never any fun out there. Finding the electronic controls to the irrigation system and setting off the sprinklers is always a lark, and who wouldn't enjoy being goosed by Sergio Garcia? But it's not like it used to be.

Dear God, I'm starting to sound like every old fart who ever wrote about the good old days. Maybe it's because I never really understood the kind of pervert who actually enjoys practicing. Because the fact is, practice blows.

Of course, I am from a place that was hardly ideal for honing a young man's game. The practice area at Bangor Golf Club in Ireland was a tiny mud-flap wedged between the ninth and 18th holes. I'd dump a shag bag of chopped-up Dunlop 65s and begin irritating grumpy old members who sliced and hooked their way into the shabby pattern of dung-encrusted pills I sprayed in front of me. Vijay Singh wouldn't have lasted 10 minutes at Bangor—they'd have tossed him out on his ear for some grass-ackward turf violation.

Back then, hitting balls before a round was almost unsportsmanlike, and for a child to do it was evidence of bad parenting. But things were different in America—by the time Davis Love III was a tyke, his dad was parking a golf cart by a green so little DL3 could practice pitches. "Under the steering wheel!" DL2 would shout, or "Over the roof!" and the Lovelet would adjust his ball position and setup to hit the shot. Which was nothing like my own experience. My father would park himself on a stool in the men's bar while I was out practicing, and he'd shout to the bartender, "I'll have one more, Jimmy, and then I'll stay."

Today, alas, I am sore from not hitting balls. All those muscles I once used every day are thrust into violent action about once a month, and then spend the next month recovering from the shock. Maybe that's why Vijay keeps hitting balls long after the next-to-last player leaves the range.

He's afraid to stop. Hours later, under cover of darkness, Joey the trainer leopard-crawls onto the range, heaves Vijay over his shoulder and sneaks him into his room through the fire escape at the hotel. Because golf is like a lot of schedule-3 drugs: You have to ease your way off. Vijay can't even stop when he gets back to his room. It takes several hundred short swings with the weighted stick and a CD soundtrack of tearing Velcro to bring him down so he can go out for dinner. Even then, you can be sure that if a pea ends up in his mashed potatoes, whoever ordered the calamari rings can expect some kind of miniature explosion shot, played toward his plate with a modified fish knife.

Vijay Singh will force you to have an opinion of him. Some say he's overly cool and standoffish, but my theory is that shooting people the bird is just his way of saying, "Have a nice day." He may not have much time for the media, but the hardest worker ever—he makes Ben Hogan look like Fred Couples—always has time for his fellow players. He's a throwback that way, and maybe the greatest compliment I can offer him is to say he reminds me of Payne Stewart, always willing to watch and offer tips to anyone who asks.

Vijay's legendary practice sessions aren't just mindless nut-crushing, either. He'll hit bags and bags of full shots from fairway bunkers, just to ensure he makes perfect contact. Christy O'Connor Sr. used to do something like that—he'd hit so many drivers off the beach at Royal Dublin that you could have shaved with the base-plate on his wooden driver—but even he took a break now and then to go to the bar. Vijay just keeps on swinging, swinging, swinging. And getting better. That's bad news for the guys spending extra hours on the range to keep up with him, but hey, it leaves more room at the bar for the writers.

32

Feherty's Mailbag

Online—Published: December 1, 2004

Are you serious? You haven't played more than 9 holes in a day since '96. What's your excuse(s)? I'm glad my wife doesn't read your articles. She'd expect the same from me.

—Ritchie

I'm glad your wife doesn't read the stuff I write either. Hell, *my* wife doesn't read my articles. I get paid to talk and write about golf, not play it. McCord's the only idiot I know who still thinks he can play the game. You don't see Marv Albert shooting hoops or Phil Simms tossing the old pigskin around when he's not announcing football, do you? You think Howard Cosell used to spar with Muhammad Ali? I can still play but not like I used to when I had to in order to pay my bar tab. Besides, my balls hurt when I hit 'em now.

The wife wants to play golf. How can I dodge this bullet?

—Preston Schroer, Brewster, Minnesota

You have several options:

1. Homicide
2. Suicide
3. Self-mutilation
4. Send her to McCord/Kostis golf school
5. Make her watch THE BIG BREAK
6. Divorce her
7. Invite your regular foursome over for an intervention
8. Constantly wager with her for sexual payoffs and beat the pants off her, sort of.
9. Insist on attending her all girls bridge club afternoon

Good luck.

How many times have you heard "nice ball" since your commercial first aired?

—Mark, Grand Blanc, Michigan

Counting your message, 4,625,989, which is good. Means I'm reaching the target demographic: 18- to 55-year-old, unemployed drunks with incontinence issues who don't play golf, stayed at a Holiday Inn Express last night with a transvestite hooker suffering from self-image problems. Whoa, I've just described half the residents of Grand Blanc, which is where the Buick Open is played . . . I knew there was a reason I liked those people.

I always enjoy your writing. However, recently it seems that you take every opportunity to tell us how wonderful Monty is. I know you feel bad about sticking him with the Mrs. Doubtfire label, but you've become such a sycophant that Monty is going to need to have your

nose surgically removed from his backside. There is no doubt that he's a great player but what's the deal?

—Kevin Caple, Charlotte, North Carolina

I didn't actually hang that moniker on him; it was an English pro by the name of John Hawksworth (who is much funnier than I am). Despite his dearth of "majors," the guy is an extraordinary player, which, to paraphrase, "Nobody can deny." He won seven European money list titles in a row. And, as you've probably noticed, those guys can play. If my nose is up his backside, it's because I have come to respect the fact that he has assumed a position that has made that possible.

All I hear about Tiger is that his swing change is almost there. My question is, why change when you were the best in the world by no slim margin?

—James

Because golf is a never-ending journey, not a destination. My god, I'm deep today!

33

Feherty's Mailbag

Online—Published: December 15, 2004

A science question: I've heard that a frozen golf ball loses 20 percent of its bounce. Can you confirm this? When "thawed" does it regain all its bounce again? I store my clubs in the garage over the winter (it freezes here in Minnesota) and now wonder if it has been affecting the performance of my golf balls.

—Steve in Minnesota

Thank God you told me you were from Minnesota, otherwise I would have thought you were just deranged. I've come to expect this sort of question from people from Minnesota who seem to focus enormous amounts of intellectual energy on issues surrounding their freezing balls. Can't say as I blame them.

Your golf balls are definitely affected by temperature during the winter. Here's what I would recommend. About mid-March (March 17th is a good target date), gather all your golf balls from the garage. Wash them. Take them to your local bar. Order an empty beer pitcher and two bottles of Black Bush. This is an Irish whiskey made in Northern Ireland and possesses extraordinary curative capabilities. Place the balls in the pitcher and fill the pitcher with enough whiskey to cover the balls. Swirl the balls around in the whiskey for a couple of minutes. Use a swizzey stick if you want. Do not add ice to this mixture under any circumstance; these balls have been through enough.

Gather some friends from the bar around; you'll need them soon enough. After about 20 minutes in the Black Bush, strain the balls from the whiskey and dry them off carefully on a clean terry cloth towel. Drink the whiskey straight up from shot glasses with your friends until exhausted or drunk. Then take the balls out into the alley and set them on fire and never use them again, because they're worthless and always were. Give up golf and take up windsurfing.

I think they should put microphones on some caddies from the European Tour (especially those from Ireland). These guys are funny as hell and really tell it like it is (if you can understand them).

—John

Good lord, what a recipe for a broadcasting train wreck! Picture Lenny Bruce, Howard Stern and Opie and Anthony on speed with Irish accents dispensing bon mots like Raisinettes. We might hear something like this: "I'd like a word in your earhole, you f****** wanker. When I f****** tell you to hit a God****, f****** 5-iron, I don't want to debate the decision. I didn't come out here at 5 in the f****** morning and walk off the f******* yardage so you could hit a f****** 6 in the f****** drink. Arsehole!" It's bad enough we put a microphone on McCord.

Just read the Ryder Cup book. Nice job. I don't claim any detailed knowledge of Lefty's facial or other anatomy, but that does not look like him with Crenshaw on page 304. Looks more like Ron Howard to me. Was he a captain's choice that year?

—Dr. J

Loved you during the ABA years, you were the best. You still have the house on the course at Lake Nona? Great place.

The picture was shot from a funny angle but it was Phil all right. We recognized him from the subcutaneous fat.

There was this one round I played back when I was still playing college golf where I racked up 6 straight birdies (7 in all in the round), but still ended up with a measly 75 (on a par 72). I had 7 birdies, 10 bogeys, and 1 par. Afterwards, I wanted to jam my 6-iron up my butt. Have you ever had a round in your pro golf career where you didn't make a single par?

—Tristan Valerio, Manila, Philippines

Is that where all those envelopes come from?

I'm not sure I ever played a round without a single par, but I sure as hell remember a double bogey. By the way, if you're going to shove a club up your ass, a 6-iron is the wrong selection. Trust me here, I've had many, many a club up my butt. It usually happens when I fall down on the practice range. Too much loft will cause more spin than you want on the way out. I don't want to get too technical here, but you really don't want too much backspin on anything to do with your arse.

While I truly enjoy watching the PGA Tour on TV I will say they are ruining recreational golf. The speed at which these morons play golf is horrific. My suggestion is to have a world ranking of the slowest of the slow. Put the habitual offenders' names in lights. I see 12-year-old kids at my course lining up putts from 14 different angles, it is a joke. HELPPPPPPPPPPPPPPPPPPPPPPPPPPPPPPPPP!!!!!! I can't take it anymore. What is your take????

—W.W. Willy

If that's your real name, your parents are heroes to me.

Wanna speed it up? Have everybody punch in when they get to the first tee like they were going to work on an assembly line. Then charge them in accordance with how long they were on the course. Set a par for time, say 3 hours, 40 minutes. Anything less, you get 20 percent of the green fee back; anything more, you get charged by the minute.

34

Season's Bleatings

Golf Magazine, *10565493, January 2005, Vol. 47, Issue 1*

It's upon me again, the most depressing day of the year. Christmas Day pips my birthday for that honor because I've now reached that stage in life where I can choose at least one of my own birthday presents, which means I'll get one thing I actually want, rather than a bunch of boring crap I need. Like the Bowflex Ultra that She Who Must Be Obeyed gave me last year. It took me several months to get her to send it back, and that was only after she realized I would never attain the necessary strength to put it together.

My favorite gifts are from my daughter, Erin, who still makes small things for her dad with her very own beautiful, podgy little hands. (Though I've got to be honest and say I'd take a really nice 20-gauge, too.) So this year, dear readers, in the spirit of Christmas, I thought I'd make something just for you with my own podgy hands. I hope that at least some of you like it, and that those who don't can cope with your obvious personality disorders.

'TIS THE SILLY SEASON

If I were the fairy on top of the tree,
Despite all the pine needles up my hy-nee
(Granted, we're off to a fairly poor start
But so far, so good—I've not mentioned a fart)
To Tiger I'd give Oregon (like he'd give two farts;
He now owns Bermuda, St. Kitts and St. Bart's).
For Vijay and Teddy, who own IMG
(Which pisses off Tiger and terrifies me),
A mobile, inflatable, suede practice tee,
And to show how I lurrve them, nude photos of me.
A green jacket for Ernie, for his frustrating year,
With pockets to hold at least 17 beers.
A hunting dog's collar is what Phil is getting.
So Amy can shock him and say, "Down boy, no betting!"
For John Daly, another Open at St. Andy's. What a plus!
He could buy himself spinners for the wheels on his bus.
For Jim Nantz, who stays calm when we're all in a lather,
With a wave of my wand he'd be in for Dan Rather.
Bill Macatee, best-looking man in TV,
Gets hair dye to last him till he's 83.
For Lundquist and Enberg, who've been on the air
Since Ali was Christian and Bradshaw had hair,
I'd give two pairs of knees and two matching bathchairs.
Lanny Wadkins? I'd give him the sense just to quit.
How long can he keep playing that kind of s——t?
For Oosty a chest wig, flared pants and some flowers;
Then he can pass for a big Austin Powers.
For McCord (what a princess, he's so hard to buy for),
Rubber spatulas, strange pants . . . and slingbacks to
*   die for.*
Two things he must have, and the first is a pup,
The second? The good sense to shut the hell up.
Bobby Clampett? Not golf balls; some marbles instead,
Or a curative blow to the back of his head.

Peter Kostis, my friend who knows all 'bout my job,
Gets a whole day at work with no shouts of "Hey, Bob!"
Tim Finchem's a tough one, and I don't know why,
But I think that I'd give him a South Park necktie,
So the next time the pros whined, he'd stand up and cry,
"Zip it, you grassholes—RESPECT MY AUTHORI-TIE!"
"But what of this fat, bearded Feher-y," you're thinking,
"With the tree up his arse and his lights all a-blinking?"
No, no, my dear readers, don't worry 'bout me.
The truth is that I'd do this back page for free.
It's the stiffs at Golf Mag *who are now looking solemn.*
Merry Christmas to all—I got paid for this column!

35.

Feherty's Mailbag

Online—Published: January 14, 2005

I have never read your column. However, my husband does refer to me as "she who must be obeyed," so I am enamored by your wisdom. I have a question. Why is it that my husband watches a golf tournament, videotapes the same golf tournament, watches TV highlights of that golf tournament later that evening and then reads about that same golf tournament in the newspaper the next day? This is a consistent pattern of behavior that happens not only for the majors, but most golf tournaments. Does this make any sense? Did he not "get" it the first time? Why spend time watching highlights about something you already saw? Why read about something you saw and also videotaped so you could see it again? Is there something wrong with my husband? Should I have his brain comprehension tested by a professional? If you have any insight into this behavior I'd be forever grateful.

—Respectfully,
"She who must be obeyed #2," La Jolla, California

Well diagnosed, my good woman! And thank you for not reading. You are a paragon of perception in a veritable sea of imbeciles. What has happened here is that your erstwhile mate has supplanted sex with golf. My guess is he is around 46 years old. This is the age when men find their primal urges declining for reasons they don't really understand. As their desire wanes, they replace it with complicated substitutes that require vast amounts of close study. The reason golf is so attractive at this stage is it may be the only sport left in which they can actually compete with any sense of accomplishment, unlike say, tantric sex. That's because golf is not really a sport and just about any dolt who can fall down a flight of steps drunk can achieve some semblance of expertise.

My advice to you is to rekindle his basic instincts in his once thriving libido. Get a hold of some steaming hot lingerie, set up a video camera, film the dastardly act then write up a report detailing his performance (this part may require some clever editing). Then in the morning before he gets up, no pun intended, have it ready for him to read at the breakfast table. Then set up the video to play when he turns on The Golf Channel when he gets home at night. I predict that in no time at all, our boy'll be bursting through the door, ravishing you with astonishing regularity. Oh, he'll still watch all that golf too, but I suspect at that point, you'll be grateful for the break.

With the NHL strike still unresolved, I wonder, what would aggravate PGA Tour golfers enough to go on strike? Who would cross the picket line?

—Kim Geikie, New Brunswick, Canada

Not to put too fine a point on it, because the result's the same, but it's a lockout, not a strike. Tour players could withhold their labor for any number of reasons. The ones that come to mind are: the free food at the country club they are playing that week was not as hot as it should have been; an equipment manufacturer tried to invoice them for a club, a pair of shoes, a glove, a shirt, rain gear, a bag, pants, a belt, a visor, or a Rolex;

their courtesy car didn't have a GPS system on it and/or the gas tank wasn't completely full, the tournament group refused their request for 400 clubhouse badges, preferred parking and skybox access for their manager's or their caddie's first wife.

The second question should be, who would be on the picket line?

It dropped into the low 30s today on Hilton Head Island . . . very unusual. I have several friends who REFUSE to play golf anytime it is not 70 and sunny. I say strap on the bag, pull on the gloves, and get out there. What is your limit for playing in cold weather?
—D. Moore, Hilton Head Island, South Carolina

Dinty: (I assume that's your name)
    Half a bottle of Bushmills.

My father and I and some of our degenerate golf buddies are planning a trip to Scotland next summer (St. Andrews, Prestwick, Troon, Turnberry, etc.). My father said that while he was still vertical it might be a good idea to get in a few rounds (golf, not Guinness, David) in Ireland while we are in that part of the world. I might be able to get two or three days of golf in prior to Scotland. Any suggestions? I was thinking about Old Head, but it seems that most of the other great golf courses I'd want to play are on the West Coast. Or I could just go to Dublin and work my way from pub to pub trying to discern who has the freshest Guinness. Please let me know your recommendations.
—T. O'Connor Johnson, Richmond, Virginia

If you've only got two or three days stick to the Dublin area. Old Head's down in Kinsale and it's the only course of any repute in the area. Actually the golf course itself isn't great, but the vistas are stunning. And you know what they say: Old Head is better than no head. Play Royal Dublin, County Louth and

Portmarnock in the Dublin area. The beauty of this plan is the reduced travel time, which allows for more consumption of the finest adult beverages in the world.

Recently, pgatour.com did a matchup of well-known golfers who looked like well-known celebrities . . . Phil Mickelson—Hugh Grant, etc. I was wondering who you thought you looked like (with goatee). My first thoughts included that Katsumoto guy from "Last Samurai" (Ken Wantanabe) or the other end of Mr. Ed. Since you never answer my emails, I'll assume, in advance, I'm being insulted.

—Bob-Rob, Algonquin, Illinois

Bob-Rob—do you make your friends call you that?

I would never insult you in advance. I prefer to insult you in real time you steaming pile of French pig waste. How's that?

By the way, I happen to be a dead ringer for Brad Pitt. My friends tell me this all the time.

36

Feherty's Mailbag

Online—Published: January 26, 2005

I have a daily calendar of "Amazing But True Golf Facts" on my desk at work. Interestingly enough, the entry for 11/25/04 (Thanksgiving) reads as follows: "The Turkish Tourism Office touts 'the cradle of civilization's exotic luxury golf' being offered at affordable prices. One of the courses is a David Feherty design and is set within view of biblical landmarks, ancient ruins, and historic shrines. Festival activities range from yachting to 'camel wrestling.' " After reading this tidbit, two questions came to mind:

1. Have you designed any courses here in the United States that may be a bit more accessible for us average folk?
2. How did you fare at camel wrestling?

I enjoy your work very much, both in broadcasting and in print. Thanks for the lighter side of golf.

—Mike Welch, Bradford, Pennsylvania

1. After seeing the designs I built over there, no American course would let me design their ladies' locker room let alone their precious golf courses. If

you want to play one of my gems, which the Turkish liken to the work of Alistair MacKenzie, you'll have to take a camel to where ever the hell those biblical landmarks and ancient ruins are. Actually, the whole back nine is now officially an ancient ruin.

2. Camels do some things really well but they can be annoying to wrestle. First of all, they spit a lot. Then they tend to view their opponent as an object of which they feel compelled to gain carnal knowledge, all of which is very disconcerting. Once they've covered you in expectorant, they get a little frisky. To answer your question, I lost the match but won a friend for life. He still writes me during Ramadan.

I just finished reading your thoroughly enjoyable tome about the history of the Ryder Cup. The book was not only educational and entertaining, it added muscle tone each time I carried it from the coffee table to the bathroom. I did notice that counting the book's front and back coverleafs, as well as spine, your name appears no fewer than eight times. Is this what they mean by subliminal advertising? Keep up the great work.

—Mark L., Houston, Texas

Nothing subliminal about it. It's as in your face as we could make it. I wanted to insert one of those pop-up cardboard cutouts of me that jump out when you open the book or at the least, offer a pullout, life-size foam board likeness of me, but they said the damn thing weighed enough as it was.

Who's this "Fat Person" to whom you dedicated your Ryder Cup book?

—J. Bowen

His name is Jimmy McGovern, and I love the fat bastard even though I've never met him. I offered to dedicate the book to anyone who would pony up $50,000 for the privilege and this bozo bit. I couldn't believe somebody would be that stupid, but I jumped all over the dough. By the way J., in case you're interested, I've a new book coming out sometime this spring. I have a few prime positions available. Let me know.

Where do you hide your single malt while "walking the course" commenting on TV? You have so much gear on you look like the PGA marching band.

—Bobby K., New York City

The earpiece I wear is actually a flask. I am able to suck the nectar through the mouthpiece. It's beautiful. If you think I look ridiculous, you should see Kostis when he puts his gear on naked, which he usually does in his room while he waits for the room service guy to get there. Then he doesn't have to tip.

Some of our favorite golf celebrities post their schedules for the new year around this time, and I was wondering if you would/could post yours. Just wondering if your work/speaking/charity schedule will be bringing you to the greater Toronto area in 2005. All the best to you and yours for a happy, healthy, holiday season! BTW, any resolutions for the new year?

—Rebecca Brydges

Only one resolution: Try to stay the hell out of the Toronto area in 2005! That way I'll probably only be there about a dozen times. Most of the gigs I do are booked by my useless and unbelievably obtuse agent, Barnaby Turdlington. I don't know where I'll be tomorrow, let alone 6 months from now. Besides, my shtick is a little rough for the distaff side of the house. But you're welcome to come if I'm in town provided you pay the freight for the charitable cause. As for now I don't have a web site with my schedule. Perhaps I should consider it.

37.

The Cider Cup Fool

Golf Magazine, *10565493*, *February 2005*, *Vol. 47, Issue 2*

I'd never been on an organized golf holiday until a few years ago, when I conceived the Cider Cup, contested in England between idiot friends of mine from both sides of the Atlantic. After conception, I ran from responsibility. Mitch, my great pal and ex-agent, took care of the arrangements, from travel to lodging to tee times, and it went smooth as Nantz's bottom. But for the second go-round, I wanted the boys to see my native Northern Ireland, so heroically I took the organizing upon myself. It was just 20 or so morons drinking and golfing—how hard could it be?

You know those nauseating golf novels in which the mystic game serves as a bilious backdrop for one man's journey of self-discovery, leading to the hurlingly obvious reaffirmation of that which he already knew to be true? This is the short version. Yes, friends, by taking the reins, I confirmed that the biggest moron I know is still me.

I booked 10 rooms at the five-star Culloden Hotel. No problem there—until a snotty staffer called a few days before the Cup to demand more info, else I'd have to cough up for any no-shows. I was in the market for a little flexibility—six of these pillocks were going to arrive on a Gulfstream G4 when-ever they damn well pleased—so after getting the Heisman, I politely lost my reason and told them to insert the rooms where the sun doesn't shine, which in Ulster gave them plenty of options. I called the friendly Royal Hotel, which is within blundering distance of Fealty's, the best pub in Bangor, my hometown. . . . Brilliant!

OK, so the lads weren't thrilled with the rooms, or that I'd showed up at the wrong airport to fetch them, but never mind the minor details. Golf beckoned, and we tore up a lovely wee course called the Ava at Clandeboye. Then we all got bullet-proof at Fealty's, the lads stumbled back to the Royal and I took a bracing walk home around the seafront to Mom and Dad's house, pausing to get up off the ground only twice. Things were going swimmingly.

The next morning, I arrived at the hotel with a 24-seat bus and a pickled tongue. Searching for bodies in last night's wreckage, I came up four short. A broken steam pipe had turned several rooms into a Turkish bath, and the G4 swine had escaped to the Culloden!

So, the pleb-filled bus set off to Royal Portrush, but halfway there, the driver, overcome by cigar smoke, Guinness farts and Bushmills belching, took a wrong turn and went to Ballymena. Somehow, this was my fault. Anyway, the G4s took a cab there, no one broke 100 in 50-mph squalls and we fled back to the Royal, where I almost soiled myself when I realized I hadn't paid the greens fees!

A cell phone and a credit card doused that fire, but my operational hell got even warmer when the G4s were forced to move from the Culloden to the Belfast Hilton and my pal Hollywood Anderson finally arrived, finagling a room at (where else?) the Culloden. Hollywood was wearing a laven-der cashmere sweater with matching lavender FootJoys and a positively dangerous pair of slacks that I thought were peppermint but he dubbed "sea foam." (Sea foam is a brown scum where I come from.) Liberace was hitting the links.

But I digress. We played Kirkistown Castle the next day—another 17-vehicle, three-hotels-in-different-towns daytime nightmare. The official tour guide was catching heavy flak. Tomorrow was the final day, at the incomparable Royal County Down, and the nicest name I'd been called all week was "dork-wad." I beseeched Allah, Jehovah, Buddha and Dr. Phil: Decent weather please, or maybe an invisibility cloak.

The next morning, at the only moment I took my bulging eyeballs off the road, the damn bus took another wrong turn. The drive to RCD is about 45 minutes—we took twice that. But while I was cursing Dr. Phil, it happened: As we rolled into Newcastle, County Down, the sun rent a hole in the clouds over the Mountains of Mourne and spread gold over the purple dome of Slieve Donard and on down the hill through the forest and over the town and slowly began to light up the Irish Sea. Mouths hung open as we trundled into the parking lot. Then the wind died, and the day turned into a fairy tale. Suddenly, the tour guide was a hero.

But I am never, ever doing it again.

38

Feherty's Mailbag

Online—Published: February 15, 2005

Golf has changed tremendously here in our country. We hosted the 1999 World Cup won by Tiger Woods and Mark O'Meara, and the Carlsberg Malaysian Open is now a feature on the European Tour. Do you see the possibility of Malaysia (an Asian country) hosting the Ryder Cup in future? Perhaps the Yanks may perform better without the pressure of their home crowds.

—Joe Carlos, Malaysia

In answer to your question, no. The Ryder Cup will always be contested in the U.S. or Europe. It's kind of an old-fashioned tradition. Think of moving the Iditarod dog race to Iraq, and you kind of get the idea.

On a more serious reflection on the Ryder Cup results I would argue that the Official World Golf Ranking ought to be revised so that European Tour tournaments should receive higher points. Would you argue against, or would you be in the forefront of this truly worthy cause?

—Ren Andersson, Veberd, Sweden

I don't know how the World Rankings work, and I don't want to, in case someone asks me a question about it. I think they probably get the top half dozen or so in vaguely the right order at least some of the time, maybe. Or not, who knows? I hope this clears it up for you.

Sitting here in the backwater of Worcestershire, I am a little behind the times, having a computer which gives me yesterday's news, weather and events. So to ensure that I get your reply at approximately the right time would you join me in congratulating the victorious 2006 European Ryder Cup team. This result is as big a shock to myself as it is to my regular American four-ball partner who cannot understand how a team of underdogs without a major between them have done it again!

—Kaitiea

First of all, don't be so hard on Worcestershire. I love that stuff on my steak, although I have to admit I've never mixed it with backwater, whatever the hell that is. Second, get a new computer. They're not so expensive these days, you know. And lastly, why are you playing with an American with four balls? Are you nuts? (Little joke there.) Look, get rid of this guy, he's no good for you. I'm thinking of starting an advice to the lovelorn column for Cosmopolitan soon. What do you think?

I love your work in the booth as well as what you write for GOLF Magazine. My question is why don't you write a book about the old Euro Tour. The stories you have told in your column are classic and I would really like to hear more. By the way, I personally would like to see a head-to-head match with you and McCord.

—J.T.

The people involved in a book about the European Tour are still alive and I don't think I could survive the lawsuits that would result. I don't play golf with McCord. Hell, I don't play golf with anybody, but absolutely not with that cross-dressing bedwetter.

There are a blue million golf resorts that are doing all these package deals. Where do you recommend an 80–90+ shooter to go for a golf vacation?

—Big Bertha Bill

Deer Valley, Utah. During ski season.

39

Feherty's Mailbag

Online—Published: February 25, 2005

Great stuff at the Tommy Bahama Challenge! I'm curious, what flavor was the pie you took in the face? It looked like a plate of Edge Gel or Gillette Sensitive Skin Moisturizing Foam.

—David Castle, Garland, Texas

I'm pretty sure it was a Bushmills frappe. The problem with it was the plate it was on. If you were going to hit someone in the kisser with a pie, wouldn't you want it on a paper or a foil plate? Not McCord. The moron went ceramic, and almost broke my nose, which wasn't in the best of shape to start with.

When are you going to lose that goatee on your face? You look like a cross between Lucifer and Shecky Greene.

—Chris D., Rochester, N.Y.

P.S. Love your books.

Without it I look like a cross between the Pillsbury Dough Boy and John Lovett.

Besides, I think it makes me look like D'Artagnon.

P.S. I love your money.

I have just finished reading one of your recent mailbags, and I wanted to say I think you're MUCH more handsome than Brad Pitt. Your face reflects character, humor and joie de vivre. (Did I spell that correctly?)
—Theresa Turner

Thank you Theresa.

Yes I am, yes you did, and for God's sake get into therapy.

Caught you at the AT&T, and great job as usual. You were excellent at pretending to care what CBS celebs had to say about the tournament. I was also stunned by your newly thinned physique. Where did you get the tapeworm? Do you have any diet advice for those of us still laboring under our excessive girth? Have you forsworn food and gone to an all-liquid (read Bushmills) diet?
—Kellan, Chicago

I increased my output, decreased my input, sped up my throughput, ignored any feedback and ate more fish than a harbor seal.

Dammit, I knew someone would ask me this. Okay, I quit drinking. Kind of had to really, what with it taking me having to get started on a second bottle of Bushmills just to get a buzz. I quit for the same reason I quit golf—because I was so good at it, it no longer felt like a challenge. I now have the body of a 25-year-old and the face of a hockey goalie, although I did have my annual physical last week and my liver function came back normal. I'm thinking of sending it to Cooperstown.

What is happening to David Duval? I remember when he was battling Tiger for the top spot in the World Ranking. I couldn't believe the scores he put up at the Bob Hope. Is he battling an injury?

—Lance

I wish I knew and could wave a wand and fix it for him. It started with some physical problems and now seems to have evolved into difficulties between the ears. Whatever it is, I really hope he works it out and gets his freak back on. This game is just too weird.

40

Charity Case

Golf Magazine, *10565493, March 2005, Vol. 47, Issue 3*

By definition, a charity pro-am is a six-hour ordeal on the golf course followed by a deep-fried nightmare of heavy hors d'oeuvres and a cocktail party designed to get the punters hammered so that they sniffle at the heart-rending video of crippled Timmy and reach for their wallets when the minor celebrity emcee auctions off assorted signed crap they'll eventually give as Christmas presents to people they don't like. But like I tell people when I'm the crap auctioning minor celebrity emcee, the best way to weasel out of next year's event is just donate the crap back when they're asked to play. That way, they don't have to invent a pathetic excuse like, "I'd love to play, but my wife is recovering from prostate surgery." If the cocktails are huge enough, people don't notice that the wine tastes like lighter fluid and dinner is a lump of gray meat, accompanied by a strangely familiar slab of salmon, whose fishiness is mingling with the ubiquitous divot of burnt yardbird, along with a trio of violently undercooked tubers, all topped off with an anvil-like wedge of serious injury by chocolate.

I know, I know, I know: These are wonderful events run by magnificent people in the name of worthy causes that go to the very fabric of our great game. But for years, I've dreamed of running a pro-am event that's throbbingly different. All I needed was the right running mate—you know, someone who shared my outlook and moral values.

Then George came along. George Lopez, that is. I've been a fan of his for a long time, ever since Robert Gamez lent me a CD of one of his early standup routines, called *Alien Nation*. George challenges his fellow Latinos to see the ridiculous side of their culture, to stand up and be counted, and think of themselves as valuable members of society. There's even a similarity between salsa and Poteen. Both are homemade and put into old bottles. As George says, "You don't have to tear off the old label—it jumps off by itself."

The Lopez-Feherty Foundation for the Prevention of Teen Pregnancy, Gang Violence and Stupid Names for Mexican Fast Food Celebrity Pro-Am* will be different. There will be a 30-second limit on speeches, a one-minute limit on the crippled Timmy video, no boring auction (because it will be horrifyingly expensive to enter), no posed photographs and the golf will be limited to 12 teams of one celeb, one pro and two amateurs. As I write, I haven't asked anyone to play, but the event is very real, and here's my dream list. (If any of the following are unfortunate enough to be reading this and would like to play at the Vaquero club outside Dallas on the 16th of May, please contact me via the magazine or at tourtalent.com. Also, any stupidly rich amateurs who are willing to cough up $20,000 for a team of two plus 10 tickets to hear George that night can also give me a shout.** I will call you back personally—and talk dirty, if you like.)

---

* We're still finalizing the name. But proceeds will go to Texas Scottish Rite Hospital for Children in Dallas and SpiritHorse Therapeutic Riding Center in Corinth, Texas, which improves the lives of disabled, abused and at-risk kids by interaction with horses.
** Anyone who enjoys taking more than three hours and 45 minutes to play 18 holes need not apply, no matter how stupidly rich they are.

Let's see . . . Willie Nelson, Jack Nicklaus, Wayne Gretzky, Lee Trevino, Ray Romano, Kevin James, Cameron Diaz, Dr. Phil, Tiger Woods, Ernie Els, Bobby Orr, Todd Hamilton, Gary McCord, Phil Mickelson, The Donald, Samuel L. Jackson, Lorena Ochoa, Annika Sorenstam, Arnold Palmer, Keith Richards, Bill Murray and anyone else George can bribe.

Just like the Irish did 150 years ago, Latinos are building this country. When a Mick dropped dead of yellow fever while draining the swamps in New Orleans, another one popped up to take his place at eight cents an hour. We were worth less than slaves and portrayed as monkeys in the newspapers.

These days many immigrant workers are treated pretty much the same, and just like the Irish, often their families have sold everything to give one child a chance of a better life in a new world. The key to that better life lies in education. Latinos need poets and writers, musicians and scientists, business people and leaders, and comedians like George Lopez, who teaches all of us the most important lessons of all—never take yourself too seriously, and don't be bitter, be better.

41.

Feherty's Mailbag

Online—Published: March 11, 2005

If you could come out of retirement and win one major, which one would it be?

—Dave Hodgson, Vancouver

This isn't some kind of "deal with the devil scam," is it? Like if you let me win the major of my choice, will I have to spend an eternity scrubbing skid marks out of McCord's boxers? What's your real name, Dave, Mephistopheles? Beelzebub? I'm not falling for that old ruse, you bastard. Besides, if I came out of retirement, I wouldn't settle for less than the Automotive Grand Slam: the Buick Open, the Bob Hope Chrysler Classic, the Nissan Open, and the Ford Championship at Doral. I need cars, dammit, not claret jugs.

This is not a golf question as much as a golfer question. Recently someone in my family went to one of those genealogy websites and found out we were descended from a long line of Scottish lunatics, and that we are distantly related to Monty. My question is, in your opinion, what are the chances of him finding out where I live and asking for money?

—Sincerely worried, T. Montgomery

Hey, after the wife from hell got through with him he was lucky he still had most of his internal organs. But I'm predicting he'll win a major this year and he won't need your money, not that there's much chance you would give him any, you Scottish tightwad.

OK, Feherty, fess up. You stole the phrase "she who must be obeyed" from the BBC series "Rumpole of the Bailey" starring Leo McKern and written by John Mortimer!! I expect nothing less than a full confession on national TV. Then maybe I'll buy your books.

—Larry Nanook, Lapeer, Michigan

Nanook of the North:

I'll confess as soon as John Mortimer admits *he* stole it from the leader of a matriarchal tribe in Bophutaswana, Africa. A real fence doesn't steal stuff; he redistributes it with prejudice. That's what Mozart did with Vivaldi anyway.

When are you going to pass around the single malt so your sidekicks will stop calling you FERRETY as in . . . and on the course DAVID FERRETY . . . or is there a FERRET involved somewhere???

—Bob Koz, FDNY (the hot corner), New York City

It's so close, it's hard to call. Hell in New York, your buddies probably pronounce your name "KAZ", and somebody needs to explain Brett "Favre" to me, like I could give a fart. FEE-HERTY doesn't roll off the American tongue all that easily, and as long as they get it right on the paycheck, they can call me whatever they want, as long as it's after 10 a.m. And it's still a

damn sight better than what they called me back home. My
father couldn't even agree with my uncle Jack on how to pronounce it.

To say I am disappointed would be an understatement. I placed an
order on amazon.com for your book "A Beastly Turn of Events." I must
have dropped the ball last year because I don't remember this coming
out. When I first read "A Nasty Bit of Rough," the woman sitting next
to me on my flight must have thought I was a raving lunatic, especially
after I almost threw up from laughing so hard while she was sleeping.
But enough of that. I wanted to read the new book. Is it released?
Thanks.

—Chris

Ah yes, "A Beastly Turn of Events." Thank you for bringing it
up, you bridge troll. I've missed that deadline by about three
years, a fact of which my publisher occasionally reminds me.
But thanks for trying to buy it. I do have a new compilation
titled, "An idiot for all seasons," which will be out in a month
or so. Hopefully you'll blow chunks again.

42.

Feherty's Mailbag

Online—Published: March 25, 2005

I thoroughly enjoy your on-course coverage, and your segment on TGC's Playing Lessons with the Pros at Whistling Straits is one of my favorites. My question: what do you have to do to get the club selection from the caddies during your telecasts? Thanks for making golf coverage fun.

—Gary M.

I give them legal advice. I help them with their divorces (like how to *avoid* custody), and a lot of trumped-up porn stuff. I also help them with medical issues such as gerbil problems, those pesky four-hour Woodrows after washing down 12 Cialis tablets with a six-pack and four doobies, and how to find a Doc to help fill out those workman's comp forms in every state.

Okay, it's hand signals.

I've been reading GOLF MAGAZINE for a few years now and it never fails. Each time I finish the last page I say to myself, "gee, I could use more of that." That's when I noticed the web address at the bottom of the page (being from Canada and perhaps somewhat slow due to low temperatures). I ran to my "PUTER" and I began to surf. I read all that you had to offer in one sitting and as soon as the temp. rises above −20 degrees, I'm off to the mall to get your book. My question: Why, when I'm playing "Tiger Woods 2005" do you tell me that the break to the cup is "starboard" when in fact it's to the left? Hmmm, perhaps I should stop listening to you. Keep up the great work.

— David "Swingcat" Pastuck, Winnipeg, Manitoba, Canada

Because I only said "port" when I wanted a glass of it. And I know starboard is to the RIGHT, you half-wit. So that means someone at EA doesn't. I can't complain, though. We're about to do 2006 and we'll almost certainly muck something up for you in that one.

I am in the military, stationed in Turkey. I won the last two events at National . . . nice course. I'm originally from Dallas and miss Texas terribly. Once I retire I want to be around the game—caddie, course management, whatever. How does one position himself to caddie for a living? I suspect it's an inside connection of some sort. Just want your thoughts. Thanks.

— T-Bone
p.s. Village Idiot is a masterpiece!!!

Boner:

I guess Turkey's better than Iraq, huh? You're the only person I've ever heard from who has played one of the two courses I had a hand in building. I actually hand-dug one of those bunkers in front of eight locals leaning on seven shovels. Hey, I'm Irish, I can't help myself if there's a spare shovel lying around. As far as caddying for a living, you'll have to acquire a taste for strong drink, but chances are if you're in the Air Force stationed in Turkey, you're more than likely well on your way there. Drugs, gambling, more than one divorce and a three-strike felony record are also prerequisites, but that's only if you want to get to the top of your profession.

Hi David, you're doing a fine job. Enjoy your wit immensely. I have a cultural question about the Irish. I saw "The Boondock Saints" movie the other day and a few days later a documentary on James Joyce; are all Irish supposed to be nuts?

—Serge, Quebec, Canada

And this from a guy in a province that wants to secede from Canada so they can sit around and eat frog's legs and snails. Best hockey players in the world though. I wish they were playing.

Look, any movie with Willem Dafoe and Billy Connolly can't be all bad, and what can I say about James Joyce that wouldn't take a fortnight to finish? Oscar Wilde was fairly normal . . . rampantly gay or not. You're picking on some of my favorite crazies here. I love these guys.

Did you know my dad, Norman Sutton, a fixture on the old British PGA circuit?
    Regards and keep up the good work.
—Ken Sutton, Cobourg, Ontario, Canada

I did know old Norman. What a guy. Still owes me 25 quid from a bet we made that I couldn't empty out a pub in Northamptonshire with one fart. Give him my regards and tell him I'm still looking for the money.

43.

Better Golfing Through Chemistry

Golf Magazine, 10565493, April 2005, Vol. 47, Issue 4

I was at my psychiatrist the other day for the old yearly mental, and we got to talking about drugs and sport. It's a hot topic, what with Barry Bonds admitting that he "unknowingly" pumped up his biceps and probably shrunk his nads with 'roids, and all the jawing about whether his records and others' should have an asterisk.* Maybe Mickey Mantle's records should have one, too, because he was almost certainly hammered when he set them. Sprinters have obvious anabolics in their spandex, cyclists swap blood (now that's just weird), snowboarders inhale laughing gas, and golfers . . . What's out there for us to straighten it up and get it to the hole? (Rim shot, please.) I highly doubt any Tour pros are doing 'roids. But if, say, Charles Howell III were to dabble, it would be obvious—he'd gain a whopping four ounces, and someone like Corey Pavin could surprise himself and finally tear a piece of toast in half with his bare hands.

So, having been a firm believer in better living through

---

* The author advises strongly against the taking of any drug that doesn't make you feel better.

chemistry since the '70s (or maybe it was the '80s—details are sketchy), I thought I'd make a suitable guinea pig. I have been prescribed pretty much every drug for pain ever made, and I always keep a few around in case of emergency, like a blister on my typing finger. Golf is unquestionably painful, so I thought I'd start with codeine, which is strictly entry-level when it comes to making you feel different.

I took a bunch and fell asleep in the cart waiting for four morons to clear the third green. Strike that one off.

The next day, I tried hydrocodone, which showed promise—I played splendidly. But then at the turn it took me 30 minutes to take a leak. The guy in the next stall thought I was peeing a distress signal in Morse code. I couldn't remember for the life of me what I scored on the sixth, which is kind of important. Nix that one, too.

I had one Percodan left over from knee surgery, and took it the following morning. This one would have worked if I could've figured a way to back out of my driveway without cracking myself up. I never made it off my property but had a splendid day nonetheless.

Psychiatrists will tell you that prescribing medication for people who just aren't right is a trial-and-error affair. One of my early errors was Adderall, a drug usually prescribed for attention-deficit disorder (called "stupidity" when I went to school). Anyway, I had some lying around so I popped a couple and hit the links. I struck the ball very well but took 74 putts and sweated like a fat girl at her sister's wedding. Also, the round lasted only 47 minutes.

Clearly, we needed something less speedy, so next up was Toprol, which I already take for stratospheric blood pressure. Beta-blockers were highly touted back when I was competing, said to lower the heart rate and reduce skeletal trembling. It did bugger-all for me—I still kept spazzing out over 18-inchers, and we were only playing for a 10-spot.

I wondered about the existing research on this kind of selfdiagnosticism, which isn't even a word, but the Adderall had worn off, so I lost interest. The bottom line: There's no drug that can help anyone play better golf. Believe me, if I'd discovered one, you wouldn't be reading this crap—I'd have mules out selling dime bags in country club parking lots. If there were a substance that took shots off handicaps, I'd look like Pablo Escobar.

You don't have to be strong to play golf, or particularly aggressive, or be emotional and have tiny little genitals. But you do have to be awake, even just to talk about golf, which brings me to my final cautionary tale. A few years ago, before a telecast from Castle Pines, I was rummaging through my pill bottle for a Lipitor, to make sure my cholesterol didn't kill me halfway up the 17th. I swallowed it and headed to work. At least I thought it was Lipitor—it was actually Ambien, a similar-looking pill that I call the velvet sledgehammer.

I did the broadcast from a coma on the flatbed of a cart, and to this day McCord claims it was my finest work. But don't try it at home; remember, I'm an athlete.

44

Feherty's Mailbag

Online—Published: April 13, 2005

As an avid sod-thrower, ditch-digger and abuser of the fairway (and rough, tee box and anything else that happens to get in the way of a wickedly swung 5-iron), I have thoroughly enjoyed your columns and books. Of course, the very idea that you are being paid disgusting amounts of money to write about, not even play, a game makes me insane with jealousy, but I digress.

I hail from a horrid patch of useless clay known as "Kansas." We Kansans are not completely bereft of all that is golf, but I do weary of discerning rules interpretations for tumbleweeds and prairie dog holes. Have you ever played (and I use that term loosely) golf in Kansas? While we don't have the driving rain, cold, hills and drunk locals careening about the course—no, wait . . . scratch that last bit—that you had in Ireland, we can easily match the wind. If you have had the debatable pleasure of bouncing a lofted wedge off a rock-hard prairie green to the next fairway, where did you play?

Keep up the good work. You continue to bring smiles and even, dare I say it, a chuckle now and again.

—Brian Buselt, Wichita, Kansas

I don't for the life of me understand why all of you idiots like me. Doesn't anyone know how to complain any more? It's not as if I'm not a total a-hole either. If you've bothered your arse to read any of this crap, you'll notice that I'm insulting, irritable, illiterate, and ill. You're right about one thing though; the amounts of money I'm paid are disgusting. I need more and I need it more often.

Never played in Kansas. The Wizard of Oz scared the hell out of me; still does. I have either played with on the European Tour, worked with at CBS Golf or met on airplanes, pretty much everybody in that movie. The only one I ever thought made any sense was Toto. No, no my friend, if I go anywhere near Kansas, I will be carrying a gun and looking for John Ringneck (for my idiot editor, that's a pheasant rooster).

I have played in a golf league for a couple of years. I have a buddy who I always bet with. Well, because I am an incredible talent, I generally pummel him. Now he doesn't want to bet me anymore. As someone who used to get pummeled regularly on tour, could you recommend some new bets so that I could continue to pummel him.

—S. Allison

Either he's an idiot or your "incredible talent" is sandbagging him, which still makes him an idiot. What kind of cad takes delight in pounding the handicapped? Why not try boxing the blind, tossing the midget, or bowling against shut-ins? Or, you could try losing a couple of times and hold yourself for a price as they say in horse racing.

I've only been playing golf for a couple of years, and I'm trying to play the right way. But my golf buddies seem to play a different type of

game. Should there be a set number of mulligans during an 18-hole round? I say one per six pack, per player. What's your opinion?
— Bill Nellums, Louisville, Kentucky

I knew a lot of guys in Ireland named Mulligan but we never had to set any limits on how many we played with. What happens if you can't find *anybody* named Mulligan that week? Do you still play? Oh, hang on, I get it. You're talking about free shots, do-overs and that. I believe in reverse mulligans. In other words, whenever you want a player to take a shot over again, he should have to. Say like if he makes a 40-foot putt for eagle; make him do it again. It's more fun. Hell, any schmuck can follow up a bad shot with a good one. Try two good ones in a row.

You are such a funny man. Love your answers. Here's my question: Since they have vested knighthood on some rock stars (Paul McCartney, Elton John, etc.) is there an English golfer to ever have that title? Sir David Feherty sounds good to me.
— Tesoro D. De Guzman, Jr., Lake Forest, Calif.

I've always fancied the old knighthood thing, but I think the royal family are mostly idiots, so it probably won't happen.

Are you an official big-time personality now or were you always one? First, it was a book and the obvious speaking engagements. With your wit and eloquent tongue, those things are expected. Next, you get what looks to be a nice endorsement with Cobra doing their commercials. Then you are talking to the celebs at Pebble Beach and one of them says he called you to help him with his Belfast accent for an upcoming role. That has "big time" written all over it. Please say you are still just an average Joe. Thanks!
— David Castle, Garland, Texas

Hey, I'd just like to have an average Dick.

45.

The Gerbil from Hell

Golf Magazine, *10565493*, *May 2005*, *Vol. 47, Issue 5*

I was always pervertedly fond of the way Corey Pavin played, even though losing to the Chaplin-esque chopper is like getting your ass kicked by a grinning garden gnome. He was listed at 150 pounds, but I never believed it. In his heyday he looked as if breaking wind on his downswing might cause him to fly out of bounds. Occasionally his caddie would absentmindedly try to put a headcover on him and stuff him into his own bag.

But he could certainly get it around a golf course with that ghastly-looking, low, skanky cut of his, which was especially disagreeable after you'd watched it a few times and realized he was actually trying to do it (by which time you were about three shots behind him). He could get in your face, too, like he did in the '91 Ryder Cup at Kiawah, charging out from behind the sandhills like Hobbit O'Rommel, pumping his horrible little knotted fists and sending the crowd into orbit. As a member of the European team, I was on the wrong end of that one.

Not so long ago, the game was harder for really tall guys like Weiskopf and Oosterhuis, because a golf club that fitted people their size had the attributes of a tire-iron, and was similarly balanced. But with lighter shafts and heads, the spikes are now on the bigger feet. (That's why there are more good left-handed players these days, too: their equipment no longer sucks.) To trade punches with today's heavyweights, the little guys have to hit the exact center of the clubface pretty much all of the time, and be able to get it up and down from everywhere. You have to admire the wee ones, like Jeff Sluman and Fred Funk, who could share a pair of Ernie Els's Y-fronts, and Pavin, who could hide under his hat; each is living proof that on a good day, a determined flea can still bite the Tour's big dogs. But the guy who takes golf to the next level will probably be a giant, and the small in stature will be left playing uphill and into the tide.

This brings us back to Pavin, who thank God has decided to play on. I say thank God because I find it much safer to talk about the ratbag than compete against him, and for a while there I was sure he was after my job. Following a stint for ABC a couple of years ago, he seemed destined to flounce the fairways with a microphone before long. The little swine was good at it, and the last thing I need is Pavin, the beastly, shaven-headed gerbil from hell, gnawing at my vitals again, or (horror of horrors) Nick Faldo, who is sucking up to ABC with a transparently obvious foreign-accent ploy. How pathetic is that? At least Azinger has the decency to sound American. Even though they're pimping for another network, I hope every one of these devious reprobates suffers an immediate resurgence in his game. Not that I'd want to appear mean-spirited, but if they fired Edward R. Murrow, I have a feeling that they can almost certainly dispense with me.

Anyone smarter than a sack of bad shellfish would notice that my act is getting old. I wouldn't want any of this to go on the record, but I am the single laziest, most irresponsible, ungrateful journalist/announcer I know, and most days I don't smell particularly good either. I had to quit drinking several months ago, and now I'm in a permanently crappy mood, completely unreceptive to any more change. It has become throbbingly obvious that the only way I can continue to get away with this job is to do my best to ensure I'm surrounded by imbeciles like McCord, Clampett and, of course, the staff of *Golf Magazine*. I do have a minor problem with Oosterhuis and the rest of the CBS crew, but I've calculated that the mercury I'm putting in their tea should start to kick in around The Memorial. The fact that Maltbie is on board with USA Network isn't going to hurt either. I can't wait to work with him. He'll make me look both smarter and thinner, although I have lost almost 50 pounds in order to ensure that I appear even more magnificent than usual.

However, I am still experiencing a feeling of general unease. The next thing you know, Faldo will be writing a column full of smarmy wit, fart jokes and self-deprecation. Bugger it! That's the problem with raising the bar. Even the big guys can get underneath it.

46

Kill Your Slice

Golf Magazine, 10565493, May 2005, Vol. 47, Issue 5
By David Feherty, Greg Midland, and Angus Murray

I have a confession: I love being a hooker. Deep down, I bet you'd love to be one, too. I know this because I feel your pain. During my playing career, my ball flight went from a slight fade (when I was at my best) to a low skanker that couldn't resist the right rough (when a microphone became the sexiest thing I'd ever seen). But that's all in the past. Thanks to my instructor, Mike Abbott, I kicked the bad habits that caused those big benders to land somewhere to the right of Rush Limbaugh. By learning how to hook it, I now keep the ball in the fairway more often, and I hit it farther too. Here's how I did it. For once, this is a good time to follow my lead.

Abbott: "Curing a slice means first going to the other extreme: You adjust your grip and posture to quickly hit a big hook. Then you can gradually move to hitting it straight, because you've learned how to rotate your hands and arms to square the clubface."

Feherty: "To a recovering slicer like me, an ugly, screaming duck hook can be as lovely as watching Cameron Diaz bend over to get a ball out of the hole."

Get a grip: Like most slicers, my left hand was too far under the club with the handle set in my palm. This weak grip means the left wrist can't hinge on the backswing. You're forced to lift, which leads to a steep downswing. Sound familiar? Then rotate your left hand more on top of the grip. This sets the club in your fingers and creates more cup in your wrist, so you can hinge and not lift. Hold the club out in front of you and cock it up and down a few times to get the proper feeling.

Change your aim: This is a familiar defense mechanism: The more I sliced, the farther to the left I aimed. And that caused even bigger slices. That's easy enough to fix if you understand how to tilt your upper body away from the target, so your left shoulder is higher than your right. This aligns your shoulders and stance parallel to the target line, instead of 30 yards left. It also helps flatten out your swing—now you can start hitting hooks.

TIP SHEET
1. Strengthen your left-hand grip so the club sits in your fingers.
2. Cup your left wrist to hinge the club up on the backswing.
3. Set your left shoulder higher at address.

Swing it back straight: Fixing my grip and posture made it easier to groove a better takeaway path. When the club reaches parallel to the ground it should extend straight back, with the toe pointing to the sky. Check your takeaway by pausing at this checkpoint. Hold the club steady and then turn your body and feet to face it (below). The club should be oriented in front of you the same way it was at address—straight ahead, bisecting the triangle between your arms.

Abbott: "Slicers rotate their hips open and drag the club too far inside. That's a killer move that destroys the path of your swing."

Feherty: "Mike would hold my hips in place while I swung the club back, which both straightened out my takeaway and got me a little excited."

TIP SHEET
1. Keep your hips quiet, like they're in cement.
2. Pause the takeaway when the shaft reaches parallel to the ground. Make sure the toe of the club points up.
3. Turn your torso and feet to face the club. It should look to you the same way it did at address.

Shift and step: I was worried when Mike said my downswing needed to be more athletic—do pint curls count? But it all boils down to forward momentum: Slicers fall back, the result of a reverse pivot, while better players shift forward. Try the Gary Player walk-through drill: Step forward with your right foot after impact. Translate this feeling into your swing, and you should feel your weight finish over your left leg. This indicates you've released the club and your body, so you can fly your drives past your buddies.

Underneath your backswing: I made this my one and only downswing thought, and you should, too: Swing underneath your backswing. Come into the ball on a flatter path, and you avoid the over-the-top chop, which sucks power out of the swing by making only glancing contact with the ball.

TIP SHEET
1. Do the walk-through to groove a proper forward weight shift.
2. When you swing, be sure to finish over your left foot.
3. Swing flatter on the downswing to come from the inside.

47

Feherty's Mailbag

Online—Published: May 6, 2005

Don't tell me you gave up drinking. That's like saying McCord has given up being a dork. And if you feel like defending him go watch Tin Cup. Anyway, every once in a while our group needs a 4th and most of the time it's a work buddy or somebody's brother-in-law. I know brothers-in-law are supposed to be annoying, but what's a good way to let somebody know their etiquette sucks without looking like a jerk and offending the real friend who brought the flag-dropping-while-I'm-putting-22 handicapper? I really enjoy all that you do . . . with golf.

Hugs and kisses, Case in Denver

Case: (and everyone else who asked about my "Lifestyle Change")

Okay, okay; I know this is hard for you to get your heads around, but I have indeed given up the gargle. She Who Must Be Obeyed pointed out that staggering amounts of Bushmills, my poison of choice, were causing me to, well, stagger. This was a personal, and necessary, decision on my part and I absolutely promise I will not preach, bore to tears, bray about the benefits, share the horror, force anyone to bear witness, or offer testimony. Neither will I proselytize anyone to do the same. Look, we all get a finite amount of alcohol we can consume in one life. By the time I was 32 I had exhausted my allocation and was working on several non-drinking dead people's supply. Enough already. And that's all I'm going to say about that . . . except that it sucks.

As to that annoying prong who occasionally joins your group, I find nose blowing, burping the alphabet, shooting beer out of your nose and, of course, the old standby—projectile farting at the top of his backswing—will usually get the point across. Good luck.

I'm sorry, I thought I just read that you stopped drinking. I must be drunk.

—Dean, Canada

If there's a God in heaven you are.

My father is an avid golfer (avg. 72–74). He has played (and loved) Pebble Beach and St. Andrews. I want to send him on another trip— where would you suggest in the U.S. and abroad? Thank you!

—K.C.

My God. How the hell can he be 72 one day and then 74 the next? Just call him 73 and be done with it, and send the old goat wherever you want as long as it's not near me. I have enough problems with my own father, who thinks he's Camilla Parker-Balls.

Great job in the booth. I don't believe you and McCord don't play golf together. You both sound like pals and I'm sure you two are a hit in the

19th hole. What's your favorite golf course, playing or working? Thank you and much continued success.

—Jeff

Thanks for the kind words. I have been known to feign strokes and heart attacks in order to avoid having to hang around McCord in a bar. I rarely play golf anymore, but my favorite to play is Royal County Down in Northern Ireland. My favorite to work is anyplace that's short and flat, like Colonial. I actually don't particularly like the booth, I prefer to walk, hence the short and flat preference.

Enjoy your on-course and off-course commentary, have done so since I took up golf (about 5 years) when I turned 55. My question is: Why do I see a lot of the pros wearing steel spikes when a great number of courses require SoftSpikes? Thanks for your time.

—Garry Fraser, Canada

How desperately sad that you had to take up such an affectation at your age, you poor, misguided bastard. As for the spikes, the PGA Tour has no requirement with respect to footwear. They considered it once when Doug Ford and Ken Green showed up with their obscene brogans years ago, but alas, took no formal action. The real reason that many of the pros choose to wear nails is that it can get pretty expensive to fall on your ass at the start of your downswing.

I just wanted to tell you how much I enjoy your writing and TV work. I always go to the last page of GOLF MAGAZINE first. When you write about getting older it's always hilarious. Too bad it's true. You always seem to get it right. I spent my 50th birthday in Afghanistan on a deployment with the U.S. Army National Guard. I know, after 32 years,

I'm getting too old for this s—t. Hopefully, this will be my last one. You have a lot of new fans over here because even the guys that don't know anything about real golf love to play Tiger Woods PGA Tour on their computers. I'm always telling them that those guys on there are real announcers on TV. I will be going home soon and I have been buying a lot of new golf equipment on line over here so I can still keep up with the young guys (too bad you can't buy a new body). My question is: How do I explain all this new stuff to my One Who Must Be Obeyed?

—Rod, BAF, Afghanistan

Thank God for men like you, who put their lives on the line to look after pu—ies like me. Don't confuse "She Who Must Be Obeyed" with "She Who Must Never Be Lied To." Tell her you won the stuff in the hundreds of card games you played over there. Get back safe and hopefully soon and don't be going back again at your age, you idiot.

48

Feherty's Mailbag

Online—Published: May 20, 2005

At the aptitude testing foundation at which I work, we test for each client's eye dominance. I can remember once reading Jack Nicklaus write that it may be an advantage for a right-handed golfer to have a dominant left eye, and vice versa for a left-handed golfer. Any truth to this theory?

—Rob Panasik, New York City

No doubt about it, your theory is correct. Virtually every successful golfer in history has had the opposite eye dominant advantage. I don't have a dominant eye myself and as a result my nose, which lies in neutral territory, had to take over the whole putting thing. This was particularly vexing on windy days when it was often impossible to smell the longer putts. Sometimes I would have to close my eyes altogether and snort like a mule on crack to get the line. Once I got it though, dear God but I was deadly. A by-product of this phenomenon was that I never needed a handkerchief while playing. However, I had to withdraw if I had a cold.

Sadly, the advantage has proven useless in sporting clay shooting, which is my real passion. Try as I might, I am unable to perfect what I call olfactory shooting. Therefore, in order to overcome the dominant eye factor I have taken up mounting the butt of the gun directly on the bridge of my nose. The recoil is a bastard.

Your column is the best. It's the first thing I turn to when my magazine arrives and I split a gut every month. But I can't help but wonder, is there a reason why CBS doesn't let you talk more?

—David Whalen, Saginaw, MI

Whale: It's not CBS that restricts my dulcet tones, my boy, it's the players. They get really pissed if I talk in the middle of their putting stroke. Since I'm usually pretty close to the action, I have to be mindful of my talking.

I'm sorry about your gut. That's gotta hurt.

You still earn (insert laugh here) your living from golf (columns, books, head talking, interviewing, guest speaking etc.). If you were to insert your income into the yearly PGA tour money list, how pleased with your ranking would you be?

—Geikie, Canada

A damn sight more pleased than I would be if I had to earn the same amount playing this stupid, useless, annoying game.

I was recently downsized by a large financial services company and thought perhaps you could help me get a job as an on course golf reporter. With the popularity of reality shows I believe the golf viewing public would love an ordinary golfer type guy calling the action in a style that they could relate to. I would use insightful descriptions like "Holy crap, how did he do that?" and "The rough is really, really deep here." We could even film segments with me attempting to hit shots that the pros would be faced with during the week to see how an ordinary golfer type guy would do in the same situations. Hope to hear from you soon. Do you guys make much money?

P.S. I just finished "The History of the Ryder Cup." All I can think of is seeing one of the current pros, coming off the course after his round, going into the press tent and explaining that his play improved drastically after the turn, thanks to the "formidable turd" he released in the locker room. I've never laughed so hard in my life.

—Jim Severance, Richmond, VA

Sorry about your job, but what the hell did you expect with a name like Severance? Jesus, man, change your name to something more positive like "Raise" or "Bonus" or something.

I'm sure you'll do well as a golf announcer with those pithy observations you describe above. That's repartee and badinage of the first order, that stuff. It's certainly a damn sight better than anything McCord comes up with. And Nantz is the only one making any money on this deal.

Having just witnessed your ads for Cobra I'm still impressed how you've managed to keep that wonderful Irish twang after all your time on the other side of the pond. However, I'm worried that your waistline has definitely gotten all "American." Do you still go walking the fairways for CBS? Because maybe you should try jogging them a little and lose the odd pound or two. Keep up the good work!

—Garry Adam, Stonehaven, Aberdeenshire, Scotland

Ah, the famous crushingly direct Scots! Never one to mince words, that bunch. By the way, I've been to Stonehaven. What a beautiful part of the world. Too bad we can't move it somewhere where the weather's nicer, like Hawaii.

Obviously you haven't seen the new version of me. I'm down to 170 pounds soaking wet with an erection, and holding an Ailsa Craig curling stone in each hand.

49

Groundhog Daze

Golf Magazine, *10565493*, June 2005, Vol. 47, Issue 6

For me, every great major championship golf course has a great major champion who will always be associated with it, a matched pair if you like: Hogan and Carnoustie, Weiskopf and Troon, Nicklaus and pretty much everywhere, and of course Payne Stewart and Pinehurst. Mind you, I associate that swine—Stewart, that is—as much with a La Quinta hotel we both happened to be staying at. Every time I drive by it I see his face, innocent as a choirboy, and I feel a little ache that I never got to pay him back what he was owed.

The groundhog incident typified the sort of evil-minded idiocy, blind luck and comic genius that was pure Payne. Employing one of his favorite tricks, he had picked up my key card off the bar the previous evening and replaced it with someone else's. I stumbled back to reception, muttering and cursing, when I found the key didn't work for my room. But that was just the start of it. The next day Payne was driving back to the hotel after a morning tee time when he hit an unfortunate groundhog with his courtesy car. Ever the humanitarian, he stopped to see if the poor beast needed to be put out of its misery. It had croaked. William Payne Stewart was not the kind of man who would let a perfectly good dead ground-hog go to waste, however, so he tossed it into the trunk and pressed on with malice aforethought. When he got back to the hotel, he retrieved his rodent and headed directly to my room, where he deposited it.

I arrived back tired, sweaty and too many over par, blundered into the room and dumped my clubs into the corner with a clatter. And wouldn't you just know it, from underneath the desk a groundhog lunged straight at my nads. At this stage in my magnificent career my senses were Samurai-like, and I automatically recoiled into a crouching-tiger position that would have sent most adversaries reeling back in awe, if the move hadn't been accompanied by an involuntary Girl Scout shriek and a small southern raspberry.

I tried to ward off what seemed like certain emasculation at the fangs of the rabid herbivore by wailing like a banshee and jumping from one piece of furniture to another. The furry little bastard was wearing a pair of my underpants, which, looking back, were in considerably better shape than the pair I had on. I was standing on the desk, holding on to an electrical cord that I'd ripped through 18 inches of ceiling, when Punxsutawney Phil finally keeled over, snorted, and died. After an appropriate period of mourning, I gave the corpse a prod with my wedge. There was a knock at the door. I gathered myself and opened it to find the housekeeper standing there with a roll of toilet tissue in her hand. How kind, I thought. I wonder who could've requested that? The whole episode had probably lasted only a few seconds, but the horror was permanent. And it reeked of Payne, that worthless, steaming pile of Stewart, who would be mine. Game on.

When there are no witnesses to such an assault, there is only one way to conduct the investigation: pretend it didn't happen. Wait for curiosity to get the better of the perp, who will then reveal himself. I acted cool at the bar that night, as if nothing had happened, after nervously spilling most of my first drink into my crotch. But Payne was unmoved. When I changed tactics and stated the facts of the case coolly, he maintained an air of indignation that made me look like a lunatic. Over the years that followed, I tried several times without success to filch his key card, but the best I managed was to hide his courtesy car in the woods, an act made moot by his reaction, which was to steal mine and drive it back to our hotel, leaving me standing in the parking lot with a bag on my shoulder and two arms the same length. One down again.

I think of Payne often, and occasionally imagine him behind the wheel of that car, chewing gum and cackling to himself, and I see the juvenile mischief behind the facade of his stoic straight face. To win at Pinehurst, you have to keep it straight and narrow, which should have ruled Payne out, because that man was seldom straight, and never narrow. I miss him.

50.

Feherty's Mailbag

Online—Published: June 24, 2005

Hello David, thanks for all your witty, intelligent commentary on the fairways; it makes for a nice yin and yang contrast with that evil McCord. My question: Having traveled a lot, do you speak any other languages: Gaelic? McCordian? Hubspeak? Thanks for your time.
—Serge Alain, Saguenay, Quebec

To begin with, Gaelic is not really a language. It's a bastardization of High Norse, Arctic fox yelps and sheep bleating spoken by drunken Galway idiots who get slitty-eyed and shirty after a few scoops. They claim it's a legitimate language in the West of Ireland, but everyone knows it's just a subterfuge whose main reason for existence is to confound the legal system. Under the law of the Republic, a man accused of a crime can demand a trial in Gaelic. Since no one really understands a damn word, the trials are invariably dismissed. It is unpronounceable, defies any attempt at spelling, possesses no grammatical architecture, and can be neither interpreted nor comprehended. Therefore it will come as no surprise that it is the only language my therapist will employ and is widely recognized as the official language of PGA tour caddies.

First off, I always enjoying reading your columns/rantings, they are the greatest. It's the first thing I turn to while sitting in my reading room, i.e., on the throne. While, like most Americans, I've never met Payne Stewart, I just wanted you to know that articles like yours endear him to me more. I always thought that he was a great golfer but reading stories like the one you told make him seem more down to earth too. I'm sure you feel privileged to have known him, and I'm privileged to read what others have to say about the personal, albeit sometimes sadistic, side of Payne. If you have more stories about him, please run them in the future. Thanks for the story and I hope for many more years of your columns to come.

—Jeff Davidson

I loved that man, that's for sure. But my stories about him are like wine, only to be let out of the bottle when the world is ready for them.

Given your access to a large number of golfers, especially some of whom I will undoubtedly find playing in a group ahead of me sometime in the future, I would like you to address the issue of golfers urinating on the course. The idea that my golf ball would be dampened by another's recycled beverage is particularly disturbing given my tendency to take deep divots and clean my golf ball with the "lick the thumb, wipe the golf ball with the thumb and repeat" move. Should there be a penalty assessed against the offenders or should I just change my swing path and my golf ball cleaning move? I would sincerely appreciate your input on this issue. Thanks in advance.

—B. Wilder, Houston, TX

Could you B. any Wilder?

Don't be so squeamish, you paranoid, panty-waisted hair-dresser. Peeing on the golf course is a time-honored tradition, like slamming your club into a ball washer in the middle of your opponent's backswing. Let's take the positive approach and see this behavior as an opportunity to consider the type of beverage consumed. If it was wine, what kind was it? Red or white; a nice cab or a burgundy; hints of berry and chocolate; tawny but not pretentious? Or is it just salty? How about beer? Domestic or imported; lager or dark; bottled or canned? There are all kinds of permutations to be considered here. But most of all, have fun with it. All I want is to be able to pee a full stream again.

I am a boogie golfer . . . looking for game improvement clubs. My question . . . what is the difference in graphite versus steel shafts in irons and who should use either?

—rckmorse@yahoo.com

How appropriate your ISP is Yahoo. Boogie golfers should play at night so it doesn't really matter what shafts you use. You should be looking for "game improvement" lessons, not clubs, you moron.

Hi David, I recently read that the rule makers are considering changing the golf ball in tournaments so that it will not travel as far since golf is becoming "too easy" for the tour pros. What a great idea! They should also put extra weights in Olympic runners' shoes so they won't run so fast. Perhaps they should let some air out of Lance Armstrong's tires so he'll quit winning the Tour de France. Come to think of it, those NASCAR cars are going really fast these days. Maybe it would be helpful to decrease the number of cylinders the engines can have.

With hopefully obvious dripping sarcasm,
—Ben Falk, Portland, OR

Your sarcasm dripped all over my writing thong. I think they should throw Jello in the pool to slow down Michael Phelps. But actually, if you think about it, the IOFC (the International

Organization of F——king Cretins) does probe cavities for performance enhancing chemicals, the Tour de France does legislate several aspects of bike construction and NASCAR places strict limits on design and engineering elements of the vehicle. I watch these guys hit driver, sand wedge on 465-yard par fours every weekend, and all it does is make me feel worse about my own projectile dysfunction. Sad, really.

51

Me and Big Al

Golf Magazine, *10565493, July 2005, Vol. 47, Issue 7*

So I walk into my doctor's office the other day and say, "Hey Doc, I've been feeling iffy for the last couple of weeks—I feel like I'm turning into a moth." He looks at me and says, "Well you shouldn't be here, you need to see a psychiatrist," and I say, "I know . . . but your light was on."

I thought if I were jovial enough I might be able to slide another dodgy physical past the medical vice squad, but my blood work results were in, and The Doc had the look of a coroner. It was going to be a struggle to get away with a few nods and promises this time. "Seriously," he says to me, "these numbers belong in Cooperstown. Just how much are you drinking?" It was the question I didn't want to answer, but I sucked it up and told him anyway. I was glugging a bit more than 2 bottles a day, but on the bright side I was doing it very quickly. "Of wine?" he says. "Uh, not really," says me. "Bushmills, Jameson's, Redbreast, cleaning products . . . you know, whatever's handy."

The Doc sighed and said, "David. 2 bottles a day? Have you ever considered getting some help?"

"No," I said, "I can drink it all myself."

That was the last of the joking, and the last of the drink, too, but the real reason I quit is my 6-year-old daughter and my wife, the Two Who Must Be Obeyed. The night before, I was in my usual half-man, half-mattress position, horizontal in the recliner with an almost empty bottle on the table beside me, when my girl clambered on me, held me by the ears, and put her forehead on mine. Then she grinned and said with the wisdom only children have, "Dad, you need another bottle." She Who Must Be Obeyed Sr. just looked up from her book and smiled at me sadly.

"Holy crap!" I thought, rather like St. Paul on the road to Damascus after his wee donkey suddenly exploded. "I do need another bottle." So I sent her to get me one (no point in quitting if you're only halfway to where you need to be) and resolved it would be my last. The following day was the longest of my life, and the morning after it, I woke up with the strangest feeling. For the first time in 25 years, I was hung under. I tried to shave, but I had the yips. I started on the right side of my mustache and then tried to even it up on the left, but it was clear that if I didn't stop trying, in about five minutes I'd look like Adolf Hitler.

That I'm an alcoholic can't possibly be my fault. I reckon it was the damn golf that did it to me. It takes about three and a half minutes of actual swinging time to play a round, so what the hell else was I supposed to do with the other four and a half hours, huh? A curse upon the roving beverage cart that wafted miniature whiskey bottles past my cavernous nostrils every other hole, and a pox on the idiot Scot who had the first thought of something to do after chasing a sheep into a sandy hollow. Now how am I going to explain why I'm ordering a Bushmills on the rocks, hold the Bushmills? But wait. I can tell everyone I have to quit because of the Irish curse. Like every green-blooded bogtrotter, I have the inbred ability to hurl a vat of whiskey down my neck without collapsing like a deck chair. By the time I quit I had to be through my second bottle to get a buzz, and the last time I got truly drunk the price of Irish Distillers stock went up 14 percent.

I have a lot of friends who have over-gargled themselves to the stage at which I now find myself. One good thing about it is the quantity and quality of the stories they have to tell about their years spent cuddled with a bottle. Like PJ, who got obliterated one night in Dublin and was walking down the banks of the Liffey when he lurched to a stop beside an old man. He offered him a swig from his bottle but there was no reply, so PJ got humpy, threw a punch, and promptly passed out. A few hours later he woke up covered in starling turds with a broken hand, lying under the statue of Patrick Kavanaugh that he had attacked. "There's no such thing as a recovering alcoholic," he tells me. "You're either drunk or you're not." Right now I'm not, and though I can't be certain of how I'm going to do, I'll tell you this: I will never drink again . . . today.

52

Father Knows Less

Golf Magazine, *10565493*, August 2005, *Vol. 47, Issue 8*

So I'm down at the courthouse with son Shey, my 16-year-old traffic-ticket-on-wheels. His violation was a moving one all right, and at this moment I feel moved to strangle the little fuzz-magnet. We're standing behind dozens of useless children and their apparently useless guardians, sullenly avoiding eye contact. Contemplating my own parenting skills, I'm wondering how the human species has managed to avoid extinction. Looking around this dungeon, it occurs to me that most children (including mine) do well just to survive their parents.

Not that raising kids is a breeze, mind you, all you have to do is look at the animal kingdom to see how awkward it can be. A mother tiger has to hide, feed and teach her cubs to survive predators, the most dangerous of which is often their own father. Which brings me to the Sean O'Hair story, you know, the kid who finished second at the Byron Nelson, the one with the father threatening to, in his widely quoted words, "crucify him in the media" in retaliation for the fruitless years he spent coaching, publicity-seeking and investing in his son.

Before I get off on a rant here, I would qualify it by stating that I have no intention of acting like a therapist. I've paid dozens of the bastards $150 an hour to tell me I'm-right-but-that's-irrelevant, but I'm not daft enough to think it actually makes me one of them. I could give a small dog's trousers about your kids; I have trouble enough with my own.

But it must be very cool to watch one of your own kids suc-ceed at the highest level in anything, especially a sport. Most of us have sat through hours of God-awful recitals watching other people's children who seem a lot less talented than our own and are pretty damn gawky too, for those few shining moments our undeniably beautiful prodigies give us. Most par-ents are happy with 10 fingers and 10 toes. Marc O'Hair wants his 10 percent. And Sean will have over a million dollars in earnings in his rookie season by the time this column appears.

We might want to blame Earl Woods for the Control Freak school of prodigy-raising, and though Tiger's daddy is a tough old fart, that's where the comparison between him and Marc O'Hair ends. Beneath Earl's gruff exterior there has always been a hopelessly obvious dotage. It was always about a little boy whom he knew was destined for great things, of which he needed no part. In short, Earl Woods made sure his dream didn't turn into his son's nightmare.

I walked with Sean O'Hair for the last two rounds of the Byron Nelson, and he might be the most talented young player I've seen since Tiger. It's been that long since I saw a kid hit half and three-quarter shots under that kind of pressure. Sean is any parent's dream—or almost any parent's. (Hey, Mr. O'Hair: This is the media. How's the old crucifixion thing coming along?)

My dad is 80 now, and I see him all too seldom. Like Sean, I turned pro at 17, and though my dad didn't make a lot of money, he gave as much as he could so his son could have the best possible chance to succeed. I've never felt able to repay him for his faith in me, but he has always said that my success is reward enough.

Giving up your career for the sake of your children is noble

all right, but it's not exactly unusual. People do it all the time—
they're called mothers. After their children set off into the big
bad world, mothers are usually happy enough with a hug, or a
card and a bunch of flowers once or twice a year. Some of them
even go back to work.

53.

Feherty's Mailbag

Online—Published: August 3, 2005

I remember a time when after the pros hit a tee shot, you'd hear somebody yell out, "You da Man"? I guess those days are gone. While watching the U.S. Open on TV this year, I heard the replacement yell for "You da man!" It was a belching "Git-'R-Done!" I had to admit that it was pretty darned funny. But then again, I thought McCord's bikini wax comment about Augusta's greens was funny as well. Do you think "Git-'R-Done" could somehow be worked into your on course commentary?

—Randy, Pascagoula, Mississippi

Look, I think "Larry the Cable Guy" is funny, but "Git-'R-Done" is the exclusive territory of NASCAR, hush puppies and frog giggin'. And if you don't know what that is, you're not from Mississippi. No, let's not try to replace "You da Man" with anything, thanks. In fact, let's not yell it either.

Did you enjoy the train wreck that was the last round of the U.S. Open, or as an ex-pro is that kind of golf too painful to watch?

—Dave Hodgson, Vancouver

It was definitely too painful to watch. And excruciating to
listen.

Alright, I didn't win the contest to play at Pinehurst, but I still got a
bottle of Oban waiting for you. Let's get together at a local dog track
with a bunch of New York firemen who would love to show you how to
get over your pressure issues!

—Bobby K . . . the hot corner . . . FDNY

Sorry, partner, I tried to fix it but they wouldn't let me. And just
for the record, I love you guys, but I don't think I want to
resolve my pressure issues with a bunch of guys who run up
85-foot ladders so they can dive through into the window of a
building, the interior temperature of which is 2500 degrees.
And Oban is a Scotch, and when I did drink it was Irish, but
thanks anyway.

Keeping this short and sweet. What is your take on the "Golf for
Dummies" DVD starring Gary McCord?

—Steve, Bethlehem, PA

You have to be something of a dummy to play golf, so I think
the DVD works for everybody. The only thing wrong with it is
that McCord is actually *in* it.

54.

Feherty's Mailbag

Online—Published: August 24, 2005

I thought Michael Campbell was one of those infuriating hot and cold could-be golf geniuses who kept us tantalized with his talent. But after reading some of the sages of the American press (and listening to Johnny Miller on television), whose knowledge of world golf is so profound, I've realized he's just a no-talent bum who had his 15 minutes of fame at Pinehurst, is bad for American golf and we'll never hear from him again. As a good Texan, it must be tempting for you to stick the spurs in as well.

—Tom, Victoria, Australia

Michael Campbell might have surprised you by winning the U.S. Open, but more importantly, he surprised himself. Maybe he just found out how good he is, who knows? By the way, he finished in the top 10 at St. Andrews. And the way I read it, that was a very nasty thing to say about Johnny. For the record, his 15 minutes of fame was in 1973, and I think we'll be hearing from him plenty.

A colleague asked recently what sport I was into. Golf. I asked about a sport he scoffed. He admitted to never have tried golf (except mini-golf, ha!), but there was no way to convince him that an activity not involving a team of running, jumping, sweaty men chasing a ball "in motion" could be considered a real sport. I figured the guy was a bonehead, anyway, but have found myself since, searching for a short, insulting and yet convincing answer that would wipe off the smirk from the golfomus ignoramus bonehead face. I know you are the best man for the job. Please, do provide one.

—Thanks, Vladimir

Clearly, English is not your first language so winning an argument with this moron might be difficult. But I'll have a go for you. Tell this nimrod to go down to the local range and hit 100 balls. He'll have so many blisters on his hands afterwards that he won't be able to have sex with himself, which is probably the only sport at which he's any f—king good. I've changed my mind. You win.

About three months ago you wrote about "a better game by chemistry." I'm 35 years old and recently was diagnosed with ADD. As I started taking some medication my golf game improved dramatically, obviously as a result of better concentration. I know Mark O'Meara went through the same situation in 1998 when he won both the Masters and the British Open. Is there any more material about this subject, more evidence of medication as a game improvement tool, are there more pros on the tour with ADD?

—Guillermo Ariza, Caracas, Venezuela

Hey I know you're in Venezuela, but stop chewing the leaves. Payne Stewart was the best ADD player I ever knew, and I've always suspected Jesper Parnevik. And if there actually were meds that helped, I'd have mules out selling dime bags.

Sir, what do they mean when they say "his swing was over the top"? Also explain the reverse V—and how long do you hold it or release it? Thank you.

—Michael Ward

Don't call me Sir, you disingenuous fartwit. I have no idea what anyone is talking about when it comes to the golf swing. I just make this crap up. And the only person I ever knew who had a reverse V was a girl on our 11th grade field hockey team, and I never got to hold it.

Do you really believe the hype regarding the new low spin golf balls? Is it really going to help my game by dropping $50 on Nike's newest release?

—JB

JB and a splash of water:

You might as well drop $50 into the nearest lake. That's where the balls will end up anyway.

55

A Visit with St. Nicklaus

Golf Magazine, *10565493, September 2005, Vol. 47, Issue 9*

In my youth, I dressed up and pretended to be Jack Nicklaus. I had a couple of advantages when I was 12, like a squeaky voice, and the fact that in the early 1970s it was okay for a kid to wear the absurdly flared polyester nut-squeezers favored by Tour players. (Looking back, the tightness of Jack Nicklaus' trousers might well account for the fact that I had a total lack of pubic hair until I was 27, and why I can still yodel with the best of them.)

In the deadly serious world of the 12-year-old Tour player, getting first pick in the hero role-playing department was a lot more important than who got to hit first. The name Nicklaus struck fear into the quivering spleen of Lee Trevino, who had a speech impediment and only four clubs, and positively pureed the bowels of Gary Player, whose mom used to drag him squealing off the course by his ear if he hadn't done his home-work. Being Jack usually meant victory, but it was a total drag when he lost, because Jack had to be graceful in defeat, which was tough to pull off when Arnold Palmer was dancing glee-fully around the 18th green, flashing you his pimply bum. As I recall, Tom Weiskopf could be a complete swine, too.

Then I grew up (okay, that's crap) and turned pro, and after several years of desperately chopping my way around every Nicklaus course I played, I began to think my childhood hero was a landscape gardener on acid. Every time I set foot on the first tee of one of Jack's golf courses I lost 70 points off my IQ, and my confidence hit the deck faster than Paris Hilton's pants. I decided that this couldn't possibly be MY fault: there was an obvious design flaw in Jack's work, a theory I frequently shared with the tabloid pencil-squeezers with whom I drank after such disasters. Feherty's play was usually more quotable than notable, and I became known as a Nicklaus-basher. But I never really worried about that. I mean, it wasn't likely I'd have to look the man in the eye, right?

Uh, wrong. I moved to America and started to play badly on every golf course. I evaporated into broadcasting and then, before I knew it, found myself sweating like a vole in a toaster as I waited to INTERVIEW Jack Bloody Nicklaus. When he sat down beside me he might as well have had one giant sky-blue Orwellian orb in the middle of his damn forehead: in that instant I felt Nicklaus knew every damn thing about me. But the man didn't even have the decency to get shirty with me. He was warm and friendly and funny, even endearing in a Golf-God-like way. I felt like a mean-spirited little crab in the presence of a really nice dolphin.

Okay, that last sentence was a bit weird, but it worked for me. Moving right along, I need to say this: I actually love Jack Nicklaus, and I have since I was a little boy. You love him, too, of course you do. He's the greatest winner of all time, and more importantly the greatest loser, and best of all, he had the decency not to retire at the top, so that we could all see that he is human after all. The decline of Jack's game has been sweetly painful for every golf fan, his occasional flashes of glories past have been magnificent rages against the dying of the brightest light in golf.

God, I wish that I had played with him just one time. In my

career I got to play with almost every great player in the modern era, but never with Jack. In my current state of perfection, I probably couldn't play a round if Stryker Orthopedics gave me free ceramic hips and a year's supply of Percodan. (It's the pain, you know, from a debilitating pelvic condition diagnosed by my doctor as "there's nothing wrong with you, you whiner, and, no, you can't have any more narcotics.") Jack Nicklaus is the bingo I never got to shout, the missing last card in my royal flush, and probably the only person on the planet who might be able to lure me back onto a golf course. Even if it was one of his.

56

Feherty's Mailbag

Online—Published: September 19, 2005

I enjoy your commentary and your columns. I especially enjoyed your "stick of dynamite and a sand wedge" comment on Phil Mickelson's lie in the rough on the 16th hole on Sunday of the PGA Championship. My wife, who is frequently subjected to watching me play Tiger Woods 2005, almost shot her drink out her nose and promptly exclaimed, "I can't believe he just said that! I thought he just said things like that on the game!" My question: My father-in-law really enjoys golfing with my brother-in-law and I. About a year ago he was in a horse riding accident and broke seven ribs. He is now golfing again, but he starts to get tired after 12 holes or so. Any recommendations on how to keep energy up in the latter holes of a round? P.S. If you're ever in Salt Lake City, we'd love a fourth.

—Justin McBride, Salt Lake City, Utah

You don't own that boot company, do you? Man, I love those boots. By the way, when your bride shot her drink out her nose, I hope she didn't get any on the dog. They hate that; don't ask me how I know.

Slip a Cialis tablet in his beer on the thirteenth tee, have your

Mom call him on his cell and make suggestions as to what may be waiting for him after the round. He'll perk right up.

Thanks for the invite, but I try to avoid Utah. The Mormon Tabernacle Choir scares the crap out of me.

I firmly believe television golf analysts will be the first up against the wall when the revolution comes. I particularly curse the one who first told us to put a mark on the ball to line up our putts. I have a friend who now religiously marks and lines up every six-inch putt. He is still on 27, he still putts like crap, but now it takes us five hours to get round. He also uses a club to line up his feet AND his shoulders on each fairway shot—more tips from television analysts. Please, please, tell them to stop it right now.

—Steve, Brisbane, Australia

Hey, here's a radical idea for you (I'm yelling here), GIVE THE POOR BASTARD THE SIX INCH PUTT AND MOVE TO THE NEXT F——KING TEE? You're killing me here.

However, you do have a point which I will award you with respect to television lessons. There should be a disclaimer like on those car commercials that show some clown jumping the Grand Canyon in a Neon while on the bottom of the screen they're telling you he is a trained driver (by who, Robin Williams?), it was on a closed course and you should not attempt. No s——t, really? The bottom of the screen would say something like: "If you're foolish enough to believe that you can be taught golf by watching this moron on the television, at least disguise your stupidity by NOT emulating this useless drill on the golf course." Tips are for waitresses.

I have a question about which title to use in polite society when referring to Annika Sorenstam. As you know, Annika is the only woman to shoot a 59 in a LPGA event. She has been known ever since as "Mrs.

59". Since she is divorced should I continue to use the Title "Mrs. 59" or should I change to "Mz. 59".

—Politically Correct, Upland, CA

Ah, California . . . Arnold hasn't proselytized all of you yet, eh?

First of all, you should avoid polite society at all costs. There is nothing to be gained from hanging around these stiffs. They're fartless, belchless, scratchless, humorless wankers and some of them are completely sober Democrats. Oh, and by the way, I think I discovered the cure for depression—beating the s——t out of Tom Cruise. It would certainly cheer me up.

As to Annika, she should never have been referred to as Mrs. Anything to begin with since she didn't change her name when she got married. In any case I prefer hyphenated women. I shall call her Ms. Sorenstam-59.

I had the great experience of getting an up-close look at the PGA Championship (working for a local media outlet gave me some sweet access). As you strolled past the gallery (mob) following Mr M. on the fourth on Sunday, folks were yelling "hey!" and stuff and you were stonefaced . . . perhaps the headset was noise canceling? And have you lost a bunch of weight? You look like it. Finally, the Mrs. gave me a ration because during the rain weather delay on Sunday afternoon she saw you doing an interview then called me and begged me to have you call her on my cell. Being a complete pro, I refused. She was still pissed. We (me and Penelope) enjoy your work!

—K. Corey, East Windsor, NJ

K & Penelope: (Don't want to ignore her again!)

Oh yeah. How would you enjoy having 5,000 people in your office screaming at you while you were trying to listen to your boss on the phone and your career might depend on your reply? I will occasionally mix it up with the fans (who I adore by the way) during commercials, but I have to stay in the moment.

McCord spends all of his not-inconsiderable free time dreaming up ways to catch me asleep at the mike switch. I've got to be ready for anything out there.

Hello Mr. Feherty, your insightful and professional commentary is always something to look forward to when tuning in to a CBS golf broadcast. However, television poorly conveys the contours of the course as well as the trajectories of the shots. What are the advantages of going to see a tournament firsthand compared to a telecast?

—Serge A., Jonquire, Quebec

Serge, you insane hoser-frog. Who are you kidding? Now that hockey is back you won't be watching golf at all. However, if you were:

No commercials for starters. The best way to see everything is to go to the tournament and get invited to, or crash, the title sponsor's trophy suite. They have great food, wine, cold beer and gorgeous hostesses that fawn all over you. They're completely enclosed and have televisions all over the place so you can watch the action all over the golf course in air-conditioned comfort with plush seating and your own private john. If you really want to see all the contours first hand, flag down a CBS employee driving his own cart and ask him to take you out to wherever you would like and wait for you so you won't have to walk back. Tell him you're a close buddy of McCord. Park in the CBS compound too, why don't you? Nantz's spot is usually available since in his new contract he gets a limo and driver everywhere. You should see what they have to put in his suite. Makes the Rolling Stones dressing room look like a cell at Rikers Island.

57

If Old Tom Really Did Come Back

Golf Magazine, *10565493, October 2005, Vol. 47, Issue 10*

I love John Cleese's Titleist ads on the telly. But they make me wonder how Old Tom Morris, now under the sod for almost 100 years, would play if he actually DID come back.

Scene 1. Inside the clubhouse at St. Andrews, several members sit, sipping pink gins and talking. None of them is John Cleese. A ghostly vapor appears on the window, the condensing breath of Old Tom, who materializes holding an old wooden spoon. He is screaming:

"Hey fellas, any chance of a wee snifter for the auld boy here, or am ah still no' allowed intae the f——kin' clubhoose? Yez don't need tae wurry aboot the sheep here, she's female, so ah'll be leavin' her ootside."

The members look shocked, but one of them motions for the old man to come in. The ancient keeper of the green walks through the window and sits down. He waves at the bartender. "Hey Jimmy, ah'll have a glass of the Macallan 25-year-old, although it'll still be fairly new tae me so ye might as well make it a pint." He cracks up laughing.

"Oooh, that wuz a wee beauty, wuz it not? Ah'm killin' maself here." He looks around the group. "Whassamatter? Yez all look like y'uv seen a ghost or something. D'yae fancy watching the old boy playin' a few wee holes or wud yez rather sit there like poofters? Come awn, an' we'll do the whiskey loop."

Scene 2. The first tee, where a cluster of members has gathered. Old Tom loosens up with his old spoon. He looks toward the group. "Hey Snodgrass, gimmee a pellet there an' make sure it's a ProV1. F——k the NXT, ah need the good stuff." The member tosses the ball, which Old Tom catches and tees up in one movement. "Okay lads, how much are ye payin' an why is it so little?"

They decide on a fee of £1 over the whiskey loop, aka holes 1, 2, 17 and 18. Tom settles over the ball and makes an elegant swing. The spoon goes right through the ball, leaving it resting on the tee. "Shite! Ah forgot ma clubs are dead too. Y'ez cannae count tha' one. Hey Wilberforce! Gimme tha' big smelly-lookin' Cobra driver there an' ah'll take another dig at it."

Old Tom snatches the driver and looks at the head quizzically. He walks over to the pathway beside the tee, picks up a handful of gravel and rubs it vigorously into the painted finish. "Too bloody shiny this thing is. It'd give a man a headache." Then he takes another swing, and this time the ball flies sweet and true down the middle of the vast fairway. But he reels back off the ball, holding his ears. "Christ, what wuz tha'? If tha' thing disnae deafen ye, it'll start a f——kin' fire. Ah remember the ball comin' aff with a wee squelch."

Scene 3. Old Tom has borrowed a wedge from one of the members and is over the ball. He swings, clips the ball neatly off the tight turf and turns to the crowd. "Suffer tha' one, ye losers." The ball lands 10 feet short of the hole, takes one bounce forward and zips back violently into the Swilcan Burn. "Bollocks! Did you see tha'? Tha' ball must be haunted or something. In my day the bastard went forwards."

Scene 4. Tom is standing ankle deep in the water. He stares at the ball, confused.

"Okay boys, somebody needs t'explain tae me why this piddly

wee trickle has a concrete bottom. It's supposed t'be 'watery filth,' ye know? An wha' is this ye've handed me?" He looks at a sand wedge, fingering the sole. "You must think ah'm away in the heed. This has a wee bumpy sole tha'll never let me under the ball, so gimme a 9-iron." He opens the face of the club and plays a neat little splash shot to a yard from the hole, covering himself in slime. "BOLLOCKS!"

Scene 5. Tom has decided that four holes is too much like work, and he needs to get back to the Macallan, so he goes to the 18th tee, where he makes an elegant swing with the big driver. The ball takes a bounce on Granny Clark's Wynd, shoots forward and runs into the Valley of Sin.

"Holy pints of McKewan's, tha' wuz some bounce! Granny Clark made the haggis ye know? The problem wuz she ate it too, and tha' path used to be deed grass tha' she killed as she wuz just walkin' along."

With that, Old Tom turns his back on the members and begins to make his way toward the clubhouse.

58

Feherty's Mailbag

Online—Published: October 28, 2005

Q: Michelle Wie took the money from Nike, Sony and other companies and is running right to the bank. Do you think she made the right move turning pro? What would you do if she were your daughter? Part of me understands that you can't turn down millions, but then I hear guys on TV saying stuff like, "You can't re-live your childhood . . . she's making a mistake."

—Howard Mullin, Evanston, Illinois

Howard:

I turned pro at 17, so I think it would be hypocritical of me to knock Michelle for what she's doing. The difference was I didn't get any offers from Sony or Nike. My sponsor deals were from an acne company (for headwear), a codpiece manufacturer, (for my trousers), the Polish car maker Skoda, whose cars would actually disassemble themselves if you closed the door too hard, (my courtesy car) and a funeral home/pub combination in Bangor by the name of Danny O'Dead's, (for my shirts). There wasn't a lot of money involved, but my complexion cleared up and kicking me in the nuts was futile.

As for my lovely daughter, Erin, whose picture graces the back of the dust jacket of my new book, "An Idiot for All Seasons" (*which is available in bookstores everywhere you bastards*), my guess is I would want to keep her as close to me as long as possible because I know I'm going to be broken beyond repair when she leaves, and I don't want to face that moment until I absolutely have to. Which will be never. If Michele were my daughter, I'd have serious words with She Who Must Be Obeyed, because I'm pretty sure we don't have any Asian ancestry.

Q: I've heard that the PGA Tour is talking about shortening the season. What would you do with a little extra time if all of a sudden the season ended in September, hunt more?

—Peter Sheppard, Lake Charles, Louisiana

Peter:

My season ends in September now. ABC takes most of the autumn schedule as it is, so I'm normally off for a good part of the end of the schedule. I spend most of this time studying quantum mechanics and nano-technology, performing open heart surgery on underprivileged kids in Beverly Hills, designing rubberized underpants, translating the Dead Sea Scrolls into Spanglish, nude topiary, and, of course, shooting at anything that happens to be more than six feet off the ground. Like Oosty's ears.

Q: David, I remember that *Golf Magazine* once wrote that the milk shakes at Castle Pines are awesome and that the hotdogs at Westchester Country Club are insanely good. You are on tour a lot and seem like the kinda guy who knows how to use a knife and fork. Which tournament do you think has the best grub?

—Steven Nesbit, San Francisco, California

Steven:

All of the ones CBS doesn't do. Incidentally, the best use of a knife is to stir your cocktail (it provides a greater surface-to-lick quotient afterward), and a fork should be employed to pick the excess ice out of your drink.

The truth is I rarely eat in the clubhouse. CBS provides us with a catering truck and Henry (my personal trainer) does a great job cooking up grub for us. Besides, it's a rare country club that would permit the likes of McCord or me in their hallowed halls. McCord's been escorted out of more clubs than a card counter in Vegas. And that goes for restaurants, too. His idea of a tip is "Seabiscuit in the seventh," and he's got a pocket full of fishhooks, too. Last time he picked up a check, American Express fraud prevention services called his wife at home to report unusual activity on his card.

Q: I literally started to cry when I saw John Daly miss that 3-footer in the tiebreaker with Tiger Woods at Harding Park. You know John, how do you think he's doing? Is this going to be just another footnote for the big guy whose life is like a country/western song or could this be a career-changing event?

—Chris Schultz, Alpharetta, Georgia

Chris,

Don't worry about John, and stop being such a big girl's blouse. Johnny's like my beagle; two seconds after he lays a steamer on the kitchen floor, he's forgotten it and he's on to the next adventure. Where's my ball? Is that stinking squirrel out there? Let's get him! The only thing that would bother John at this stage of his career is to lose the Hooters sponsorship. That would surely break the man.

Q: Okay David, here's my laundry list: What's your: 1.) Shot of the Year, 2.) Player of the Year, and 3.) Predictions for the 2006 PGA Season?

—Adam Weinstein, Orlando, Florida

OK Adam, here you go,

1.) Mickelson's second at the PGA Championship on the 14th(?) on Sunday out of the knee deep rough to 12 feet for birdie. Beyond belief.
2.) Chris DiMarco for his Presidents Cup play. He was fearless, dominating, relentless, enthusiastic and humble, and he had everything to lose. I thought he was brilliant.

And as far as predictions,

- Clampett checks into language rehab
- Nantz gets caught with Bush 41 playing naked mumblypeg with Hillary
- Vijay attends a media day. (not)
- Golf Channel gets caught placing foam core spectator cutouts at European tour events so it looks like there are more fans there. One of the cutouts wins *The Big Break*.
- Mike Tirico goes postal and beats the crap out of Azinger and Faldo.
- Kent Jones gets surgery to create a chin. "I'm sick of it taking me 45 minutes to change a pillow case."
- CBS drops Yanni, goes Asian with theme music. Sean McManus says, "It sounds as if an eighteen wheeler full of wind chimes smashing into a Jamaican steel drum band at a bird calling contest. Holy Crap."

59

Get Scrooged!

Golf Magazine, *10565493, December 2005, Vol. 47, Issue 12*

Pouring a cup of holiday jeer:

These holidays reek, they're about nothing but money.
They make me feel sullen and gloomy
St. Patrick ain't funny, nor that Easter Bunny,
And Valentine's Day can just chew me.
I'm sick of this swinging and putting and pitching,
And Santa (that fat drunken hack).
I'll pilfer his costume and pick out the stitching,
And have Blitzen pinch loaves in his sack.
Those pros down in Proville are making me heave,
Their cheating percentage is zero.
I like the fudgers, and mean nasty nudgers
(That man Barry Bonds is my hero).
Today's players are wholesome and strong and athletic
(Apart from John Daly and Lumpster).
Somehow my sandwich seems really pathetic
As they have their lunch brought in a Dumpster.
My heart has been shriveling; it's down two full sizes,

But my liver's as small as Wyoming.
If I had my way there'd be nickel first prizes,
And the commissioner's mouth would be foaming.
This kindness, this giving, this charity crap.
Much more and I'll soon lose my lunch!
I need some dirt, a real scandalous flap,
From this horribly generous bunch.
See, this year I'm meaner (and sober to boot!)
Like the Grinch on top of Mt. Chunkit.
So Sergio Garcia can kiss my pitoot
And into my pool he can dunk it.
I'd float in his pool wearing only a thong,
With butter my shoulders he'd rub.
I'd steal Ernie's crutches (now that's just plain wrong)
And swap Goosen's and Mickelson's clubs.
From Vijay I'd steal the hard skin on his hands.
And all of the balls on his range.
I'd fill up his bunkers with rubberized sand,
(Though even McCord thinks that's strange).
And Wadkins, pleeease, just don't get me started,
He's a blowhard at all our expense.
With the look on his face you'd think Oosty farted
Or Clampett had suddenly made sense.
On the upside he drives all the players berserk,
Which actually makes me more cheerful.
I can carry him easily, take him to work,
Though he wriggles and gives me an earful.
And Tiger, I slithered my way to his vault
To make off with a few of his millions.
I knew that I shouldn't, it was all my own fault,
(That kick in the plums from Steve Williams).
Hang on; I think that this poem may have worked!
Though it pains me to have to confess.
That always, deep in my heart there has lurked

The truth, and that is I'm blessed.
For golfers will always be different I know,
You can tell from the Drive to a Billion.
The more I'm around them the more it just shows
That I have one job in a million.

60.

David Feherty's Mailbag

Online—Published: December 8, 2005

Q: Forwilliam Golf Club, how would you rate it as compared to other golf courses in Northern Ireland and Ireland. I enjoyed playing the course. Is it the 10th or 11th hole where you have to ring the bell, to let those on the tee box know that it is okay to hit.

— Bill Sullivan, New Berlin, Wisconsin

Bill,

You mean *Fortwilliam* Golf Club on Downview Avenue in Belfast; lovely little gem. Short but a giggle to play. If I was sober, I definitely hung over and never rang that damn bell. And I'd feel like kneecapping anybody who did. If I was drunk, I couldn't ring the stupid thing in the first place. I'm glad they replaced it, though. Some of the boys and I misappropriated the son of a bitch one night after a few snifters and mounted it top of Declan Meagher's dad's car. Every time he hit the brakes the whole neighborhood would drop to their knees thinking the Queen had grabbed her hat (died). It seemed funny at the time anyway. Apparently the Queen survived it.

Q: Practicing putting is the most mind numbingly boring thing on the planet. How do you do it?

—Earl Trigg, Dade City, Florida

Earl,

Whose column are you reading? Unless you make your living at the game, absolutely no time should be devoted to practice at all. Hey, if you feel compelled to play golf, fine, play away. But the time most people spend on practicing golf should go towards more worthwhile endeavors such as bestiality, making hats for small farm animals, curing impetigo, spaying cats, or anything else that will give some return on time invested.

Q: Do PGA Tour players play a specific ball from their sponsor based on the characteristics of the course (length, soft/firm greens, etc.) for a given week, like opting for ProV1 instead of V1X?

—Dennis Jones, Memphis, Tenn.

Dennis,

No, they play the ball that fits the characteristics of their swing and the ball flight that results. Ordinarily, the conditions of the course don't impact the type of ball they play one way or another. Balls are generally more affected in the air than they are on the ground. Once they hit the ground, gravity takes over. There are so many variables in ball dynamics that a player would need to consult with the Nobel Prize winner for physics, which, despite my enlightening paper on "The scrotal tenacity of ticks in Beagles," once again was not me this year.

Q: Okay, you must be playing a bit too much golf. Some of us are impatiently waiting for the follow-up to your great book, "Nasty Bit of Rough." Will "Beastly Turn of Events" be out for Christmas? How about spring of 2006? I have read "Nasty Bit of Rough" six times and I still laugh at the characters.

—Tom, Indiana

Tom,

God bless you, my son. You are the kind of discerning, erudite, sophisticated reader we try to cultivate. A *Beastly Turn of Events* is in the works as we speak. The reason for the delay has nothing to do with me playing golf, however. My publisher is headed up by the "tilt down guy"; you know, the third guy from the left on that evolutionary chart? The man is denser than heavy water. He thinks there should be some sort of "outline" of the story first. Has this nimrod never heard of James Joyce and "Stream of Consciousness"? I think not. Did Yeats work on a deadline? Don't think so. But it'll be out by the end of next year [I lied] and a moron like you will love it. Uncle Dickie and the boys are at it again. In the meantime, why don't you fill your useless, empty hours perusing my latest tome "An Idiot for all Seasons." The email questions between the chapters are worth the price of admission. Some of the most brilliant work I've never produced.

61.

Take Me to Your Leader

Golf Magazine, *10565493, January 2006, Vol. 48, Issue 1*

I was thinking [Hope that didn't hurt too much —ed.] about who might replace PGA Tour Commish Tim Finchem if he finally snapped, took his $4 billion pension and walked out in a huff. Here are my lop 10(ish) candidates

1. **Snoop Dogg:** He's into golf these days, and on the shizzle side he'd certainly introduce a beverage and booty cart. Maybe even a left-handed cigar bar at the turn. All therapy in the fitness trailer has a happy ending. Bad shots are hysterically funny, but oddly difficult to count. Or even remember. Wanamaker Trophy is replaced with ruby-studded pimp goblet.
2. **Rush Limbaugh:** Three hooks in a row lead to summary execution, boosting TV ratings by more than 400 percent. Not unlike Snoop's reign with regard to medication. Brian Gay would have to quit the Tour. Any dip in TV ratings blamed on Hillary Clinton.
3. **Richard Simmons:** Brian Gay reinstated but Greg Norman is out—too butch. There are fines for clashing colors and poor accessorizing, and every

caddie wears mesh and goes barefoot. Prize money is distributed in accordance with how hard you try, not where you finish. No cuts—that's not nice! Saddle shoes look even fruitier. Pleated khakis out; ass-high shorts in. PGA Tour cards replaced by Deal-a-Meal Cards.

4. **Hillary Clinton:** Michelle Wie gets a lifetime achievement award and Martha Burk replaces Ed Moorehouse as lead counsel. Barbra Streisand takes over Tour Productions and abandons first-round coverage altogether in favor of horrifying musicals. Christopher Lowell retained to work on window treatments in TPC clubhouses, and new "winner's tax" exceeds actual earnings—though Clinton herself accepts millions as an advance on her next book, *It Takes a Gated Village*.

5. **James Gandolfini:** Rocco Mediate is finally made after 20-year Tour career, and anyone who heckles DL3 becomes part of an abutment on the Garden State Parkway. Sabbatini rule lets members take out a contract to whack slow players. No one goes anywhere near the Pine Barrens to look for their ball. Steel spikes allowed only in cement Foot-Joys. Italian-American players fined for eating at Olive Garden.

6. **Charles Barkley:** No Q-School: If the brother wants to play, let the brother play. Rules officials can be wedgied, short-sheeted or Tasered at any time. If green speeds are more than 11 on the Stimp, a backboard for the hole is deployed. Uphill putts of more than 25 feet can be blocked, and Charles Howell III is fined for being too damned skinny.

7. **Rosie O'Donnell:** All Tour officials are fired. (Who are they to say what's right and wrong?) Except rules official Slugger White, because he looks like that cop in the Village People. *Tiger Has Two Daddies* is

produced by the Tour's new publishing house, and
Gary McCord finally feels comfortable enough to wear
hose on the Champions Tour. Feigns crush on "cutie
patootie" Adam Scott, then sends roses to Danielle
Ammaccapane. "These Guys Are Good" catchphrase
replaced with "Doritos Are Good."

8. **Lanny Wadkins:** Playing away from a flagstick is
disallowed, tee times are allocated in relation to the
number of shotguns a player owns and there are
heavy fines for shirts not professionally laundered.
The wolf game on Tuesday is worth more than the
tournament, and all players must live below the
Mason-Dixon line.

9. **Paris Hilton:** No meetings before 11 a.m., and players
are penalized for having their ankles less than three
feet apart at address. First commissioner to offer
room service, she resigns after only 125 days when she
runs out of exempt players.

10. **Dubya:** Rules disputes are settled by skeet shooting at
the ranch (and rightly so) or by who can bag the
biggest spotted owl. Uranium is discovered under the
17th green at TPC Sawgrass, ushering in Tour's new
mixed-use land policy. Dick Cheney takes up residence
in a bunker at Pinehurst No. 2 and Arjun Atwal is
strip-searched before entering all locker rooms.
Disappointed that he's not greeted as a liberator by
cheering crowds of golfers. Inspects newly svelte
Darren Clarke for weapons of ass destruction.

11. **Ken Lay:** Purses immediately jump to $14,000,000 but
first prizes average just $137.65.

62

David Feherty's Mailbag

Online—Published: January 19, 2006

David,

I have noticed NFL kickers compress the ball with their hands before kicking off. Why do they do this, and should I consider doing it as part of my pre-shot routine in golf?

—Brad Titus, Calif.

Brad:

NFL kickers, like professional golfers, are an incredibly superstitious gaggle of geese. Although I don't have a personal relationship with any NFL kickers, I did get a Garo Yepremian jock strap from Gary McCord for Christmas one year. But I digress. The reason they squeeze the ball before they kick it is to exorcise the demon that possesses all Wilson balls. No kick has ever been returned for a touchdown after a kicker has successfully exorcised the ball-devil, (known as a Rozelle) in all the pro pigskins. So what I'm saying is, squeeze away at your balls if they are manufactured by Wilson. I don't know if they're haunted or not, but if you're going to hit them with a golf club anyway, a little squeeze could hardly hurt.

David,

Why is it that hockey players make good golfers? Considering that you can't whack someone with your 1-iron across the shins after a bad shot, you'd think the frustration would be too much for them to handle.

—Kent Salfi

Kent:

One of the smartest coaches of all time, Jacque Demers, just wrote a book revealing he can't read. That's why hockey players make good golfers; they're incapable of rational thought. A good golf swing requires an empty mind (ask Sandy Lyle), and hockey players are supremely suited for the task. By the way, who says you can't gash your opponent with an iron after a bad shot? The hockey players I play with, hook, slash, board and bodycheck and that's only when we're shooting sporting clays.

David,

Gary McCord's facial hair is starting to resemble a billy goat on steroids. I don't know if you are really his friend, his mentor, his working sidekick or his bedfellow but can you talk to him, man to goat, and get him to shave that thing?

—Mike Noah

Mike:

Get all those animals on board yet? How do you get zoning authority for an Ark? My conversations with McCord never involve his facial follicle growth, which he originally grew to hide his Adam's apple in gay bars. Over the years, he has deluded himself into believing that it, and that nose-shrubbery of his is attractive, although to be fair, there is one novelty store in Scottsdale that has had tremendous success, using a picture of him to sell toilet seat picture frames.

David,

Just started to read the columns and emails. Didn't know you gave up the drink. Good for you. As a guy with an Irish ancestry, I have seen both the good and bad side of the sauce. The old man was 20 years sober when he dropped dead but still had a good time in life. I gave it up for over a year and a half. It didn't quite stick with me, but I learned that thing they call moderation. As the brilliant Homer J. Simpson once stated, "Alcohol, the cause of and solution to all of life's problems." Take care, the columns and emails are great.

—Matt Monahan

Matt:

Wow, thanks for cheering me up. What am I supposed to do now, drop dead or start drinking again? Only the Irish can convince you of how lucky you are that you're being hanged with a new rope. Thanks for the kind words, I think.

63

Plan B: Why Tour Players Shouldn't Quit Their Day Jobs

Golf Magazine, *10565493*, *February 2006, Vol. 48, Issue 2*

I was at the optometrist the other day, sitting behind that odd apparatus they swing in front of your nose. The doc slipped a couple of lenses into it. "How does that look to you?" he asked me. "Well," I said, "I was hoping for something a little smaller." And then something snapped in my head like the elastic in Sir Elton John's panties. My eye quack looked suspiciously like Mike Weir playing a doctor. Which got me to thinking about these guys I work with—what would they do if they weren't Tour players? All the broadcast and journalism jobs for clinically depressed alcoholic ex–Tour players with superiority complexes being filled, they would have to find real employment and, frankly, I'm not sure that many of them would be up to the challenge. Here, based solely on appearance and body language, is my best guess at what the likes of Phil and Padraig would be doing if they had 23 handicaps like the rest of us.

Gary McCord: When McCord talks to himself, there are usually several people listening, so we have some possibilities here. He could be some kind of scientist with impossibly thick glasses and a white coat with a pocketful of pens working in a gerbil behavioral research facility, or maybe a theoretical physicist working on 10-dimensional string theory 300 feet below the Utah desert.

Sergio Garcia: He'd be one of two things: a soccer player or a matador in those tight sequin-infested pants. Either way, he'd work well on his tippy-toes.

Justin Leonard: The white one in Spy vs. Spy.

John Daly: First wildly popular director of the Bureau of Alcohol, Tobacco and Firearms.

Bobby Clampett: A tee marker at Pinehurst No. 2.

Tiger Woods: He wouldn't have a 23 handicap, and he could pretty much be whatever the hell he wanted to be—say, president of the United States.

Vijay Singh: No matter how hard I try to imagine him doing something else, the guy is still a professional golfer. Beverly Hills cosmetic surgeon, maybe, but even doing a boob job he'd probably reach for a Ping. Best we leave him in his natural habitat, out on the range.

Phil Mickelson: Phil edges out Mike Weir to be the first American elected prime minister of Canada, largely because during the explanation of his winning strategy at the 2006 Masters, most of the population of Quebec thinks he is talking in French, and about hockey.

Padraig Harrington: A shoo-in for voiceover work in Lucky Charms commercials.

Jean Van de Velde: Victoria's Secret model [ret.], then commissioner of the LPGA Tour.

Ernie Els: Captain of the South African burping team and individual world burping champion (heavyweight division).

Retief Goosen: A speech therapist, but a really bad one.

Jim Furyk: Would play Sam the Eagle on the road tour of Muppets on Ice.

Lanny Wadkins: Admiral in the Japanese navy.

Tim Herron: Figure skater.

Scott Hoch: IRS agent, sensitivity trainer or a greenskeeper at St. Andrews.

Peter Oosterhuis: Prince Charles impersonator, or maybe a giraffe keeper at the zoo—or maybe just a giraffe.

Jesper Parnevik: Designer of a fine line of Scandinavian pimpwear.

Brad Faxon: New England lobsterman, complete with wooden leg and clay pipe.

Peter Kostis: Weather forecaster for the local affiliate in Nome, Alaska.

Jim Nantz: New York City tour-bus guide.

64

David Feherty's Mailbag

Online—Published: February 22, 2006

Dear David,

I have recently noticed a few players on the tour wearing very nice shirts that don't have collars. I'm sure you are aware that some country clubs require all players to wear shirts with collars. I have also heard Greg Norman, 10 or 15 years ago, putting a dig into the PGA for not allowing the players to wear shorts especially during very hot weather. What are your thoughts on the dress code, and its evolvement on the PGA Tour?

—Bill Greene, Mechanicsburg, PA

Bill,

David Duval was the first player to wear un-collared shirts a few years back. Since then, turtlenecks have crept into the permissible sartorial envelope and the necklines have niggled down ever so slightly. Personally, I like it. Most of the guys are in good enough shape to look fine with or without a collar as long as it remains tasteful. If it ever gets down to low-plunging mesh or sheer nylon jumpsuits unzipped to the scrotum, we may have to go to uniforms.

Dear David,

I am in a dilemma (or am I having a dilemma, which would be a dilemma in and of itself). Having a name that sounds similar to yours, especially when spoken by your television cohorts, I feel compelled to voice my opinion during golf broadcasts. The problem is the only one who will listen to me is the dog. How do I get him to stop howling?

—David Heraty, Chicago, IL

David (if indeed David is your real name),

First let's clear up this dilemma crap. Being "in" or "having" a dilemma is the same thing, you pinhead. If you're in a dilemma as to whether or not you're actually in a dilemma, you're plugged in a conundrum. Drop yourself out under penalty and play frickin' on.

I have some suggestions on how to unburden yourself of the problems resulting from the name thing:

1. **Teach the dog to talk.** He may be howling because your observations are idiotic and that's just his way of communicating his disagreement with you. Or alternatively, the pitch of your voice may simply be too high for humans to hear.
2. **Get other dogs in the neighborhood to listen to you as well.** If they all start howling, it's your problem, not theirs.
3. **Stop talking during golf broadcasts.** I am a paid professional, after all.
4. **Change your name to McCord.** The dogs will still howl but they'll be joined by the "Village People."

David,

I purchased a new set of irons last spring. Boy, is new technology great! Unfortunately, I'm in snow up over my knickers and it's time to store them away. "The One Who Must Be Obeyed" is convinced that regular exposure of the clubs and bag to golf course pesticides and weed killers is not a healthy thing in the house. Personally, I would like to keep the clubs in the bedroom and HER in the garage! Oh well, what about the clubs?

—Gregg K., Parma, Ohio

Greg:

Is that where that "Parma" ham comes from? I love that stuff on melons.

The truth is your wife spreads more germs than your clubs do; unless you're picking your nose with your wedge all winter long. If it makes her feel any better, dip the boys in a beaker of Crown Royal Manhattans before you park them in the living room. When you're done sterilizing them you have a delicious cocktail waiting for you. Hey, your next kid might have a tail, but what the hell? My dad always says, "As long as there are Indians in New Delhi going to bed sober, you should never waste a beer." I'm betting your kids look like NFL linebackers when they leave the house to ride their bikes.

Hello David,

Considering the vast amount of money you get paid for sharing your profound and entertaining thoughts on golf, written or verbal, I've been wondering if you've ever kissed the Blarney Stone?

—Serge, Saguenay, Quebec

Serge:

You're getting to be a frequent correspondent, aren't you, Serge? Things a little slow up there, old son?

To really understand this Blarney Stone phenomenon, you should know the legend is that anyone, but particularly an Irishman, who lays a lip lock on the Blarney Stone will be deeded with the "gift of gab." It's a nice concept, but it's, well, blarney. What makes the Irish so brilliant with words, written or otherwise, is fear. Even Cromwell was reluctant to lop off the head of someone in mid-sentence. We figured if we could keep talking, the English would eventually give up and gallop off in frustration looking for someone a little less loquacious to impale.

But the real truth is I'm petrified of heights and that's why I've never bussed the old boulder. The Blarney Stone is located in Blarney Castle in County Cork. The line is a half mile long and winds up the most claustrophobic four stories of decaying, shoulder scraping, wet, cold and miserable steps you've ever seen. As if that's not enough fun, the castle is almost completely disintegrated. The roof is long gone and when you reach the top level where the stone is located, you have to circumnavigate the entire outside rim of the castle, inches from death. When you finally get to the damn thing, you have to lie down on your back and lean down into a hole with some iron bars to keep you from slithering head first to the rocks below. Two Irish gargoyles hold onto your legs and a couple of leprechauns snag the money that falls out of your pocket. Now for the magic moment; you're upside down staring at a snot-encrusted rock. If you listen closely, you can hear the E-coli, dengue fever and other lovely viruses having a party.

No, I've never kissed the Blarney Stone.

65.

Here, There, Everywhere

Golf Magazine, *10565493, March 2006, Vol. 48, Issue 3*

With apologies to Johnny Cash and Willie Nelson, I've been everywhere, man, and it's that time of the year when I'm somewhere again. I'm not looking forward to flying, but now I think I have the check-in and security procedure worked out: I'm traveling naked. I'm taking off all my clothes and my watch and packing them in one of my two carry-on bags. Screw checking a bag. Then, in my lightest pair of wand-repelling underpants, I'll just swan through security and get dressed on the other side. Yes, if I were a country singer I'd be Charlie without the Pride, and this would be a song about my love-hate-detest relationship with these places.

Worst airport traffic system: Philadelphia International. If you miss the cleverly concealed signs (and you will) you have to circumnavigate the entire complex over again. I think this airport was designed by Pete Dye and built by Rube Goldberg.

Best airport shoe shine: No airport shoe-jockeys anywhere can touch the crew at Lambert Field in St. Louis. Perverts fly through Lambert solely to see up the skirts of the women in front of them without having to use their cell phones.

Best airport pretzels: Philly. Put German mustard on these big softies, and the hairs in your nose will combust. Be sure to get a Coke or something with it, or 10 minutes later your tongue will taste like Gandhi's flip-flops.

Scariest landing: Hong Kong. Approach is in between rickety apartment blocks strewn with nasty-looking laundry. If the pilot gets 6 inches off-line, there are skid-marks on the outside of the airplane, too.

Worst airport experience (on ground): Off-property rental car centers. Shoot me in the kneecap, but something's wrong when the ride to pick up or drop off your car is longer than the damned flight.

Worst airport experience (in plane): Being stuck for hours on the tarmac because a bolt of lightning was seen 50 miles away. If I'm going to be held hostage, it'd better be by terrorists, not some comb-over with a silly hat and stripes on his coat sleeves.

Happiest airplane: Anything to Vegas.

Saddest airplane: Anything from Vegas.

Best coach section: The only way you're getting me back there is if I get a chance to give my seat up front to a boy or girl in desert camo. I'd sit outside for them.

Worst possible in-flight experience: Pencil-thin inter-city jets with interiors designed by Hervé Villechaize. You have to de-plane just to change your mind. Opening my laptop once, I knocked three teeth out of the lady sitting next to me. But she was nice and agreed to work the left side of the keyboard for me.

Worst name for the business traveler: Road Warrior. Tell a Marine you're a Road Warrior, and then try to get your laptop out of your ass.

Worst innovation: Those horrible little Bluetooth earpieces for the Road Warrior who has too many important things to do with his hands while he strides through the concourse. (Ladies, this device is an early warning of someone who is unable to have sex without a TV remote in his other hand.)

Best taxi drivers in the world: London. They know 10 ways to get to anywhere, and they don't have to ask you where anywhere is, because they know. "Ear, uvbin teafrow free tahms awreddy t'die." Translated: "My good man, I have been to Heathrow three times already today."

Worst taxi drivers in the world: New York City cabbies smell awful and drive like lunatics (which is a requirement in NYC). But they do get you there ASAP. If you want to see actual insanity, go to Zambia, where I once got in a cab that had a live ostrich in the back seat. It was tranquilized when we set off, and sharp as a razor when we arrived. The driver got my luggage as a tip.

Best place to ask for directions when you're lost: A donut shop. Inside you'll find a cop, a mail carrier, or both.

Best hair stylist out of town: There isn't one, anywhere. I don't give a damn if you look like Cosmo Kramer, let your hair grow until you get back home. No matter how explicit your instructions, if you go for a road-do, you'll come out feeling like you should have panties on your head.

66

A Whole New Skins Game?

Golf Magazine, *10565493*, April 2006, *Vol. 48, Issue 4*

The race for TV ratings seems like a silly business, but what human beings find entertaining hasn't changed for centuries: a dash of public humiliation or triumph is best, with risk of serious physical or mental injury tossed in. Not that long ago, we gathered in droves to toss rotten vegetables at some poor sod who'd been locked in the stocks for, say, playing the lute really badly. For the average pox-addled villager, an opportunity to mock the fallen warmed the cockles the same way that *American Idol* does today. Please, don't try to tell me that show is about winners. It relies almost entirely on stupid people who have either no friends or mean friends. ("Hey dude, I think I can sing, d'ya think I should try out?" "Go for it!")

We've had a couple of reality shows in golf, but so far none of them has had enough of the old squirmage factor to fit into the *Idol* category. I have high hopes for *The Daly Planet,* the first episode of which airs as I write. Big Johnny should leave a trail of rich white trash behind him that's visible from space, covering the humiliation aspect, and the guy's just brilliant enough to win another major.

Now I have a shot myself. I'm hosting the St. Joseph Pressure

Challenge (May 14 and 20, 2 p.m. EST, CBS, just prior to tele-casts of the Byron Nelson and the Colonial), produced by this very magazine, and I intend to inflict suffering of biblical pro-portions upon the Regular Joes therein. Verily, there shall be pestilence from above and heckling from beside these poor souls as they attempt to make pars for increasing amounts of cash. If they make nine in a row, they win $250,000. But there's a *Who Wants to Be a Millionaire* catch: After each par, they can pocket the money, or risk losing it all with a bogey on the next hole. While the contestants will view this as their chance of a lifetime, I'm thinking of it as a useful outlet for all the pent-up vitriol I have up my kilt after 10 years of watching the pros. The problem with covering the Tour is that I never get to see crappy golf. It's always right at the flag or the middle of the green. I'm bored.

Which leads me to wondering how much the world of golf might change when everything on TV is packaged like a reality show—a couple of seasons from now, I mean. The sweet spot seems to be humiliation combined with maximum bare skin, and since golf already has plenty of the former (whiffs, whoop-sies, shanks, duffs, flinches, flubs, etc.), right away we'd have to start getting the tackle off. It'd be a whole new kind of skins game: For every bogey, the naughty golfer would have to remove an article of clothing. "Tiger, 4-over with three to play, is one shot away from the leopard skin plum-smuggler, but now let's go to the third where big John Daly is playing his 11th shot! Dear God, he's going to have to shed his spinnaker!" It wouldn't be pretty, but neither is *The Biggest Loser.*

And I see good things here for the LPGA, equal-opportunity-wise. With the trend toward physical fitness spreading into the women's game, and players getting younger and better-looking by the minute, the ladies suddenly might give the men a run for the ratings on Sunday afternoon. Advertisers know that until someone makes me a pair of underpants with oppos-able thumbs, I'm never going to stop putting my hands in my pockets to adjust my coin purse, and doing all the other guy things guys do, like looking at attractive females, which is, admittedly, disgraceful. On behalf of the 99 percent of the men who are reading this and feel exactly the same way (author's estimate: probably a little low), I apologize. But the bottom line is this: If I need to see a triple-chinned, wobbly breasted salad swerver attempting an athletic endeavor, I'll play golf with Roger Maltbie.

Would it work? Well, the closest thing we have to reality-based golf today is the AT&T Pebble Beach National Pro-Am. Never mind which pro is in the lead, what people want to see is Kevin Costner looking windswept and magnificent with his tie tucked into his vest, topping one off the cliff at the eighth, and George Lopez refusing to rake bunkers in one of his frightening argyles. Now, if we could just throw in Kevin James, one duff away from his birthday suit, maybe that would give *Fear Factor* a run for its ratings.

67

David Feherty's Mailbag

Online—Published: April 18, 2006

David,

After the unfortunate and uptight attitude shown to Gary McCord by the Masters for his comments regarding the fairway undulations, how difficult was it for you to keep your wickedly sarcastic sense of humor in check while being part of the announcing crew this year? It seems you had to check your nads at the gate.

—Bill Busch

Bill:

Let's clear up the "check your nads at the gate" thing first: My entire package, including my nads and my unit, never leave the house. She Who Must Be Obeyed stands guard at the back door, ziplock freezer bag in hand whenever I head for the airport. Only after I deposit the jewels in the bag may I leave the house. She puts the bag in the freezer and I get everything back upon my return. My normal voice is much deeper than you hear on TV; I go up an octave when I'm on the road. The good news is I rarely have to shave when I'm away and I don't seem to mind joining McCord antiquing or shopping for new dust ruffles and throw pillows. Occasionally we go to the pool and shave each other's back.

And I never discuss the Masters. Ever.

Dear David,

I was rooting for Phil until recently when I heard that his nickname on tour is FIGJAM. Any truth to this? Or is this just a case of a minority of also-rans just bellyaching?

—Patrick

Patrick:

Well most of the time he'll tell you and not bother to invite you to ask, so I'm not sure FIGJAM fits, but for everything I love about Mickelson, he's not perfect. Let's face it, when you've won as much and as often as he has, it's hard not to order some bigger hats.

Two other factors: 1) Jealousy and 2) Misinterpretation. It's natural for some of the boys to resent his success. Phil knows that and I don't think he ever knowingly or purposely throws it in anyone's face. And sometimes people, especially those with an ax to grind, might hear a perfectly innocent remark and interpret it in a way that suits their already formed opinion. If you ever have a chance to meet Phil, I'm pretty sure you'll come away with a positive opinion. Continue to root for him unabated.

Dear David:

Do you think Tiger would withdraw from the Masters if his dad died during the tournament?

—Chris Garbord

Chris:

Absolutely, you morbid idiot.

David,

I find myself going to the last page of the magazine (your article) as soon as GOLF arrives. This has become, and continues to be, either an obsession or superstition. With my handicap, you would think I would read the instructional articles first. What can I do to remedy my actions?

—Mike Giel, Lawrenceville, GA

Mike:

Why can't it be both? Most obsessions start out as superstitions to begin with, but that doesn't make them mutually exclusive. Having said that, failing to heed superstitions usually results in some dire consequence. For instance, I know for a fact that if I don't have exactly three tees, two Irish penny coins in my pocket and shift my right testicle one inch to the left before I hit a drive, it's going dead left. By the way, that last statement will have every bit as much effect on the outcome of your swing as all the instruction articles ever written. So look, pal, if you want to waste your time searching for the answer to your golf problems by reading those idiots, be my guest. But I'm afraid I have to insist you continue to read my article first. Only then can you possibly be in the right frame of mind to tackle an instruction article that will have you bent into a pretzel in no time.

Better yet, start buying my books, you pantload.

Dear David,

I was always a big fan of David Duval. Do you think he will ever be back on top? Or at least near the top with the best players in the world.

—Jamie Waynesburg, PA

Jamie:

Every now and then David will post a low number and we will all get excited. It's like a guy who's been in a coma suddenly sitting up and reciting the Gettysburg Address, only to suddenly splash back down and not move for another year. It's soul-destroying to watch. Maybe we could arrange a space and channel the old David back. I wonder if Copperfield would do it.

68.

And It Stoned Me

Golf Magazine, *10565493, May 2006, Vol. 48, Issue 5*

The whole issue of booze and professional sports has become a
touchy one in these righteous times, as Bode Miller found out.
Apparently, a person who dives headfirst down an icy cliff
wearing a spandex jumpsuit is supposed to celebrate with a
nice glass of tea. We all know when one drinks tea, one must
extend one's pinky finger. Bode drank the Long Island version
and extended the wrong finger, that's all. Personally, I thought
he was refreshingly brisk, eccentric, and just plain different.
But these days a jock with a tendency to celebrate needs to be
doing post-career laps on the media circuit before he pulls the
trigger of truth. That way he's not a bad person, just a colorful
character. Sorry, but that's bollocks—and this is one of those
rare occasions when I know what I'm talking about, trust me.

Why do many people believe that today's athletes have less
character than those of the past? Think Mickey Mantle, Joe
Namath, Wilt Chamberlain. Answer: It's not the jocks—it's the
journalists. In those days writers traveled, stayed and frequently
got wrecked with the players. They had a vested interest in
each other's occupations. There was an unspoken code: The
pencil-squeezer didn't rat the player out, period. The scoop was

never worth the price of the relationship with an athlete. I don't know when it started to change, but journalists today face much greater pressure from editors, who in turn answer to media moguls hellbent on satiating our appetite for scandal. Upside: Juiced ball players and 'roidally enraged wife beaters are exposed. Downside: We've traded in the chance to know what the rest of the characters really think, and who they really are.

Mind you, I was one of your golfers with a tendency to celebrate. I never knew Jimmy Demaret, but I bet I would have loved him. In 1962 he was playing the Crosby at Pebble Beach when he flung open the drapes to find a blanket of snow on the ground, at which point Demaret said, "I know I got loaded last night, but how the hell did I end up in Squaw Valley?" Imagine Ernie Els going with that line today? One of my favorite people, Tom Weiskop-with-a-lowercase-f, is a founding member of the hangover hall of fame. (The fact Tom isn't in the real one indicates the wrong people vote.)

In his waaay-heyday, Saint Tom of Columbus would have a few (hundred) drinks and go to bed feeling fine, but of course he'd feel like a bag of crap when he woke up. The big T concluded his problem wasn't the electric soup, it was the sleep, so with beautifully simple logic rivaled only by his swing, he chose to stop sleeping. Bert Yancey once said that some of the greatest rounds of golf he ever witnessed were 71s and 72s from Tom Weiskopf. But one year at the Tournament Players Championship in the 1970s, Tom went drinking with Edgar Sneed and the great writer Dan Jenkins, both of whom bailed out around two o'clock in the morning. Tom forged on through the night. Early next morning he blundered through the first two holes with a pair of 6s. Before he hit his tee shot on the third, he called for a ruling. PGA Tour official Eddie Griffiths was stunned when Tom claimed he couldn't go on unless Eddie brought him an egg sandwich, a vanilla milkshake and three aspirin. Eddie, stout man that he was, had the remedy by the time Tom reached the green, and Tom went on to make nine birdies in the last 15 to shoot 66. When Dan and Ed went to the scoreboard to see what Tom had shot, Jenkins declared that it was "the greatest round of golf ever played by a dead man."

We're talking about trying to get a ball in a hole, or sliding down an icy hill on a pair of planks—games. And people who like games often like a drink afterward. For Tom Weiskopf, the only life or death involved was his own, and he hasn't had a drink since Jan. 2, 2000.

How many times has an innocent man been sent down because Jack Daniel's was a witness that only a hungover judge could hear? Call me old-fashioned, but that judge is the real bad example. If Bode Miller and Tom Weiskopf are bad influences too, then I'm registering as an offender at the nearest police station. Keep your kids away from me, neighbor, because I was a bad example to those guys you think are bad examples today.

69

The Naked Truth

Golf Magazine, *10565493, June 2006, Vol. 48, Issue 6*

I spent the two days after the AT&T in Pebble Beach shooting Cobra commercials in Palm Springs. I had to bounce on a trampoline in a cheerleader's outfit, and was worried that something might pop out, you know, like those female Russian weightlifters in the 1970s, so I had doubled up and worn a pair of men's briefs underneath my big yellow panties. As it turned out I needn't have worried; the panties were industrial polyester, designed to keep zitty teenage boys out, and so tight it was all I could do not to yodel.

Later, back at the hotel, I was in the bathroom to take a pee, which didn't go well. You see, it felt *soooo* good to take my panties off—men: it's almost as good taking your own panties off as someone else's, really—I forgot I was wearing the safety pair underneath, and had slipped my boxers on over them, and then my jeans. Having to dress as a teenage girl all day had been traumatic enough, but when I went into my jeans for little Dave and found nothing, I screamed, and wet myself a little bit too. It was the end of a long strange day, and tomorrow didn't look like it was going to be any better: I was going to have a nude photo taken. (The picture is farther back in the magazine, but don't go there now . . . Oh, what's the point?)

And welcome back, sorry if you're disappointed. Few people my age ever see a mirror they like, even when they have their clothes on. I'm almost 48. Given the way I've lived my life, I have the face I deserve. If you factor in the 12 years of sleep I've missed, I look a net 60. So I was worried about this photo. A large-format film camera with a one-second exposure is designed to reveal flaws in brutal detail. I had an irrational fear I might get one of those dreadful four-hour erections and no one would notice, but the main thing was that I can't do serious expressions—I'm too self-conscious. If I try to be serious, I look exhausted by constipation.

Before the shoot, my ruthless agent, Basil O'Turdlington, pointed out that this is the last year of my current contract with CBS, which may or may not make it the best time to admit a long struggle with mental illness. But as I told Basil, my out-to-lunch-ness probably hadn't escaped the attention of my employers. Why not flop out the wobblies for the camera just for good measure? I informed every relevant party of my intentions to bare both my soul and my ass, and the reason why. Not everyone, actually. This is where the wisdom left me, for because I was sore afraid, I neglected to tell She Who Must Be Obeyed one tiny detail: that I was taking my clothes off. It's no big thing, I thought. Just a photo. Of me. Naked. It's symbolic. Artful. She might be a little miffed at first, but it'll be nice, and it'll help people, and, dear God, please don't let her kill me.

I thought she was going to kill me. Turned out I had left out another tiny detail, that the photographer, Karen Keuhn, was a woman, and, worse still, a female one. I had incurred the wrath of my 95 pounds of Mississippi madness before, but when she saw the first photo, I felt like I was in a scene from *The Exorcist*. Her eyes turned plutonium-rod-water green, and

I thought she was going to vomit at me, but it was much worse than that. She went straight for the woman's weapon of mass destruction. She pretended to be fine. It was quiet around our house for a while, but after three weeks, my best friend—which is why she must be obeyed—finally looked at the stack of 8-by-10 photos, and picked out the twisted one that appeared in the rag.

Turned out all she wanted was to know the truth and to be included. If you read the story you'll realize I owe her a lot more than that—my life, for a start.

So, to review: I had dressed up like a cheerleader (think Molly Shannon, but hairy), wet my pants and then got naked on a photographer's set that was closed about as often as Lee Trevino's mouth. I also thought that my wife wouldn't be upset about it, and some of you might be surprised to hear I have struggled with mental illness. And this is my life when I'm well? I must need my f——ing head seen to.

70

David Feherty's Mailbag

Online—Published: June 22, 2006

Dear David—

I'm another EURO transplanted in the USA, smitten by the golf bug but incapable of playing a decent round without the idiot I am playing with coughing or otherwise distracting me. By the way, I recently saw McCord butt naked, streaking across the 10th fairway wearing nothing but a sombrero and a pair of heels, but I digress. The fool also laughs if I miss a short putt. Can one hire Uncle Dickie and his men to hide behind the pot bunker on the fourth hole at my course to beat some golf etiquette into my playing partner, the moron?

—Petrovich, Boston

Petrovich:

Welcome to the land of the free and the home of the brave; damn glad to have ya. If this guy's an American, you can't stop him by showing that he's getting to you; that'll only encourage the bounder. The best way to cure him is to wager ridiculous amounts of money on every conceivable outcome on every hole: Longest drive, closest to the pin, longest putt, etc. When your tab gets in the several-thousand-dollar range after the match, tell him you never intended to pay him and the next time he coughs, hiccups, farts or rattles his change you'll hit him square in the nut sack with a Vokey wedge. Uncle Dickie and the boys don't do wet work.

And that couldn't have been McCord you saw; he wears fluffy mules with his sombrero.

Mr. Feherty,
What the hell is up with the picture of you on the banner of this website? You look like you're trying to impress a lonely looking llama from across the room.

—Mike, Toronto, Canada

Mike:
Actually, you have a point, but hey, have you got some problem with bestiality, pal? How'd you like to spend nine straight weeks on the road with only Kostis to hang out with? Last week it got so bad, I took a chick called Bobbie Clampette to dinner.

David "F-ING" Feherty,
You seem to know a little about golf, so here goes. Is it immoral to take a few practice balls from the range? How about one of the mats? Thanks for your guidance.

—Brad Titus, Carlsbad, Calif.

Brad,
Hell no, it's fine to pilfer a few balls from the range, pinch the odd mat or two, no worries. In fact, those little range pickers make great dune buggies once you get them revved up. Who told you any of that's immoral? Illegal, yes, but immoral? No way. And just for the record, you can steal those BullsEye putters at the Miniature Golf place as well.

Mr. Feherty,

I am a 30-year-old staff sergeant in the US Army with three years till I get out. I have always loved golf and finally have the ability to afford clubs and play. When I first started I was shooting 136, now I am in the 90s after only three months of playing. I want to get out of the army and play golf for a living. Is this unheard of? Can I still try to go pro at this late stage of my life? I just want to make a living for once doing something I truly love. Thank you for your time.

—Brian G. Burwell, SSG,
U.S. Army Infantry

Brian:

I'll give you the straight skinny, as they say in the Navy, which is like the Army, but on a boat. (Don't ask me how I know what they say in the Navy, it's a sordid story involving inflatables.) First the broad view: Sure, anything's possible. You could get your tour card and go on to blow by Snead's all-time tournament wins, Jack's major record and Byron's eleven in a row. However, the odds are similar to me becoming President of Cuba. If I were you I'd think about trying to get into golf TV production instead. The idiots I work with play all the golf they want and get to watch the good stuff close up too. I'm always glad to help out the guys who really ship the cheese around here, and you, my friend, are one of them. Thanks for your service to all of us.

Dear David,

When I really need to exercise my stomach muscles with a good laugh I seek out your column. When did your humor get formed and did overbearing, knuckle-whacking nuns have anything to do with it?

—R. Franklin, Chicago

R.,

I have a school report that starts, "David is not a particularly intelligent boy, but he can take a punch." The mere sight of a nun made me soil myself. My daughter and I were watching *The Sound of Music* only yesterday, and it happened again.

71

Criminal Negligence

Golf Magazine, *10565493, July 2006, Vol. 48, Issue 7*

Investigative journalism (that is, the Woodward-Bernstein variety) involves two things I try to avoid, investigation and journalism. I see no future in either. But I do enjoy a good crime scene, and sometimes curiosity overpowers my natural instincts, as it did in the strange case of the World Golf Hall of Fame. It turns out there are some bodies missing from the Hall, and the perps haven't left a clue (because you can't leave what you don't have) to explain why Lanny Wadkins, Curtis Strange, Hubert Green and Tom Weiskopf, for example, who won six majors and 73 Tour titles among them, aren't in. Weiskopf has never even made it onto the ballot! This gumshoe wanted answers.

I tightened the belt of my battered raincoat, turned up the collar, tilted a gray fedora down over my eyebrows, and lit up a Lucky Strike. All of which was pointless because I wasn't going any farther than my study and cigarettes make me blow chunks, but, hey, I like to play dress-up.

I called in some favors from my golf snitches to find out who does the voting for the Hall, who chooses the voters, and what these idiots are smoking. Within hours I had my answer, a cleverly coded two-word phrase ending in "off," which suggested that my questions had struck a nerve.

It looked more and more like I was going to have to do some real detective work. So I punched "PGA Tour Hall of Fame" into Google, moved Ziggy the beagle off the desk and put my feet up. Now we were getting somewhere. The search results shocked me like a headcheese belch in a Wisconsin deli. There were absolutely no men in the Hall, only women! Then it dawned on me . . . the L is just slightly below and to the left of the P on my keyboard. Yeah, I do in fact type with beagle paws.

I splashed cold water on my face, and glanced in the toothpaste-spattered mirror in my bathroom. It had been a grueling few minutes, and the evidence was on my face. Like a goat staring at a wristwatch, I just couldn't understand. And it looked like I might have to eat it. Although it burned my raisins to have to do it, I called the Park Avenue cube farm that produces *Golf Magazine* and asked for some help working the thingy. They were polite and all that, so I fired up another Lucky, puked in the trash can, and waited for a call back.

It turns out that the PGA Tour voting body is made up of journalists, with a side order of historians and dignitaries, some of who are still alive, and holding grudges. It didn't take me long to figure out that the missing victims have one thing in common: in their big-dog days they all had a tendency to tell journalists, historians and dignitaries where to stick their pencils, history and dignity. Straight talkers, my kind of guys. So now we had a motive. For $50 a day plus expenses, you can wrap me in Scotch tape and tear it off slowly, but I'm beginning to think someone is afraid that this character Wadkins might approach one of these voting stiffs from behind and try to slip a C-note into his tweed underpants.

The Strange guy was the best player in the world when he won back-to-back U.S. Opens in '88 and '89, and Hubert Green won one of his majors under a threat, and is surviving another one. And the word on the street is that there's a good chance that someone will kill Wadkins every week. Whatever. They should all be in this World Golf tin of peas, including that big gun-happy weirdo, Weiskopf. These guys aren't in the same category as Barry Bonds or Pete Rose. You can put an asshole after their names if it makes you happy, but not an asterisk. And while I'm yelling into the phone at you, I can tell you for a fact that Fuzzy Zoeller is not a card-carrying Ku Klux Klansman, either. For God's sake, the man's middle name is Urban. Now I'm gonna see if I can get this freak Weiskopf to glue a possum on his head, and pretend he's holding something that can cut you. It might get him on the ballot. Don't laugh, it worked for a skinny Puerto Rican called Chi Chi. At least, that's what the evidence tells me.

72

A Style of His Own

Golf Magazine, *10565493, July 2006, Vol. 48, Issue 7*

There's something different about Darren Clarke. Maybe it's because he puts a high premium on fun. Or maybe it's the sadness at home. Or perhaps, as fearless gumshoe (and the only man to whom Clarke would grant an interview) David Feherty discovers, it also has a little something to do with being Irish.

A decade or so ago, Darren Clarke was forging his way onto the world golf stage, just as I was falling into the orchestra pit. We're both from Ulster, so it's often difficult for me to steer clear of openly rooting for him. But support is one thing the big lad has never lacked. His warm fuzzability and willingness to buy a round of pints have made him a crowd favorite wherever he plays. And those pants? Well, it's kind of hard to ignore a man in lavender plaid who, from behind, looks like he could kick-start a jumbo jet. In the early part of Darren's career he was, by his own admission, too hard on himself, but the last three years have been different. His beautiful wife, Heather, puts up a spectacular fight—daily—against breast cancer, and it takes a vile toll on him. But thankfully, Ulster folk are experts at dealing with heartache and getting on with the job. Recently, I had a chance to talk with my friend and countryman about everything that used to matter to him, and the only thing that's important to him now.

So then, is the British Open at the top of the list of tournaments you'd like to win?

The Open is always No. 1 on my list.

Given that it must feel like a home crowd to you even though it's always in England or Scotland, do you feel a bit more pressure there as opposed to the other three majors?

I feel it is the major I have the best chance of winning and because of that there is possibly a bit more pressure, but I'm used to it by now.

What's the first thing you'd do with the Claret Jug if you won the Open?

Kiss it.

Have you played Hoylake?

I have played Hoylake and it is a very good test. And my memories of it are happy ones because I won a pro-celebrity tournament there in the early 1990s.

Why do you think European players haven't had more success in the majors?

That's a good question that comes up a lot and there's no real explanation for it, because we do have a lot of really good players. I think one obvious answer is Tiger's domination and because we play better on teams.

Is that why Europe has been so successful in the Ryder Cup?

Probably because of the team spirit. I think you know that, David, as well. We have that spirit that pulls us together. Everybody wants everybody to help each other. It's just part of the European Tour culture. We all travel together and stay at the same hotels.

Does it mean more to a European player to get on the Ryder Cup team?

I think so. The PGA Tour is the biggest and best tour in the world, there's no debating that. But in the U.S., it's much more of an individual sport. In Europe, it's different. I don't know quite how to put it. The Ryder Cup is almost the pinnacle of a European Tour player's career. You just feel so much for your teammates and work so hard because you don't want to let them down. So yeah, it is a big difference.

What do you think it will be like playing in front of the home crowd in this year's Ryder Cup (at the K Club in Ireland)? Do you think it will add to what's already an insanely pressure-packed few days? This will be your fifth Cup. Does it get any easier as you go on?

No. It doesn't get any easier. It will still be the same sleepless nights. I'm looking forward to it and I'm hesitating at the same time. Ireland will be a sensational venue for it and the atmosphere will be like nowhere else before. I think the crowd will be very fair. The Irish and the Americans are very much linked and because of the camaraderie I think it will be a fair and fantastic time.

When you first went to the Ryder Cup do you remember thinking to yourself, "Holy crap, I'm on a Ryder Cup team!"?

Yeah. It's kind of like having your first child: Unless you've done it you don't know what to expect and you can't explain it. That's exactly what it was like. I played with Monty on Saturday morning and I think he'd spoken a couple of words to me by Friday. After my first tee shot I ended up having to play through a tree or under a tree, so I had my first shock right away.

Did Seve [Ballesteros] look at you differently when you got your first Ryder Cup point? I know he did with me at Kiawah Island. I made a putt and all of a sudden this guy was my friend. He had never spoken six words to me before.

I don't recall. There wasn't a lot of communication between the two of us.

Do you think we'll see more of the Lee Westwood–Darren Clarke pairing?

I hope so. I think if you take a look at our results it's a pretty good pairing. We travel a lot with each other and play a lot with each other and we drink more than enough with each other. Probably too much, but we have a good time and we enjoy each other's company.

Talking about Ryder Cup celebrations, what's the most fun you've had? I remember using you as a sofa at the Belfry. I have a photograph of me and Jesper Parnevik on the dance floor leaning up on you like you're a dead water buffalo on the floor.

I wouldn't deny that in the slightest. I know the last one was particularly bad. I remember on the Monday morning Mr. Westwood and myself were up and we didn't get any sleep that night. We just had to carry on and go to the airport to get the flight back home. Westwood was a little bit more intoxicated than I was—which was an awful lot. We bought a couple of cowboy hats at the airport, and wore these ridiculous cowboy hats with the European Tour uniform getting onto the plane.

Even drunk you were able to accessorize. You've always been really good at that.

At what? Drinking or accessorizing? We flew home on Virgin Atlantic from the Ryder Cup and there was a bar on the plane. The flight was 10 hours and I think we spent nine of them at the bar. So just in case I didn't have enough the previous evening, I decided to carry on all the way home. A few of my teammates propped me up when we were meeting with the press after we got off the plane.

You had a great match with Tiger Woods in a match-play tournament two years ago [the 2004 Accenture Match Play Championship, which Clarke won] and you handled him pretty confidently. Would you have the same confidence in a Ryder Cup match? Bottom line is he doesn't have a great Ryder record.

He doesn't and it's very strange. If you take a look at his U.S. record it's second to none, but in the Ryder Cup I don't think—and he readily admits—that he has played golf in his best form. But anytime you get a chance to compete against Tiger, who's the best player in the world, you have to take a look at the challenges that come with it to improve your game. If you manage to come out on top then you know you're doing the right thing.

The season Tiger had that year is among the best in golf history, but you got the better of him. Is there a moment that stands out with the two of you that day? I remember Tiger going to the range in between rounds and you going to the clubhouse for a cigar and a cheeseburger.

Yes, I enjoyed myself. I thought there was no way I was walking down that hill to the range and back up again. We had breakfast together that morning and you know how Tiger gets when he gets pumped up about something and he's got his fist pumped and he's running around the greens. So I said, "Now if you hole a chip and start fist-pumping around the green, I'm going to run after you and hit you." Tiger said, "You can run all you want 'cause you won't catch me."

Will you consider your career a failure if you don't win a major?

I will be extremely disappointed, yeah.

I was kind of coming off the Tour as you were coming on and our careers barely overlapped, but I know you used to be really hard on yourself. You're an Ulsterman, so you're a special kind of Irishman. We have a low threshold of tolerance for ourselves. You've been different the last couple of years and I know your priorities have changed with Heather [Clarke's wife] being sick. Is golf less important to you?

Much less important to me than it used to be. It used to be the end-all-be-all and I'd lie in my bed at night and analyze every shot that I hit that day, thinking about what I messed up and what I needed to do to make sure I didn't make the same mistakes over again. Now, I go out and try to play as well as I can. If I do, I do. If I don't, I don't. When I'm done I have a couple of beers. It's my job and I enjoy it most of the time—not all of the time, but most of the time.

What's the worst time you've ever had on the golf course?

I've had a few. We've all had a few. Where have I messed up

really badly? Oh, years ago at the European Open, which is held at the K Club, I shot 60, and 66 the following day, and then 75 the last day. Lee Westwood shot 64 the last day and beat me.

The rotten bastard!

Tell me about it. That was a real low point because nobody had won at home in Ireland since John O'Leary had won the Irish Open [1982], and I played so well all week and I was going into the last round with a six-shot lead, and I managed to completely mess it up and didn't win. That one hurt an awful lot. Not that Lee had won, just that I disappointed myself and all the people who were there. But then two years later I returned and won at the K Club [in 2001].

Do you think the new crop of flat-bellies out there have enough fun in their lives? I mean, you're kind of carrying the torch for me.

Compared to us? No. I think one of the good things about the European Tour is that it's a global tour and they play everywhere. There's nothing like going all over the world playing and experiencing different places and cultures and different aspects of misbehaving.

You've got a reputation for being a guy who enjoys himself with some pints and cigars. Has a late night ever cost you a few shots in a Tour event?

Oh, most definitely.

Has it been worth it?

Definitely.

That's an acceptable answer. How much have you cut back on booze and cigars? I mean, Heather's not well, so does that ever cross your mind? Like how should you balance the way you want to live your life and making sure she's going to be OK?

That's a very good question at the moment for me. Heather's been battling very hard now for the past couple of years. She was first diagnosed with breast cancer and then she got the all-clear for a year and a half and then she was diagnosed with secondary breast cancer, which has moved on to different areas of her body. But the fact that she's been so brave and dealt with it so well, I know I couldn't do it. I'd be a wreck. Yes, we have to get on with our lives.

How do you stay positive? These are issues that most people think about for a while and then banish from their heads, but you can't do that. You have to be there for her.

Right. We spent the week before Augusta in Abaco in the Bahamas—we've got a house down there.

Bone fishing?

Yup.

That's something we can do together. Also, you're coming quail hunting with me, right?

Oh yeah. I bought a brand-new Xtrema2 Beretta. Have you seen it? It takes 12-gauge shells and gets 'em all out in two seconds.

We're going to go to smaller gauges, 28-gauge side by side, little pop-pop gentlemen's guns.

I'm in. Where were we? Oh yeah, so we were down in Abaco and I went to Augusta very laid back. I had lain on the beach all week, done a little bit of bone fishing and spent some time with the kids and Heather. So at Augusta I was very relaxed and went and played. The press guys asked me how I was doing and I said, "Well, you know, I don't really care." Heather got home on Monday and took a look at some of the clips our housekeeper kept and said, "What's all this about you not caring? And not trying?" I told her I was just really relaxed and she said, "Don't think you're going to get away with not caring just because everybody thinks I'm too ill to do anything." And that's typically her answer for everything. She's not going to let me get away with anything. Because she's unbelievably positive, and that's good for me.

Tiger said that the golf course was kind of an escape for him with what was going on with his father's illness. Can you put yourself in that cocoon while you're out there?

Yeah, most definitely, without putting myself above mistakes. Tiger made a lot of mistakes that he doesn't normally make and you've got to put a lot of that into his dad not being well. And I'm doing similarly. We played together the first two rounds at TPC Sawgrass and not only do I enjoy playing with him but we had similar things going on so it was very easy to identify with him.

Are you a pain in the ass when you're at home?

A complete pain in the ass. I couldn't live with myself.

Is it like living with a Kodiak bear?

Worse than that. Much worse than that. You've got to get me out. It's difficult because I want to be there. I want to be at home. But at the same time I can't sit there and do nothing. The toughest time is when I'm away on Tour and we're waiting for tests and scans to come back. It's hard because you never know what they're going to say.

People feel like they have to say something about Heather, but it must be difficult for people to know how to approach you or deal with it. What is the one thing you tell people on the question of "How do you approach Darren Clarke?" I think about Heather all the time and I don't know how to balance that with . . .

I know exactly what you're saying. Just ask me how my wife's doing and tell me that you're thinking about me and that's enough. Ninety-nine percent of the guys out here say that to me. I got a wonderful note from Phil Mickelson in my locker at TPC offering to help us with anything that we needed. He offered to look after the boys. Just the littlest things make a world of difference with me.

Your appearance has changed radically in the past three years. You're fat, you're thin, you're fat.

It's a bastard for the wardrobe space because you've got to have four different wardrobes. I have pants that I save and think, "I'll get back into those later," but it is up and down again.

You've always been that way, kind of all or nothing. When you do something you do it all the way to the limit. You do as well and as much as you can and when you don't, you don't.

The best part of it has been that I can have beers again. I

couldn't have Guinness or any beers during that. So that's one good thing about not frequenting the gym as often as possible.

I kind of miss that, too.

Exactly.

I miss it right now.

I could definitely do with not eating and just drink a couple of beers.

You wear a lot of psychedelic stuff. What's the one thing you wouldn't be caught dead wearing? Have you worn a kilt yet?

I haven't managed to get into that yet.

You've got the legs for it.

Thank you very much. What will I not wear? The flowery things are getting a little over the edge for me.

You're from Dungannon. Could you imagine wearing one of those outfits that you wear right now to school?

I would have had the shit kicked out of me, which is typical Northern Ireland behavior.

Would you have gotten into the clubhouse at Royal Portrush?

Debatable. Very debatable.

Do you have a little black book with the names of people who've been unfair to you?

Oh, shit yeah, oh yeah, and I don't forget. I wait. It might take me 10 or 15 years but I'll wait and I'll get them. And there have been a couple of them that have had to wait and I've got them. And they don't know it, but I've got them and that makes it even better.

You've said guys like Tiger and Freddie Couples don't get your sense of humor. What do you mean by that? The Ulster sense of humor is dark.

Yeah, and sometimes it's hard and it cuts to the bone.

You and I grew up there and people don't understand. It's like Baghdad with shitty weather. People are tough there and in order to survive you have to have that sense of humor.

It's a peculiarly Ulster thing.

You've been in the public eye for years. What's one thing Americans would be surprised to learn about you?

They might he surprised that I actually do work pretty hard on my game. People think I spend more time in the bar than I do on the range, but that's actually not quite right.

It must be pretty close though, right?

You can't practice in the dark, but I do put a lot of work into my game.

Are you aware just how popular you are here? The people feel like they know you. You're a blue-collar guy . . .

It's different for people like Tiger and Phil and Vijay and people like that. They're always out there and they always have to perform. I'm out here to try to perform but also to have a good time doing it as long as I can. The people who come to watch give me a great deal of support. And I'm that kind of guy you can come down to the pub with and have a beer. We're no different than anybody else. Sometimes we get over ourselves and forget what it is we're doing. But, it's very easy to lose that at times. The Ryder Cup is almost the pinnacle of a European Tour player's career.

THE CLARKE REPORT

Height 6′ 2″
Weight: 215
Birthplace: Dungannon, Northern Ireland
Turned pro: 1990
Career earnings: $6,665,133
Official World Golf Ranking: 19
PGA Tour victories (2): WGC-Andersen Consulting Match Play (2000), WGC-NEC Invitational (2003)
Hobbies: Clothes, cars, films, bone fishing
How he started: As a caddie for his father, a course superintendent

Home course: Royal Portrush

Lowest score: 60, on two occasions. He put "DC-60" on his Ferrari to commemorate it.

Ryder Cup record: Four-time European Ryder Cup team member. Career record in the matches is 7–8–2. Will play in his fifth in September.

73

Trophy Hunting

Golf Magazine, *10565493*, August 2006, Vol. 48, Issue 8

I just love the British Open Championship, especially the ones played back in the days when there were more sheep on the course than golfers, and it was difficult to tell the two apart.

The Claret Jug, for which they first played in 1873, was commissioned by the Royal & Ancient from Mackay Cunningham & Co. of Edinburgh for the grand sum of £30. That doesn't sound like much now, but bear in mind that back then a bespoke pair of Purdeys (which, were I to buy today, would subsequently be used by She Who Must Be Obeyed to fill my rapidly fleeing buttocks full of No. 8 birdshot) could be stolen for a mere £15. A handmade driving club from club-maker Laurie Auchterlonie, which retailed for under a fiver in the late 19th century, fetches an unholy fortune at auction today.

My dad had a long-nosed playclub, which sat in the corner of our garage, quietly confident in its rarity value and place in golf history, until one day a 9-year-old American Indian decided that with a little alteration it would make a splendid sharp-nosed spear to throw at the snot-nosed little cowpoke down the street. The bastard was asking for it after unkindly giving the little brave the nickname "Tiny Loincloth." But as happens when an ancient treasure is disturbed, a curse fell. The relic was bad medicine, and later that Indian summer evening Tiny Loincloth's butt cheeks were as red as the dusky sky. His dad, Chief Slightly Larger Loincloth, was heap-big put out.

I've often wondered where that club might have ended up if the head hadn't been cut off and it hadn't lodged itself between the front spokes of that palefaced little arsehole's getaway horse, hurling him out of his saddle, nose-first into my Auntie Brenda's begonias. It might have made its way into a private collection, or even the R&A museum in St. Andrews. If you're ever lucky enough to wangle your way into the R&A clubhouse, you'll see beautiful trophies with silly names evoking the days when a man wasn't a man unless he had a few switch marks on his bum from a damned good public-school thrashing earlier that morning, even if he hadn't been to school for 40 years.

British golf history is liberally sprinkled with absurdly named trophies like the Antlers, the Kent Cob and the Tooting Bee Cup, which is awarded to the Brit player in the Open Championship with the lowest single round, and if that guy's not available, to the best tooter.

Upon further investigation I found out that anything the limeys could do, Americans could do bigger, better and with a middle initial. If you think the silliest name for an American tournament trophy is the Wanamaker (PGA), you're not even close. The U.S. Amateur winner's trophy is called the Theodore A. Havemeyer, for the first president of the USGA, and the Women's Open champion receives the Harton S. Semple. One of my favorites is the Crump Cup, named in honor of George A. Crump, who croaked after designing the first 12 holes at Pine Valley. Now that's a tough course. But the clear winner of the silly-name stakes is the victor at the Women's Mid-Am, who takes home the Mildred Gardiner Prunaret.

Now, I don't know what old Mildred's Prunaret looks like these days, but I guarantee you if I'd got my hands on it when I was 9, I could probably have hammered it into one hell of a bulletproof breastplate.

74

David Feherty's Mailbag

Online—Published: August 8, 2006

Dear David,

During the Western Open last weekend, it was stated by a commentator that Phil Mickelson was using the course for practice for the British Open. Using different swings, wedges, etc. . . . I find that appalling. How do you feel about a player not playing to win or be in competition?

—Michelle S.

Michelle:

Every pro practices for the next week, whether he's thinking about it or not. Phil thinks differently to any player I've known, but wherever he plays, you can be sure he's trying to win. Every time, all the time. Sometimes he even goes at it left-handed.

Dear David,

Do you know what happens to the souvenirs that are left over after the Masters? As proud as they are of their logo, I can't see them selling them on eBay.

—Ralph, Columbus, GA

Ralph:

After Saturday of the Masters, the merchandise tents are clean enough to do surgery.

Dear David,

I enjoy your Cobra commercials. I just saw a new one, and as a singer had to comment on your very nice singing voice. My questions: Why choose a selection from the Faure Requiem (Libera me, I believe)? Did you choose, or the producers?

—Mark M., Salt Lake City, Utah

Mark:

I am sooooo impressed that you picked this out! I chose the Fauré for two reasons. One, I knew the words, two, I knew the music, and three, I can't count. Trust me, my producer wouldn't know the difference between the Fauré Requiem and John Daly armpit-farting the Nigerian national anthem. I sang the *Pie Jesu* as a treble, at which time I had a voice like a bell, but sadly my aspirations to become a singer dropped with my testicles. To this day I have a great love of choral music, especially the cheery words. Here is an excerpt from the requiem mass translated into English:

I am made to tremble, and I fear,
when the desolation shall come,
and also the coming wrath.
That day, the day of wrath,
calamity, and misery,
that terrible and exceedingly bitter day.

Oh yes, haven't we all had a few of those? Well done on identifying this gorgeous piece of music, despite the dog's balls I made of it.

Hi David,

What do you think about the new PGA Tour Playoffs and the FedEX Cup?

—John B., Attleboro, Mass.

John:

Hey, do you own that Sloop John B. the Beach Boys recorded? Love that song.

I like it. The tour season used to wind down with a whimper. Thirty guys quietly competed for the Tour Championship then snuck out of town. No one cared, no one watched and no one ever knew who the defending champion was. I think it will be interesting to see how the players react when things tighten up in September. Ten mil is a lot of money and I, for one, can't wait to see who gags. I can hear the sphincters slamming shut already.

I'll give the Tour credit for trying to keep things interesting and fresh. It may need refinement but at least they're not sitting around with thumbs up their asses. My only concern is for those bread and butter tournaments and their title sponsors who have sunk millions upon millions of promotional bucks into sustaining tournaments who suffered through years of weak fields, marginal support from the Tour, rising media and staging costs, all of which resulted in Herculean efforts to maintain and increase their charitable contributions year after year. I hope that the top players remember those tournaments and sponsors that supported the Tour for so long and without whom they wouldn't be able to ponder a format like the FedEx Cup.

Dear David,

The Women's Open boiled down to *Inkie the Elder, Hurstie La Heuva Mas Grande, Annika the Ice Queen, Prannanananananan-mamma,* and *The Magnificent Blue Weenie-skirt.* I know who the men rooted for, but who do you think the women were rooting for? Or against? (I can't believe the LPGA and SOME network haven't put Weenie, Gulbis, Creamer and Pressel in a miniskirt-outfitted par-3 shootout like the men just televised. The ratings would go through the roof.)

—Jeff C.

Jeff:

Now just hang on a second there, Chris Berman . . . Men in miniskirts competed in a televised par-three tournament? And they were rooted? Sounds perverted to me. I've seen most of that pay-for-view stuff, but I tend to avoid the "alternate" ones. You carry on though, it doesn't make you a bad person. I did see Fred Funk wriggle into a skirt when Annika whipped it past him, and Lumpy let me play with his breasts once, but neither did anything for me. I like the idea, though. You could call it "The Battle of the Bee-atches" or perhaps "The Thongs Wide Open." Give Carolyn Bivens a call on it? I've heard she's hiring.

75

Sleazy Ryders

Golf Magazine, *10565493, September 2006, Vol. 48, Issue 9*

A couple of years ago I wrote a history of the Ryder Cup that was read by a total of 11 people, if you count my editor and my wife. Like most people, I figured that the first 50 years or so would be real bum-numbers—you know, the Americans won, the Brits and the Bogtrotters lost, blah blah blah and so on. So in the grand tradition of not-exciting-enough-to-be-believable history, I planned on borrowing a page from the Bible and making most of it up. It turned out I didn't need to make anything up, because going way back to 1926 when the event was first played, the truth has been more absurd than fiction.

- **1927** The British team clambers out from the Irish first-class section (the bilges) of the *Aquitania* and are met on the pier in New York by Walter Hagen, who looks and dresses like a movie star and is grinning like a picket fence. Wally promptly gets them smashed (and probably laid). By the time the matches start, the Brits are so hungover and weak at the knees that they have no chance.
- **1929** The American team practices, something the

British players, who are hanging out in the pub getting plastered and trying to get the Brylcreem off their grips, have never seen. The crowd of 10,000 applaud after good British shots and bad American ones. British writer Bernard Darwin describes American Joe Turnesa as having "the air of a poor little shivering Italian greyhound."

- **1933** The Prince of bloody Wales shows up at Southport and Ainsdale, dragging along with him a crowd of 15,000. HRH promptly announces he is a huuuuge fan of Walter Hagen. However, on the last green, Wally, who is hanging on the Prince's every word, neglects to tell Denny Shute that a two-putt would probably win the cup for America. Shute deftly three-putts, and hands the cup to the British. Hagen says later, "It would have been discourteous to walk out on the future king of England." It was the last time British royalty did anything remotely useful.

- **1947** Playing captain Henry Cotton gathers the team in his hotel room, lifts a Bible, and prays to the Almighty for help. Maybe the Almighty still had a headache from World War II, but, whatever the reason, he didn't give a rat's turd about Sir Henry's petition. Henry and the lads are hosed, 11–1.

- **1951** Porky Oliver threatens to eat Arthur Lees in the middle of the eighth fairway. U.S. wins, 9½ to 2½.

- **1953** Sam Snead describes Harry Weetman as "a bushy-haired pro with just a fair reputation." Weetman hands Sam his hillbilly ass, but the Yanks win again, 6½ to 5½.

- **1957** Tommy Bolt almost takes a swing at Eric "Up Yours" Brown, who beats him 4 and 3 and then declares, "You never had a hope of beating me."

- **1959** Everyone gets wrecked at Frank Sinatra's house, and Johnny Weissmuller almost drowns Peter Alliss in

the swimming pool. Somebody tries to pork Esther
Williams, and punches are thrown. After an 8½ to 37½
loss and too much sherry in the desert sun, Lord
Brabazon, president of the British PGA, declares, "We
are going back to practice in the streets and on the
beaches." Just in case he is referring to St. Tropez,
France offers its surrender.

- **1963** The highlight of the matches (which the GB&I
  team lost 23 to 9) was Henry Longhurst's famously
  unsuccessful attempt to say "Hunt and Coles" on the
  telecast.
- **1965** No one actually knows for sure what happened
  because, for the first time, golf writers had their own
  wooden building with a hole-by-hole scoreboard, near
  the final green, right next to the bar. So naturally, they
  all got bulletproof and made it up. Legend has it the
  Americans won 19½ to 12½.

76

Tackle Dummy

Golf Magazine, *10565493*, October 2006, *Vol. 48, Issue 10*

When you're new to a sport it's easy to get sold a bunch of crap. Take, for example, the first time I went fly-fishing. I figured I'd read a copy of *Fly Fisherman*, get down with the latest trout-speak, head to the store for all the requisite gear, and within minutes of hitting the stream I'd be ripping the lips off five-pounders and laughing derisively at my rich friends. Halfway through the magazine, I almost gave up on the idea. Christ, it was depressing, filled with nothing but stories of manure runoff, fish kills, forest fires, bear attacks and pictures of places that were only accessible by helicopter. I thought, What's the point of paying out the wazoo to be airlifted into a place where I could get smothered in crap, buggered by a grizzly and then incinerated? But there was no resisting the opportunity to abuse my fishless buddies, so I set off to get all tackled up.

Helmut, the sales assistant down at Verman Tackleberry Outfitters, looked the part in his nose-hair and Shetland wool sweater, studded with chunks of granola and a picture of a guppy on the front. They say you can tell a real fisherman by his hat, and Helmut was topped off with a beauty, a lightly toasted English muffin that looked like it had been run over by a cement truck and then boiled, probably with his head still in it.

Asking a nimrod like Helmut for fishing-gear advice was clearly out of the question, so I casually wandered around the store, nodding knowingly every now and then and making the small grunting noises closely associated with expertise in any field. But my cunning plan collapsed when I embedded a fly the size of a giant gnat in my left thumb and couldn't get the little bastard out. "It could happen to anybody," said Herr Nose-jungle, trying not to blow a snot bubble.

With the ice and my thumb now broken, Helmut proceeded to sell me a manual entitled "How to Train Your Trout-Pointing Schnauzer," several weighted trout decoys (including a 2 lb. floater), a 5-denier landing net, a pair of rubberized, barbless underpants (with front-mounted neoprene tackle-protection pouch) and an 18-foot two-weight rod. Or at least that's what the damn thing felt like.

After the first morning on the river, when I'd stopped weeping, I called the Old Woodsman himself, Tom Weiskopf, for advice. He told me fly-fishing is a sport because both sides know they are playing. If your fly hits the water like a frozen chicken on the end of a jump rope those cagey trout apparently know the difference. Worse yet, you have to be quiet, which is difficult for me at the best of times, but when I stepped onto a snot-covered rock and fell arse-backwards into the river? I may not have caught many fish, but when that 48-degree water made contact with my 98.6-degree raisins, I would have won the World Yodeling Championship at a canter. The shrieking was so high-pitched it neutered the entire wolf population of Yellowstone, and now I'm not allowed back during ski season, either.

It was a harrowing first experience, but maybe I should give it another go. I could get better, just like I did at quail hunting. I bought all the stuff for that, too—pretty double guns, orange leotards and assless chaps. I had no idea how hunting birds with dogs worked. The first time my pals Buck and T.D. took me out, I remember thinking how in the hell are they going to throw a 60 lb. German pointer high enough to hunt frigging birds? I mean, shouldn't a bird-hunting dog be something you could get a tight spiral on, like maybe a wiener? Or a Chihuahua? Idiots.

77

Feherty's Mailbag

Online—Published: October 10, 2006

Dear David,

Did Luke Donald dis Tiger by showing up with a red shirt on Sunday at Medinah? I mean that was worse than the infamous "Tiger Who" kerfuffle or what's his name saying that Tiger could be "beat" then getting his thong handed to him 9&8 at the World Match Play. Just a thought.

—Tim G., Orange Park, FL

Tim:

On the contrary, my faithful correspondent, it was Tiger who was doing the dissing when he sank putt after putt with no regard whatever for poor Luke's feelings. Luke's mom picks out his outfits for him and lays them out by day during tournament week. Although Luke is apparently a talented artist of some note, he is completely hopeless on color matching and accessorizing. Why, I once saw him wearing white after Labor Day at a polo match in the Hamptons. He was apprehended and escorted off Long Island.

Dear David,

Why is it that the European analysts like yourself and Nick Faldo overshadow their American peers?

—Kathy K.

Kathy:

Ouch; myself and Faldo in the same sentence. I'm aghast, dear girl. Faldo and I may not be the biggest assholes in golf, but when the biggest asshole in golf dies, toss in Johnny Miller and Wadkins, and the four of us might be in a playoff. I don't think it's so much what we fuzzy foreigners say, it's about how we say it—know what I'm saying?

Hello David,

Since you are now rich and famous and live in Texas, do you get to hang out with rich and famous Texans like ZZ Top or Dr. Phil? And does living in Texas rule you out for knighthood? Sir David has a nice ring to it.

—Serge, Saguenay, Canada

Serge:

You really need to get a hobby that involves actually leaving the house without your laptop. Not that I don't appreciate the weekly enquiries but you're starting to worry me, lad.

I prefer Rachmaninoff to ZZ Top and German shorthaired pointers to Dr. Phil. Texas has everything I like to do when I'm not working, which is most of the time, but I try not to hang around with people that think I'm a warm-up act for Wayne Newton.

I'm pretty sure a knighthood is out of the question for me. First of all, as I'm from Ulster, I'm Irish and British, and although I don't think that precludes the Queen from putting me on the Christmas List, it sort of diminishes her appetite.

Second, for years I've made disparaging remarks about the royal family and I suspect they don't take kindly to that sort of thing (which is a hallmark of in-breeding).

Hello Mr. Feherty,

After Phil's demise in the U.S. Open he has played poorly. In your opinion, how long will it take to come back and contend as a major contender again? Also, is Tiger well liked by the other golfers on the PGA Tour?

—Mike, Citrus Springs, FL

Mike:

It will take him from now until April of '07 to recover in time for the next major. Don't confuse Phil's play at Firestone with a lack of desire. He still approaches every competition with a fierce desire to win.

Off the course, Tiger is a completely different guy. When he's competing, he's deadly serious about his business and he looks it. But away from the game, he's just like most guys you know: he likes a good joke, even if it's about him; in fact, especially if it's about him. He likes his toys and loves sharing his good fortune with his buddies. He's well-rounded and comfortable in his own skin and yeah, he's pretty well liked by the other players. Hell, they should like him, he's making the idiots a fortune.

Dear David,

Tiger has won six tournaments in a row, including two majors, so I think it might be time for you to start a rumor that he's an alien with superpowers.

—Big Dog

Dog:

Well, let's look at the facts, shall we? Tiger was born in December. It's common knowledge that December has traditionally been the month when strange births take place; remember that "manger" business a while back? How about those appearances on *The Mike Douglas Show*? Did you notice the way he walked, with his head tilted back and his hips thrust out? Totally unnatural. And what about the swoosh? There's a school of thought that that symbol is an antenna to the mothership. Did you notice it always points up? The final proof is that Tiger wouldn't speak to Peter Kostis, who I believe may be an alien himself because he can see in extreme slow motion. Tiger was afraid Kostis would out him and he'd have to give the yacht back. Odds-on the ringleader in this whole scenario is Clampett, who is from "Nonsequitur," one of the moons of Uranus. Coincidence??? I think not.

Well done, Dog; or is it really . . . GOD?

Dear David,
     When Penn & Teller retire, Gary McCord and yourself should head to Las Vegas. I would pay to see you two perform as stand-up comedians.
                                                                —Glenn, Covington, La.

Glenn:

I'm struggling with the Penn & Teller comparison. I know McCord used to be known for his magic tricks, like making his money disappear right before his first wife served the papers on him, but I don't know as you could compare him to Penn. Or would it be Teller? Hey, if you're implying that I somehow resemble Teller, you can kiss my Irish ass.

Truth is, we're better separately than we are together. We play off each other when he's in the booth and I'm down on the ground because we have different perspectives on what we're talking about even though we're looking at the same action going on. I don't think that would work on a stage. Especially if he insists on wearing that Carmen Miranda get-up again. If a gay casino ever opens in Vegas, I might reconsider; for his sake.

78

Letter Rip

Golf Magazine, *10565493, November 2006, Vol. 48, Issue 11*

You know, it's been years since I had a decent letter of complaint. I get plenty of them all right, but they all seem to be from people who spend their free time fashioning hoods from bed sheets, each of who seems to have unusually clear insight regarding what God thinks about things, and who need to express their illiterate disgust at what they regard as my undying man-crush on one T. Woods. Well, I haven't the time or the energy to reply to people who didn't pass fifth-grade English, or are stupid enough to include their names and addresses. I'll stop being amazed by Tiger when he stops being amazing, okay Einsteins? Or is that too Jewish for you?

It does occur to me, though, that I may be doing something wrong when my hate mail is coming from only one demographic. I mean, what the hell is wrong with me? I can't offend anyone else? It's the old story, if you want a job done properly you'd better do it yourself, or at least set a good example. So, if you dislike me or what I say on TV or write in this magazine, and you feel like letting me know, here's a hate-letter template you can use free of charge. Think of it as a little inspiration.

Dear Mr. Feherty,

I am still shaking with outrage at the reprehensible and incomprehensible invective you hurled at anyone in earshot during the U.S. Bank Championship. In the old days you would have had something unspeakable inserted into you by an elderly clergyman.

Who are you, you ferret-faced weasel, to call anyone a ratbag, let alone a true superstar like Corey Pavin? Who has given you (a wretched, bitter hedgehog of a man) the right to vilify the legends of the game? How many times did you win a U.S. Open, you no-talent hack? You couldn't qualify with the 12-handicappers at the first stage with that drunken, epileptic swipe of a move you make at the ball. You look like Martin Short being tasered by an L.A. County Sheriff's deputy.

I number Corey among my closest friends (even though he used to be Jewish and I've never actually met him). I conduct weekly séances for a USGA Rules of Golf study group, and frequently get in touch with dead legends of the game like Deane Beman and Greg Norman. Occasionally we will channel through Corey, who is amazingly effective at elevating us to the next level: the fourth dimension. Just last week we spoke with Judge Smails and Glenn Ford, who, as you are no doubt unaware, played the great Walter Hogan in Follow the Son.

As if it wasn't enough to heap insults on Corey, you then felt compelled to place poor Lanny Wadkins in your crosshairs, you hamster-molesting bastard. What has little Lanny ever done to you except make you look good by letting you read the putts (as if you can)? The only break you ever got right was recess in the second grade, you bulbous-nosed Mick. And what is all that moving-boxes-at-Walmart harness crap you wear? Holy David Duke, you look like a stool-pushing Gaelic hairdresser, or Lenny Bruce in lederhosen, you wireless wanker, gliding around the golf course a foot off the grass. For God's sake, at least Lanny Wadkins dresses in a manly fashion.

Hey, I hope you regard this letter as constructive. At least I'm not one of those homophobic Tiger-bashers you hear from all the time. I like people of color, even some of the really dark ones, like Miles Davis and Tyrone Power (although to be honest I'd be pretty upset if my son

married someone like that). If you ever get to Yorba Linda, look me up.
I'll show you my collection of old balata balls. One of them has a cut in
it that makes it look just like the Virgin Mary. It's uncanny. Call me.

Sincerely,

Monsignor Michael "Spatula" Spatchatoli

Name and address withheld due to restrictions at maximum-
security institutions.

79

Losing Isn't Everything

Golf Magazine, *10565493, December 2006, Vol. 48, Issue 12*

Whether it was sport or something really important (like war), it's been a tough year to be an American playing abroad. The U.S. hockey team fell into a burning rink of fire at the Olympics, and the basketball team lost to Greece at the World Championships. Yes, the same Greece where just last year they discovered the object was to put the ball through the hoop, not throw it at the other team like dodgeball. Banana republicans won the World Baseball Classic, and the U.S. soccer team left the World Cup early with a massive wedgie. The only real success story was the tender sprouts from Columbus, Ga., who won the Little League World Series. What do you suppose their coach told them before the big game? I'll give you two choices:

A. "If you lose, you'll be letting the entire country down and you won't be allowed to play on this team ever again."

B. "Winning isn't everything, and as long as you give 100 percent, play by the rules and carry yourselves with dignity, you'll be a winner."

My money is on the latter. The problem is that by the time we don't need a hug from our mommies anymore, we're being judged by different standards. Players who make it to the World

Series or the Super Bowl are heroes for a week, but if they don't win they get branded on the ass like steers from the Big L Ranch. Somewhere between pubic hair and a legal margarita (which for me, arrived in the wrong order), our kids figure out that if they give 100 percent, play by the rules and carry themselves with dignity, they'll end up getting their asses kicked while the "winner" whines about how he's underappreciated.

The case of the U.S. Ryder Cup team is interesting. They've lost five of the last six Cups, against ever-increasing background noise that now includes moral indignation over the amount of money they play for! Excuse me? You think golfers are paid too much? Last time I checked, it was close to impossible to get one of only 50 PGA Tour cards that entitle a player to take his own money and attempt to turn it into more by beating the same 125 guys who are waaay better than thousands of other guys who made it close to impossible for him to get the damn card. And if he's really good then he might get the chance to be paid absolutely nothing to play in an event in which there's a better-than-average chance he is going to get his ass handed to him by a guy who most American golf fans wouldn't know from the tight end on the French chess team. And because of all this good fortune he'll be called a LOSER! Holy crap, does that sound like a good deal, or what?

The wee man on the lid of the Ryder Cup, Abe Mitchell, was Sam Ryder's golf coach. Mitchell competed in the Ryder Cup for the British side in 1929, '31 and '33, and he's bent over like he's about to hold his ankles for a reason. It took almost six decades for the British and Irish to get their hands on the cup with any regularity, and then it only happened because of the reluctant inclusion of a bunch of fuzzy foreigners.

The reason the U.S. has lost so many recent Cups is not because they don't care or their lives are too cushy, it's because the Europeans are a whole lot better than Americans think they are, and they have a fan-based support system that has instilled a sense of self-worth even when they have lost. Ironically, they have been helped enormously by American fans who enjoy seeing Europe win because they feel its players are less-coddled regular guys. That may be true, but when will Americans start wondering why these European guys don't win more majors, instead of why Americans don't win the Ryder Cup?

80

Letters

Golf Magazine, *10565493, January 2007, Vol. 49, Issue 1*
By David Feherty, David Kolasky, John Weis, and Andrew Seagal

HATED MALE

Dear Mr. Feherty,

I read your column in the November '06 issue, and I had to write to tell you I'm a bit confused and offended. I'm a golf aficionado and I also enjoy cracking jokes and having a great time on the course. Most of my friends would say I have a good sense of humor and a tolerance for most people. But your column was really something else. Your statement, "Or is that too Jewish for you?" offended me. I happen to be Jewish and am proud of it. I get offended when people tell anti-Semitic jokes and I fear your question and the other comments you made about Corey Pavin fall right into the anti-Semitic category. Whether you meant it that way or not, such is the way it struck me, my wife and some others who read the column. I have enjoyed your column in the past, and anticipate that I will in the future. It is the present that concerns me. Perhaps in a future column, you can enlighten us as to the purpose of those statements.

—David Kolasky, via e-mail

FEHERTY RESPONDS!

Dear David,

Thanks for your letter. I apologize if my November column offended you or any other reader, but I think if you re-read it carefully, you will see that the only people who should have been offended are the bigots who write me hate mail about my attitude towards Tiger. These people have little or no tolerance for people outside their own ethnic groups or religions, which means that I, in turn, have no time for them. That was the point of this piece, which I thought was obviously tongue-in-cheek.

Sincerely, David Feherty

81

Feherty's Mailbag

Online—Published: January 8, 2007

Dear David,

    With the New Year upon us will you be making any New Year's Resolutions? I think I'm going to stop trying to figure out what's growing on McCord's face (owl's nest?, desert brush?).

    Best wishes now and always, John

—Phoenix, AZ

John:

    While I'm not one given to serious introspection (which I suspect is one of the causes of chlamydia), I do perform an annual self-probing examination with a knitting needle, borrowed from She Who Must Be Obeyed. I follow that up with a short arm inspection from my urologist. If I pass these tests, I never make any resolutions. My theory is that strong people don't need them, as they are already in control, and weak people shouldn't make them because they only set themselves up for failure which creates more self-loathing. I'm depressed enough, thank you.

    And "Pig Eyes" McCord is scheduled for another series of plastic surgery procedures again this year, on top of the 30 or so he's already had. I'm not sure where he's going with this stuff, but he carries a picture of Michael Jackson around in his man-purse. You do the math. . . .

Dear David,

It would be a real hoot to see you & McCord in the same foursome at a Champions event when you become eligible. Any chance of that happening? Thanks!

—Russ

Russ:

Absolutely none. To begin with, when I'm eligible, Numb-nuts will be 88. Secondly, I have no intention or desire to play competitive golf ever again. My back is so fragile, I sleep standing up in styrofoam peanuts. The only turn I've made recently is wine into water.

Hi David.

I truly enjoy your work and your perspective on life and the game of golf. While watching the Q-School qualifying in December, I started to wonder how the rookies are treated when they get to the tour? Are they welcomed by the guys who are there already, or because it is so competitive, are they treated more like McCord at an Augusta National board meeting? Keep up the good work.

—John

John:

Like most things, it depends on the guy and where they are. On the course the new guys are generally respected whether they came off the Nationwide or out of "Q" school. Either way they've earned their place through the crucible of competition, and the veterans, who were all there at one time or another, know only too well the ass clenching, soul destroying, godforsaken angst they went through to get the chance to tee it up at the big show. Off the course, the FNG'S tend to hang with each other socially. But if they run into one another, the old farts are usually happy to answer any question and give advice if anyone asks.

Dear Mr. Feherty,

I am a female golfer. I've been grinding away at improving my game for about 5 seasons. In those 5 seasons, I've heard a lot of "shouldn't you be at home cleaning and cooking?" and "I hope you got all the laundry done before you came here to play." I don't take it seriously. It's just guys being guys in this man's world where I'm trying to play a gentleman's sport. I'm generally pretty witty but I can't seem to come up with a clever retort. You're the guru of witty responses. Might you be able to help me with a clever comeback?

—Tina, Massachusetts

Tina:

Well the last thing you want to do is Rosie O'Donnell them. Holy crap, if I had to choose one of them to have sex with, the Donald would be a shoo-in. I am shocked that guys from Massachusetts would act this way. You must be playing a (sniff) public course.

For the cleaning, cooking and laundry shot, you might try, "Oh, I don't need to clean or cook; the staff handles all that for me." Or: "Why would I cook when there are so many great restaurants around here and so many men dying to buy me dinner every night?" If you really want to scramble their brains and win all the bets, try: "Oh, I don't have time for cleaning and cooking. I'm a sex addict and I spend every available minute looking for large portions of the old fireman's helmet." Then look at him like he's an ice cream cone. I guarantee his next drive won't go more than 10 feet.

And if none of that works, a well-placed Foot-Joy to his scrotum certainly will.

Dear Mr. Feherty,

I am trying to find out when we can expect to see "A Beastly Turn of Events: An Uncle Dickie Novel" available for purchase at our local bookseller. I have flat worn out "A Nasty Bit of Rough"; and am dying to find out what has been going on with the gang since winning the golf match up north. By now all should be healed and we must know what can be done to save the finest golf club collection in the world.

— Mike S., West Lafayette, Indiana

Mike:

Did my publisher put you up to this? OK, OK, actually Uncle Dickie has been after me as well to get on with *A Beastly Turn of Events*. I've had a lot on my plate since the end of the CBS season. I've been working on a new cell phone directory for the Dallas area. Going door to door has been very time consuming and I'm not even close to completion. Add to that my ventriloquist lessons (in Chinese), the self-dentistry course and designing and building that new stadium for Jerry Jones, you can see my dance card is pretty full. I'm working on it and I'm glad you stayed interested. Stay on me, Mike.

82

David Feherty on Ben Hogan

Online—Published: January 12, 2007

I am a very fortunate man. Even though I never got to meet Ben Hogan, I have been lucky enough to have had the opportunity, over the last 21 years that I have been a golf pro, to spend time with some of those who knew him well.

My old coach, Bob Torrence, father of the famous Sam, taught Hogan principles, and was one of the few teachers in the game to have direct access to the great man. Bob traveled to Shady Oaks to study the modern fundamentals. I think he has in his video collection almost every shot that Mr. Hogan ever struck before a TV camera, and a fabulous collection of still photos, all of which I have had the opportunity to study. I came to the conclusion that the man was a human elastic band. It was impossible to tell where his backswing ended and his downswing started, such was the fluidity of his action. He was Fred Astaire with a golf club.

I'm also a member at the Four Seasons Resort and Club, home of the Byron Nelson Classic, and frequently bump into Mr. Nelson in the office he shares with my present coach, the director of golf, Mike Abbott. I treasure the conversation I am able to have with Byron Nelson. Even though they started together as caddies and were lifelong rivals, Mr. Nelson will tell you that he never really got to know the real Ben Hogan. He never visited his house, yet the mutual respect and admiration was always there.

In an era before gallery ropes and crowd control, and in the midst of thousands, Hogan seemed to be alone, totally absorbed by the game. Yet my friend and colleague Ken Venturi tells me stories of a different man, often generous and sensitive, nearly always modest and shy—except when he needed to win. Then he seemed to develop a disregard for his opponents, evidently capable of flicking an internal switch that enabled him to enter his own private zone. The chances are, no one else will ever enter that domain, for there are too many other activities now that occupy the time of great players today. He might be the only one to have touched golf's Holy Grail. And they say that you can't take it with you? I for one suspect that he is resting peacefully, with a wry smile.

83.

Foot-in-Mouth Disease

Golf Magazine, *10565493, February 2007, Vol. 49, Issue 2*

Trying to make a living out of golf has always been a stressful occupation, and these days, at least in terms of money, there's more at stake. Human nature ensures that an athlete's wife gets better looking in direct proportion to the amount of money he makes, but it's tough to stay married on Tour, and with the depth of talent, harder still to stay out there for any length of time. It all makes for a daytime soap opera in which, with a slip of the tongue, a rookie can get himself written out of the plot. So, for the start of the season, with every good wish for our new crop of Q-School grads, I have prepared a short list of some of the stupidest printable things I heard (myself say) in my early years on Tour. No need to thank me, boys; idiocy is my profession.

- Unless you and at least one sober witness saw a player and his wife go into their hotel room together last night and saw them come out of the room together the next morning, don't ask him how the old ball-and-chain is doing. The only exception to this is if you spot a player coming out of his room in the morning with some young strumpet in a cowboy hat who you know has been riding her way through the Tour money list like Sherman through Atlanta. Then (and preferably in her presence), it's okay to ask about the little woman. Most players think this is hysterical.

- Yesterday, your playing partner took more strokes than an eighth-grade schoolboy with a Victoria's Secret catalog, and today he needs to shoot 59 to make the cut. He has breezed through the front side in a homicidal 41 and stopped by the locker room to reserve a backward-facing middle aisle seat on the next flight out of town. *This is not the time to point out any fatal swing flaws.* Unless you feel like a visit to an oral surgeon for maxifollogical repair work, resist the urge to say "Hold it there, pardner" at the top of his swing. These new hybrid clubs can inflict a whole new level of damage to your face.

- If you're not certain how much money the guy you're playing with has made this season, do not ask—especially if you're beating him like a Whac-A-Mole. Some guys can be touchy: "Oh, real funny, asshole. I've hit more balls than Sir Elton John's chin this year, and still missed 16 cuts in a row . . . and you want to know how I'm doing? Next thing you'll tell me you just bought a 110-foot Sunseeker and would I like to go fishing, but it'll have to be on a Tuesday 'cause that's the only day you don't have a corporate gig, right?"

     172nd on the money list: "Where ya goin' for dinner?"

     23rd on the money list: "Well I was thinking of just ordering room service, but my agent's here with a bunch of offers we need to go over, so I thought we might go out to this pretentious French place I heard about; s'posed to be really good but kind of excostive, you know? How 'bout you?"

172nd: "Oh, I was thinking about room service, too, but my room's so small I put my key in the lock last night and broke a f——ing window. I let my caddie use my courtesy car to go get his bean snapped and he ran outta gas in Laredo, so I told the transportation guy something was wrong with it and they gave me another one with a full tank. Works every time. Anyway, I got a coupon for two free drinks and sides at Church's Chicken from the fat chick in the tournament office, but I'd need a police escort to go to the neighborhood it's in, so I think I'll probably see if I can get my arm far enough up the snack machine in the lobby to snag some Cheetos. If I get lucky, maybe I'll get a pack of Life Savers for dessert."

84

Spaulding!

Golf Magazine, *10565493*, March 2007, Vol. 49, Issue 3

Recently my nimrod agent secured me the chance to appear in a MasterCard ad campaign with Laura Diaz, Ben Crenshaw, Arnold Palmer and John F. Barmon. In my long and average career, I have met many famous people, but, with apologies to Arnold, the idea of actually meeting John F. Barmon made me giddier than a lone Scotsman in a bar full of sheep. You see it was Barmon who stole the show in the greatest movie of all time, with his turn as Spaulding Smails in *Caddyshack*.

For my money the true measure of a movie is how accurately you remember the scenes. Every sick bastard I know can recite at least half of the *Caddyshack* script. I don't want to come off as lowbrow here (no-siree, you have the wrong announcer there, buddy!), but *Blazing Saddles* is the only movie that gives *Caddyshack* a run.

I always wondered how a low-budget effort that *Esquire* assured its readers would bomb, about a game that no one cared about before Tiger Woods, could have scored such an ace. I picked Spaulding's brain almost clean of useless information about the movie. Barmon says that while Chevy, Rodney,

Murray and Ted Knight were the cake, it was the rest of the ensemble who provided the icing. Like the Bishop, played by Henry Wilcoxon, who was Pharaoh Yul Brynner's lieutenant in Cecil B. DeMille's *Ten Commandments*. Bill Murray's older brother, Brian, was Lou Loomis, the caddie master. Playing Dr. Beeper was Dan Resin, who was also the wee boater down the toilet in the Tidy Bowl commercials. Yeah, you knew you'd seen him somewhere before.

As the movie gained popularity, some of the politically incorrect scenes were cut from broadcast versions, like Spaulding buying a bag of weed from Smoke Porterhouse. (It was actually dandelion leaves that Smoke was shown picking out of the rough earlier.) In a later scene, also edited, Spaulding assures his pals that "It's good; I bought it from a Negro!" Porterhouse was played by Jackie Davis, a damned good jazz organist in his day, and Sarah Holcomb played Maggie, the girl who thought she was knocked up, proving once again that a comedy filled with ethnic slurs and stereotypes needs to include someone with a bad Irish accent, who is either fighting, getting drunk, or pregnant, or in this case, all three. Holcomb also played Dean Wormer's daughter in *Animal House*.

And what happened to Spaulding? It was the only movie part John Barmon ever played and he wasn't even looking to do it. It was his best pal who wanted the part, and in 1979 John tagged along with him to his agent's office. Two weeks later, his friend got the callback, which went something like, "Say, what's that geeky-looking friend of yours doing this summer?" Today Barmon says that he could probably be good at the game, but he feels obliged to play like Spaulding, i.e., dreadfully. He's a successful real estate agent in Cambridge, Mass., and says the most common misconception about him is that the movie made him wealthy. The residuals, he says, net him about "40 double cheeseburgers a year."

So, John, of all the lines from the movie that get thrown at you, which is the most common? "You'll get nothing and like it!" he screams, laughing. Ted Knight, he says, was the nicest of the stars to work with. As it turned out, the taciturn, nose-picking, spoiled country-club kid who longed to fit in with the caddies didn't get a lot from *Caddyshack*, but he likes it anyway.

85

The Drug Gist

Golf Magazine, *10565493*, April 2007, Vol. 49, Issue 4

Ever since I took my meds this morning, I've felt strangely qualified to serve up some expert opinion on drugs in sports. Of course, that might just be the drugs talking, but it seems to me that for centuries, some of our greatest minds (and apparently bodies) have been influenced by the kinds of herbs and vices that make human growth hormone look like a vitamin supplement. Thou dost take issue with that view? Perhaps thou hast forgotten that Shakespeare, Byron and Shelley were opium fiends, Charlie Parker chased more dragons than St. George, and Elvis went tits-up on the growler because narcotics make you feel like there's a 50-pound pineapple stuck in your doggie-door.

She Who Must Be Obeyed says I have no business commenting on drug use in sports because when I was playing I was usually so hungover that they'd have had to jackhammer the floor around the toilet to get enough urine for a sample. That woman is a hoot, but it's clear a decision must be made on drug testing in golf, and the trick will be isolating the substances that do actually enhance a golfer's performance (let me know if you find one). The last thing we need is to bundle in some of the stuff that'll get you and your pole vaulted out of the Olympics, like cough medicine and bum ointment. Though now that I think of it, the simple ball-diameter ring used by the Tour could be adapted to check for steroid use. Every player would be measured at the start of the season, and if at any time they slipped through on a random field-check, out they'd go. If nothing else, TV numbers would soar. "OK, Tiger, turn your head and cough."

Moving right along, the idea of drug testing is a conundrum, the solution to which I am clearly not smart enough to know. However, I do test positive for knowledge that we shouldn't involve the World Anti-Doping Agency, which I shall henceforth refer to as the WAD of A.

The head of the WAD of A is a guy named—and I swear I'm not making this up—Dick Pound. You'd think as the head of such an organization, Dick could keep his sausage-hole puckered until an athlete has been found either innocent or guilty, but this Dick is for hanging before the trial. He has even cast aspersions in the direction of Lance Armstrong, who with one plum (and who has never definitively tested positive for anything other than courage and character) is clearly a man worth a thousand Dicks.

The code of the WAD of A states that in order to be illegal, a substance must meet two of the following three criteria: (1) It is performance-enhancing; (2) It is a health risk; (3) It is against the "spirit" of the sport. Well, my tiny brain is having difficulty separating one and three, to the extent that nipping off No. 2 seems like it would help. Alcohol and tobacco are a much more terrifying health risk than some of the substances prohibited, yet in the Tour de France Lance Armstrong could have filled his water bottle with Chateau Latour and crossed the finish line smoking a massive stogie and still have been legal.

H. G. Wells once said that moral indignation is jealousy with a halo. In an interview with *Wired* magazine, Dick Pound recalled Floyd Landis's nickname as "Roid Floyd," and then covered his slime track with, "I repeat it as hearsay only." Landis's case is pending as I write, but whether he's guilty or innocent, I can't help but wonder if Pound isn't compensating for something? Most critics have one thing in common—they weren't good enough to do it themselves. Turns out Dick Pound was a swimmer who competed for Canada at the 1960 Rome Olympics and finished just out of the medals twice. Word was he didn't have the right stuff (nudge, nudge, wink, wink). Of course, I repeat that as hearsay only. Golf needs to be protected from cheats, and, just as important, from people like Dick Pound.

86.

Ass Good as It Gets

Golf Magazine, *10565493, May 2007, Vol. 49, Issue 5*

Life is unfair, and then you die. Right? You'd think that after the well-documented torture I've put my body through I would be a physical wreck. But I went to my doctor for my annual physical and it turns out I'm a perfect specimen: cholesterol 161, pulse in the high 40s, blood pressure 126/74 before they lubed me up and made me yodel. Meanwhile as I write, Gary McCord, who has always kept himself slim, fit and mentally acute, and by comparison, a paragon of virtuous sobriety, is at the Mayo Clinic in Scottsdale with pericarditis, an inflammation of his heart and the sac around it, which has filled up with fluid. In other words, he has a dodgy strawberry. The irony of his having a sac full of fluid, and it being the wrong one, is not lost on him. Apparently, his sense of humor is alive and well.

It's hard to know how to react when a friend becomes seriously ill, especially when he's a sick bastard to start off with. In this case, sympathy would alarm McCord, so I thought while he was still around to read it, it would be more appropriate to write his obituary, a luxury typically afforded only to the great, such as Mark Twain. So, in case he goes tits-up on us, the following is what I would say at the funeral of one of my dearest friends.

"Gary McCord had many endearing qualities, but my favorite was his seemingly limitless propensity toward an idiocy that made the rest of us feel intelligent. He once was striking bets with the Wadkins brothers and John Jacobs on the first tee of a practice round. He was gleefully pointing fingers, getting in faces and announcing his imminent cash winnings, and, some moments later, while he was looking for his ball in the edge of the left rough, Lanny asked him what he was doing. When McCord asked Lanny what he meant, he was informed that he had, in fact, neglected to hit a tee shot. Now that, my friends, would be a lost ball, in every sense.

"We will always remember Gary for his sense of style. He once starred in an episode of *Queer Eye for the Straight Guy* that never aired, because the Fab Five couldn't find a single thing to change. To call Gary anal would be an understatement. If he was riding in a vehicle in which the driver (who, for the sake of argument, we shall call 'Dave') broke wind, rather than inhale the perpetrator's intestinal vapor Gary would stick his head out the window like a golden retriever, at which point Dave would (accidentally) accelerate, causing Gary to be violently whipped by his own mustache. Gary bore the tears of mirth from his fellow travelers with all the dignity of a mentally unhinged early-round victim of *American Idol*, and we loved him for it.

"The accompanying illustration commemorates the last episode of our minus-rated Late Night Highlight Show, which ran on CBS for eight years during the Tour's West Coast swing. George Lopez was the host, and Gary chose the wardrobe from his signature Brokeback collection. I always admired his buttocks (in a manly way), as they looked so much more comfortable than my own, and in a final act of kindness, he has bequeathed them to me in his last will and testament. 'For posteriority,' is the term he used. It is a measure of the man's devotion to his friends that he spent the last 24 hours of his life sitting on a 50-pound sack of crushed ice, so that said buttocks would be perfectly preserved and I could have them fitted ASAP. Goodbye, my dear friend. The greatest tribute I can pay you is to say that every time I sit on your arse, I will think of you."

Footnote: The author and the subject believe that if you or anyone you care about is seriously ill, you could probably use a laugh. If either Gary McCord or David Feherty is actually dead at the time this piece appears in print, they both believe it would be pretty damn funny. Both of them would get over it.

87

Feherty's Mailbag

Online—Published: May 17, 2007

Dear Dave,

I'm a curious young guy wondering what lessons in life you have learned from your prestigious golf career? A short list will do . . . I wouldn't expect it to be long anyway. I'm sure that you have learned a lot of what-not-to-do from Mr. Poor-Excuse-For-A-Mustache McCord.

—Joe

Joe:

All young guys are curious, Joe, but I think I detect a child's portion of sarcasm in your question when you say you wouldn't expect to see a long list anyway. You have spunk, Joe. And as Lou Grant would say, "I hate spunk." Herewith my list of lessons learned from my golf career:

1. Never make a bet with someone if you are the only one who has to do anything.
2. Guinness is nothing more than a beer sandwich and it's time to quit when you pee brown.
3. The size of the check you just won is directly proportional to the size of the hammers on the

woman hanging on your every word in the bar on Sunday night.

4. It's a calumny that bartenders are authorized to perform marriages.

5. Depression is anger without the enthusiasm.

6. If you're playing a guy from the West Coast, you can double his stated handicap; if he's from the East Coast, halve it. For some deranged reason, this holds true in any country in the world.

7. Never jog, it's too hard to keep the ice in your glass.

8. If you can't fly first class, drive; except to Hawaii.

9. Clint Eastwood's the only guy who ever looked good with a cigar in his teeth.

10. Only black guys should shave their heads.

Dear Mr. Feherty:

You are extremely crude and crass. You must have had an ugly childhood. Do you realize how many people will not let their children read GOLF Magazine because of your articles and their content? The May publication was an excellent example.

—Jack McCrory

Dear Mr. McCrory:

Actually I do realize how many people won't let their kids read my articles. You're the only one. I doubt if a greased pin could be pulled out of your ass with a John Deere tractor. Lighten up. We're not curing cancer here, it's just golf, for God's sake.

Hello David,

Can you please explain to me what the term *ball striker* really means? Isn't every course a ball strikers' course? Would you also give a few examples of ball strikers' courses on the Tour?

—Doug, Lauderdale Beach, Fla.

Doug:

Next time you go to a professional golf tournament (on any tour), check out the irons in the bags of the players. You'll soon notice that the finish on them wears where they hit the ball most of the time—and that's usually pretty close to a lower middle location. The better the ball striker, the smaller the wear spot. Freddy Couples's is about the size of a fountain pen's nib. I remember some time ago a reporter asking Freddy what it felt like when he hit a shot off the center of the clubface. He looked at the guy like he was nuts and said, "Why in the hell would you hit it off center?" Ball strikers pure it almost every time.

Ball strikers' courses tend to have smaller, more-difficult greens. On Hilton Head, Harbour Town Golf Links' small greens make it a ball strikers' course. Pinehurst No. 2 qualifies because the greens are crowned and the ball has to be positioned properly for the location of the pin. A good ball striker will tend to fare better on this kind of track. A good ball striker will also be better at working the ball, which is why Cory Pavin won at Shinnecock Hills in 1995.

Hi David,

I have a title for your next book, *Lunatic on the Fringe*. What do you think?

—Al

Al:

Great idea, what's it about? I know, how about *Lunatic on the Frog Hair* or *It Takes a Village to Raise an Idiot*.

David,

Why do some players on the PGA Tour wear visors instead of hats? They are very un-manly and I have, thankfully, never seen Tiger wear one. Visors should only be allowed on the LPGA Tour.

—Mark, Big Rapids, Michigan

Mark:

Some of the guys who wear visors do so because when they wear a hat that covers their head completely, they sweat like Michael Jackson in a Chucky Cheese.

That's the reason I have always opted to wear crotchless trousers when I walk with the last group. My boys like a breeze. McCord kept telling me to use Gold Bond powder. I've only recently discovered that the stuff was not meant to be snorted, but rather, applied topically. When I have to break into a trot with the crotchless pants on, it looks like I'm sending smoke signals down the fairway. Kostis is losing patience with the whole thing. I don't know. I'm going to have to work on a solution.

Mr. Feherty,

I genuinely enjoy your commentary on the golf course and anything I can read by you or about you, but I do not find your goatee flattering. You probably enjoy that it makes you look a bit devilish, but your fans prefer your more natural look!

—Sue

Sue:

Being in awe of my former golf talent would be understandable. Being in awe of my current golf talent would be like Billy Graham being in awe of Jimmy Swaggart's preaching.

I find my face quite boring without something going on. And since I have the misfortune of having to look at the thing every morning, I like some landscaping to gaze upon. I tried a water feature but it kept ruining my shirts. I have given makeup some consideration, though. Perhaps I'll try a light blush with some discreet eyeliner.

88

Running Wild

Golf Magazine, *10565493, June 2007, Vol. 49, Issue 6*

For the longest time, I thought politics and sports didn't mix, but then I moved to America, where it didn't take me long to realize that politics is actually the bullshitter's Olympics, where every four years the athletes hope to peak like Long-horns on laxatives. If you don't think politics is a sport, con-sider that politicians are stupid enough to want a low-paying job that allows the country to shine a flashlight up their kilts, but smart enough to get away with what might be revealed, and then figure out a way to make a fortune in endorsements from corporate sponsors. Sounds like a sport to me.

I may not have a vote, but I live in Texas, and I love this country as much as any of y'all other 'Murricans out there, so I'm going to spin my cow-pattie into your corral for considera-tion. The 2008 presidential race is already garnering full-time coverage from all the major TV networks, none of which paid a communist-red cent for the privilege. That right there is just un-American. As a taxpayer, I believe we should be able to limit campaign coverage to two networks, one conservative and one liberal. For the sake of argument, we'll let only Fox and CNN cover the race, and we should be allowed to charge them both out their fair-and-balanced asses for it. Then we'd have proper American election coverage, which could be sold to the giant companies with vested interests. To sweeten the pot, every presidential candidate should have to run on a ticket with an idiot from the world of sports or entertainment. We could call it *Campaigning with the Stars*, with Wolf Blitzer as one host, and on the other side Shep Smith. (Incidentally, why the hell can't Fox come up with a better name for Shep? We've got a Wolf Blitzer on one side, and a Shep Smith on the other? Holy crap, that race is over before it starts.)

Of course, we'd need three judges to jerk the candidates around—a sweetheart woman (with big assets), a knowledge-able minority sort (with a weight problem) and a brutally honest English prick (with the sort of face you'd never get tired of punching).

Now, the fun bit would be pairing the running mates. As an independent with nothing to gain, I'd like to be a consultant. I'd go with Rudy Giuliani, who has already proven he can deal with disaster and scandal, and see if he could get out of Paris Hilton without wriggling. Or just stay out of her, for that mat-ter. Hillary Clinton could be an Olympian on leg-strength alone—hell, she could be the first president to kick-start Air Force One—so it would be interesting to see if she could shake Kinky Friedman off, or maybe Rosie O'Donnell would be tougher. Al Gore is so damned annoying, if he had an English accent, we could make him a judge, but I think I'd handcuff him to Sean Penn or Tom Cruise. Newt Gingrich deserves to be president simply because his first name is Newt. I'd put him with that political comedian Bill O'Reilly, so that if he won, his vice president could be "Toad." I like Barack Obama, so I'd give him Angelina Jolie. Nobody gives him a chance anyway, so at least he'd have a view.

If you think this idea is nuts, check your history books and you'll find plenty of eccentric, stupid, and sometimes lunatic presidents. Teddy Roosevelt shot everything that moved (and some that didn't). If JFK hadn't been assassinated, he probably would have "not have sex with that woman"-ed himself to death. An enormous percentage of presidents have been of Scots-Irish descent, one of whom, Ronald Reagan, may not have known he was president but knew he played one on TV—so this could work! Stranger things have happened, like you reading this on the back page of a *Golf Magazine* for instance . . . and me being paid for it.

89.

O, Teacher, My Teacher

Golf Magazine, *10565493*, July 2007, Vol. 49, Issue 7

Years ago, when a top player changed coaches, it was usually in a Greyhound bus terminal, but now it seems to be an affair for the paparazzi, complete with fuzzy spy photos taken from the roof of a nearby building and he-said-she-said slobberings printed as though they were (a) factual, or (b) interesting. The reality is that Tour players don't need someone to stand behind them and tell them where their club should be, they just need someone to tell them where the damn thing *is*.

That's why I refuse to teach. I never had the eye, the ability or the patience for it. In fact, when I would tell people what I thought they should be doing, and they didn't do it, I had a tendency to slap them upside the head. This worked fine with kids, but the elderly would tell on me, or worse, kick my ass.

Now, when I watch our brilliant Peter Kostis break down a swing on his BizHub weapon of mass instruction, I'm amazed at how simple he makes it all seem. So simple that I'm ready to take a crack at teaching again, but in a way never before tried, a method that might bring down the very foundation of the modern fundamentals themselves. Yes, I'm talking about reverse engineering.

I know, I know, I can see you all now, slapping yourselves on your foreheads, cursing yourselves for not thinking of it first, but you're too late. In these next few paragraphs, I shall render Dan Jenkins catatonic by revealing Hogan's secret, put the squeeze on Butch's practice balls, give Hank the Heimlich, turn Leadbetter into a bed wetter, and put forth, quite possibly, the worst theory in the history of teaching golf. You're welcome.

First, you must assume you are going to hit a bad shot with the wrong club. This covers 99 percent of all golf shots played. So it follows that your pre-shot routine should start with an outburst of loud cursing and self-abuse. Now, take the wrong club out of the bag, wave it around like the conductor of the St. Petersburg Philharmonic during the finale of Rachmaninov's 3rd piano concerto (listen to the live version by Lang Lang from the Royal Albert Hall just once and golf will never matter to you again anyway), and try to stay off balance as you walk forward a couple of steps from where your swing would normally start.

From there, assume an uncomfortable follow-through position, with your weight mostly on your right side and your chest facing anywhere but at the target, and then swing the club violently backward over the ball and stop at the top of your backswing, with most of your weight over your forward knee. (Don't worry, the chances of you actually hitting the ball are zero.) From here, make a slow downswing, stop short of the ball, pause only for a couple of reverse waggles . . . and . . . breathe.

OK, you're confused, but here's the genius of my theory! You haven't made your practice swing yet, and it is a fact that nobody, but nobody, ever makes a crappy practice swing. When was the last time you made a practice swing and staggered around the tee saying, "Shit, what the hell was that!?!" No, dear pupil, you've just got that bit over with, and the only damage done is that you really weirded out your opponents. Now all you have to do is take your normal stance, address the ball, make your practice swing, and this time let the ball get in the way! This way, you'll find out where the ball actually goes when you make a tension-free swing. It might go right, left, or down the middle, but after going through my foolproof reverse-engineered after-pre-shot routine, all you'll have to do is figure out where the hell you should aim. And that's why you'll still need Rick Smith or Butch Harmon standing behind you.

90

Feherty's Mailbag

Online—Published: July 9, 2007

Sir Feherty,

Might you don your Eye-agra and give us a Fly on the Ball perspective of these young lassies on the LPGA Tour?

—GR, Denton, Texas

Dear GR:

How come so many Texans like to be known by double initials? Just curious.

Let's see; we have Pressel, Gulbis, Creamer, Ochoa . . . (I don't think we can count Wie yet). I love 'em all. If that's what the future of the LPGA looks like, then I'd say they're in great shape. They're personable, likeable, intensely competitive and they look fabulous in the new fashion trends for women's golf. What more could you ask for? I love to watch them swing. Men amateurs would be better off watching them for swing tips than the guys on the PGA tour. I said tips, GR, *tips*.

Dear David,

I just purchased a new driver and my golf league is Tuesday night. I have a date Wednesday night. Is it wrong of me to want to go hit my driver more than I want to go on the date?

—Mike McLaughlin, Waterford, Mich.

Mike,

Well, to begin with, Mike, it's never wrong to want to spend quality time with inanimate objects or small farm animals over human beings. I'm assuming here that your golf league is predominantly male, so they fall into the same category I just outlined above.

Look at it this way:

- When you spend time with your driver, does it suddenly have to leave the table when the check arrives?
- Does your driver flinch when you move to pick it up?
- Do you feel as though you have to sit through a two-hour movie about the "Ya Ya Sisterhood," all the while reminscing about the 35-foot snake you dropped last Tuesday to win the match?
- Does your driver ever ask you if you could vote for Hillary?

I think we all know the answers to these questions, don't we, Mike? Here's how to gauge whether this girl's going to fit in your future: Take the driver on the date with you. Treat it as though it were your best buddy all night. Buy it beer; go to the john together. Let it ride in the front seat and make her sit in the back. Laugh at imaginary jokes it tells you and when she asks what's so funny, tell her she wouldn't get it. If at the end of the night she asks you both in for "coffee," marry her as soon as possible. Good luck.

David,

Have you ever farted so loud during a telecast that it was picked up by the microphone?

—Brooks

Dear Brooks:

Yes. Furthermore, the odor was picked up by the guys in the truck. Some were permanently scarred.

Dear Mr. Feherty,

I did a mental double-take when I started reading your column recently and found foul language assaulting me from the first paragraph. What gives? I was always taught a person's vocabulary was blessedly small if he had to resort to using profanity, and you, unfortunately, use it a lot, and choose very borderline publicly acceptable ones.

I hope you can make me laugh without using foul language and without resorting to very tiresome ridicule of Paris Hilton (of whom I'm not a fan, but am tired of seeing her verbally pummeled) and Rosie O'Donnell (of whom I'm a big fan and am also tired of seeing her verbally pummeled). If you've read this far, thank you. I wish you good writing in the future.

—Eleanor Green, Morgantown, W.V.

Dear Eleanor,

If it weren't for the fact you say you're a Rosie fan, I'd swear this was from my mom. But then, even though my mom hates it when I use foul language, she knows I have a huge vocabulary. I believe that language is only foul when there is an attempt to be foul behind it, and I know that not all of my humor is for everybody. I just have a healthy contempt for pomp and circumstance. I was the kid in the back of the church who was always laughing uncontrollably at the well-timed fart, you know? I can't help it, it's in my DNA.

And just for the record, I take no pleasure in poking fun at genuinely stupid people, so I would never really work Paris Hilton over, as she clearly lacks the tools to respond in an intelligent manner. And in deference to your support of Rosie, I'll leave her to The Donald. They deserve each other.

Hey Feherty,
Is it me or does Tiger's swing look like it's lost a little panache? His follow-through looks like the elastic in his bloomers broke mid-swing and he's doing what he can to keep them from falling down to his ankles. Don't get me wrong, I love him to pieces and I know he is still dominating the world of golf, but I believe the Butch-built swing is far superior to Haney's. Am I being too much of a nagging bitch?
— Lee The Critical, Thousand Oaks, Calif.

Lee The Critical,
There's no such thing as too much of a nagging bitch. The whole point of being one is to be too much of one. I mean, if you've worked hard enough to earn the title nagging bitch, it goes without saying you're too much of one. It's the nature of the thing.

Anyway, I guess I don't care what Tiger's swing looks like. I try to stay away from analyzing the bits and pieces; that's Kostis's job.

Dear David,
What happened to Fred Couples? I do not see him playing in any tournaments. I enjoy watching him play as much as I like reading your great articles. Thank you.
— Len Skuta

Dear Len:
Fred shed his second wife and has moved in with Jim Nantz. Since apparently Jim is only doing three tournaments this year

for CBS, he and Fred want to spend as much time together as possible. The tabloid press now refer to them as "Jimcup."

However, it seems there may be a little rain cloud on the horizon since word has it Fred is not too happy with all the time Jim spends inspecting Bush 41's colon. Barbara has had to console Fred by letting him hit balls into Kennebunkport Bay from the back of the compound. Stay tuned, Lenny boy, this could get interesting.

Hi David,
   Do you have any suggestions for people who want to express support for Mr. McCord?
                                        —John Lutter, Roseville, Minn.

Dear John:
   Two words: Jack Kevorkian.

David,
   Do you have a fan club? How can I sign up to be one of Feherty's Feher Ladies?
                                        —Jean Marie

Dear Jean Marie:
   You just did. Send me all of your personal information and include a video, preferably one of you on a mechanical bull at Gilly's. I'll also need a financial statement audited by Ernst & Young and a photo of all of your current residences. Seriously, I guess I'll have to take this up with my agent, the Norwegian Flash, Barry the Bald.

Dear Mr. Feherty,
   Can a golfer (much less a woman golfer!) be a snobby purist and a blue-collar average Josephine at the same time? One side of me

cringes every time I hear a bunch of drunk frat boys yelling "You da man!" at the pros after their shots, but the other half of me delights in the fact that golf is no longer reserved for only the elite. Is there any hope for me? Thanks.

—Missy

Dear Missy:
Sure there's hope, Missy. The same people who love John Daly cheer just as loud for Davis Love. I am grateful though that "You da man" has departed the scene, although "In the hole" seems to have replaced it, much to my chagrin. I hope that programs like the "First Tee" grow and prosper so that golf continues to migrate into areas formerly reserved for rolling drunks and drive-by shootings.

91

A Real Throwback

Golf Magazine, *10565493*, August 2007, Vol. 49, Issue 8

A few years ago the cover of the program for the Tour event at Colonial Country Club in Fort Worth featured a photo of Ben Hogan leaning on a club with that enigmatic look on his face, but the most noticeable thing about it was the gap between his nicotine-stained middle and index fingers where his cigarette should have been. I like to think of Hogan tossing his Gallaher's Blue to the ground as he set up over the ball—grip and posture by Leonardo da Vinci, and the last wisp of smoke trailing from his nostrils as he began his takeaway.

For the sake of John Wayne's ass, I get it—cigarettes are bad for you! But that doesn't erase the fact that some of my heroes smoked, and this sanitization of history pisses me off. How long before we remember Porky Oliver as thin, Trevino as mute, and Tommy Bolt as a Zen master?

Golf is boredom to most non-golfers, and sometimes it's on the edge for those of us who like to play and watch. I don't remember the last time I saw a player really throw a golf club. It's not like I want to go to a tournament and have a Bengals game break out. A little entertainment is all I ask, you know, for old times' sake. So, the next time you play, try tossing a club. Step into the throw Happy Gilmore–style, trailing the offending weapon well behind your throwing shoulder and hip, leaving arm and hand action out of the move until the moment of release. This is where most amateurs make the critical error of hanging on too long, resulting in a violent and often embarrassing pull, or even the dreaded backward heave.

If you decide to go totally batshit, you need worst-case-scenario plans to deal with the Tomahawk, perfected by Lanny Wadkins in the '70s, where the club is left buried up to the grip. Removal should be left to the caddie, who gave you the wrong damn club anyway. Then there are the Sideways Sikorsky and the Ass-Backwards Apache, out-of-control helicopter throws that often result in a club becoming lodged up a tree. I took counsel on the correct procedure in this situation from my good friends Dr. Tom "Total" Loss, a well known and highly suspected member of the USGA, and veteran PGA Tour rules official Sir George Boutell, both of whom gave me the thumbs-up on this decision. (At least I think it was George's thumb. He was 60 yards away, sitting in a cart eating doughnuts at the time.) Both agreed that the issues here are retention of dignity and pace of play.

Under the rules of temporary insanity, a player or his caddie may not retrieve such a club, which is deemed to be out of play, and in an interesting footnote, which I have just made up and needs to be added to the Decisions booklet (because at 600 pages it isn't long enough), both the player and his caddie are allowed to savagely attack anyone who tries to retrieve said club, until the player has holed out and taken up his stance on the next shot that denies him or his caddie a clear line of sight to where the club now rests. In other words, wait until the silly bastard can't see you anymore before you ask one of your liquored-up idiot friends to give you a leg up the tree. Under my rules, the player, having left the scene, has given up all rights to said equipment. If you get any lip from him, tell him I said so, and if that doesn't work, hit him over the head with it. Hopefully, we'll have a camera on you.

Hey, all I want is better TV.

92

An Earl of Wisdom

Golf Magazine, *10565493*, *September 2007, Vol. 49, Issue 9*

The late Earl Woods had something in common with Charlie Nicklaus. They each did a damn good balancing act in order to raise a child who had extraordinary talent. Each guided his child toward his destiny with love and discipline. Each allowed his youngster to fall and pick himself up, helped dust him off, and selflessly set him back on track. The likes of Earl Woods and Charlie Nicklaus are even more rare than their remarkable children, considering that the highway to sporting immortality is littered with wreckage from collisions between over-talented kids and overzealous parents. But, like I tell my own kids, if it comes down to it, blame the parents.

Ask Todd Marinovich or take a quick tour through the scrap heap of women's tennis, where Jennifer Capriati and Mary Pierce discovered that their enemies were closer than their friends. Even a stalker has the decency to be a member of somebody else's family! Venus and Serena Williams' father, Richard, straddled the line for a long time, with his much-too-big camera and much too short shorts, but in the end he gets a B+ because both of his girls are successful and seem to be happy. Sean O'Hair escaped a horrifying ordeal with his father, and we can only hope Michelle Wie can do the same. What happened to those days when golf was just a game for Michelle? You know, before the $20 million and being pushed one way and then pulled another. By this stage, that poor child must have the self-esteem of a Spam donut in a French bakery (although $20 mil must ease the pain a bit).

When Michelle dubiously withdrew mid-round from an LPGA Tour event on the advice of her father, B.J., and her agent, to avoid shooting an 88, it raised questions of character and respect for the game, because that number would have made her ineligible for further play on the Tour this year. Can you imagine Earl Woods or Charlie Nicklaus encouraging their respective kids to take the easy way out on that one? And the circus goes on and on like the last three rings of hell, and Michelle's the only clown, and she's crying real tears. When a child feels this way, the first people to help should be Mom and Dad, but in Michelle's case, it appears they both need to put their hands in the air and back away from the stroller. Go borrow a kid from Brad and Angelina and start over, but for God's sake, leave this one alone.

If B.J. and the missus aren't willing to do this, then someone needs to call Child Protective Services, or failing that, Macaulay Culkin. Next on the list is Larry King, or please God no . . . Barbara Walters. You know you've effed up when she rings.

When I heard that little Sam Woods had entered the earth's atmosphere, my first thought was of my only daughter, Erin, whose crush on Tiger almost rivals my own. Tiger was kind enough to sign a photo of himself to her a couple of years ago, and earlier this year, while I was reading to Erin at bedtime, she was holding it, clearly paying no attention to me. "Daddy," she said. "Do you think Tiger would like a photograph of me?" I'm not a candidate for Parent of the Year either, but I can figure out the answer to a question like that, so I said, "Of course he would, baby, but you'll have to sign it for him, too." The very next week, before Tiger teed off in the first round of the Buick in San Diego, I interviewed him for our Masters preview show, and when we were done I sheepishly handed the expectant dad a 4-by-6 of my angel, signed in her best first-grade cursive, "To Tiger, love Erin." I wished him and Elin someone similarly healthy and amazing. He went on to win the tournament, and now, the greatest prize of all—a daughter!

Who knows what great things Sam Woods will do in her lifetime, or how Tiger and Elin will do as parents? At this stage, we can only be certain that their little girl will grow even more beautiful, and her dad will fall more deeply in love with her every day. My daughter now takes credit for one of Tiger's wins, and, as bad a parent as I may be, I'm a good enough one to believe she might just be right.

93

Ruling Class

Golf Magazine, *10565493*, October 2007, Vol. 49, Issue 10

I've said this before, but the Rules officials on the PGA Tour are tops. The reason I'm reiterating this is that earlier this year George Boutell, one of the best, drove his cart into the sunset with nothing more than a sly wave goodbye. George was the grandmaster whom apprentices approached with reverence in the hope of gathering a rare crumb of knowledge (or dough-nut) that occasionally fell from the box of Krispy Kremes he would freebase in a shady spot near the port-o-lets. Yes, I'm talking about a man who once had a pizza delivered to his cart at a PGA Tour event. When a player called for a ruling it was a joy to watch George transition from what seemed like a nursing-home coma into a regimentally upright, razor-sharp, starched-white, creaseless, athletic ruling machine.

George was the Gretzky of rulings, the Federer of the fair-ways, usually invisible, yet always in the right place. I knew of only one man with a similar style, a guy named Jimmy Hemphill, from my early playing days on the Sunshine Tour in South Africa. One day in Pretoria I was paired with Nick Price and called for a ruling because I thought my ball might be embedded. As usual Jimmy was there, faster than a flick of a springbok's tail. "What's the problem?" he asked.

"Well, Jimmy," I said, trying to keep a straight face as the idiot Price slapped the bark of a nearby gum tree. "We think my ball may be embedded here, but we're not sure."

"Where is it?"

"Uh, I believe you just parked your cart on it," I said, pointing to his front left wheel. Jimmy looked down at the spot, then said indignantly, "Well then, it was a bloody waste of time calling me, wasn't it? Obviously it's a free drop." And with that, he sped off.

To the best of my knowledge, George never parked on anyone's ball. He applied the Rules to the letter of the law, performing his primary function (which was to protect the interests of the rest of the field), while leaving enough room for common sense and compassion. If there was any doubt he always leaned in favor of the player. He was a grumpy sonofabitch with a legendary hemorrhoid problem. Even if you got him during one of his bouts of pink balloon knots, you knew you'd get a fair shake, even if it did include a graphic description of the current state of his nethermost regions. When George got himself a little cancer, that merriment was briefly halted. Within weeks, George had a few feet of bowel removed and was back at work, claiming that the only difference was that his farts were now a slightly higher F-sharp.

One reason George retired early was his compassion for the people who sat beside him in coach after a week of dealing with prima donnas who wanted drops from lies where the grass wasn't growing in the right direction, viewers calling in with idiotic rulings, missing and presumed stolen courtesy cars, and frequent cavity searches at airport security. After years of being seated next to hideously cheerful "Isn't flying fun? What do you do for a living?" nimrods, he knew that eventually he was going to kill and eat one of them. In an age during which professional golf is rolling in cash, Rules officials still have to fly in the back of the airplane.

The Tour is lucky to have such great officials. Despite having recently signed a new five-year deal, they are still underpaid and overworked. Now it seems the ones with the most experience are becoming an endangered species.

It would be easy to go the Al Gore route and blame it on greenhouse gases, to which George contributed more than his fair share over the years, but it is a problem much easier solved. This column should tell readers I really miss him. His departure should tell the Tour they need to look around the world of sports (see the NBA), realize what they've got, pay up, and look happy about doing it.

94

Feherty's Rants and Raves

Online—Published: October 1, 2007

I keep telling people that I'm writing a book. I've been telling them for more than 15 years actually, but recently, these claims have had a certain amount of truth attached to them. It turns out that what was holding me back was my inability to type, and, of course, the fact that I am a lazy, fat, procrastinating, gasbag. I always had the story in me, fermenting somewhere in the bowels of my brain, and in my own defense, I did manage to pass a couple of passages from it, which stained the pages of *Golf Magazine* in the form of the "Uncle Dickie" articles. But now, it's time to announce that the entire book has been surgically removed from my system, and my body is once again working properly. It was a hardcover as well, so it really hurt.

The working title for this literary masterpiece is *Gussett of the Wood*, and some of you may remember, a long time ago I asked for your suggestions, all of which were considerably worse than *Gussett of the Wood*. So there you go. It will be available before Father's Day next year, and several publishers are fighting for the right to charge way too much for it as I write, although I will say that I'm leaning toward Kinko's, due to their aggressive recycling policy, and the softness and absorbency of the paper they use. I know where most of these tomes will end up, and nobody needs a paper cut down there, I can tell you from experience.

Yes, I read McCord's last one, too. This book will be a different experience, though. If I had to describe it, and I don't, but I'm going to, I'd say it was a story of love, honor, betrayal, lust, and incontinence, between a clan of Neanderthal Scottish cave-dwellers, a sex-crazed Jack Russell, a lubricated ferret, a Nazi policeman, a three-legged sheep, various crippled and insane ex-servicemen, a couple of gay caddies, the middle finger of the patron saint of Scotland, and an elderly superhero. I have this nagging feeling that you might have read something like it before, but hey, sometimes you just have to take a chance.

It's one of those books that you could read on a flight from Newark to La Guardia, and still have time to absorb most of *USA Today*. There will be pictures, a couple of wee maps, and a glossary of terms for those who don't understand the way that the Scottish people talk, and believe me, these people make Colin Montgomerie sound like Dan Rather.

I know that this is a cheap and transparent promo for the benefit of my own personal self, but I don't care. Mike Purkey, the editor of my magazine column, showed me how to outline the story, and cut and paste, and attach, and all kinds of really cool things, and now, I am an actual writer! I might really suck, but I wrote a book, and a lot of you out there are going to read it, if I have to go down to Kinko's, bind the damn things myself, and FedEx them to you.

That is all. I'm going back to writing in 1,500-word bursts of verbal flatulence again. Happy New Year, and by the way, does anyone know who won that match play tournament?

95

Feherty's Mailbag

Online—Published: October 10, 2007

David,

As I look back at old publicity pictures of you, you appear to be progressively taking on the look of the one and only Beelzebub. Have you sold your soul?

— Brad Titus, Carlsbad, Calif.

Brad:

Do you know when Titus was born, Brad? I'm referring to the Titus who was a Roman Emperor back before Pro V1's were available? He was born December 30, 39; 39 A.D., that is. His best friend was Britannicus. Those are the same guys that ring your doorbell to try and sell you a set of encyclopedias just as Johnny Miller's getting ready to say something unbelievably inappropriate. Do you happen to know Tiger Woods's birth date, Mr. Smartypants? Right, FootJoy breath, December 30th.

I have no idea what any of this has to do with my facial features, but ask yourself this: If I made a deal with the devil to sell my soul, don't you think it'd be so I could take over Tiger's body? Why would I settle for looking like this?

Besides, I've been told many times that I bear an uncanny resemblance to Pierce Brosnan, you fartwit.

Dear David,

Have recently fallen in love with the movie *The Greatest Game Ever Played*, starring a bunch of actors I've never seen before. They all have a better swing than Matt Damon in *The Legend of Bagger Vance*. This type of old school, pure golf stuff seems the type of thing you would relish, but I have not heard of your commenting on it. Please do so.

—Chip Bell, Myrtle Beach, S.C.

Chip:

A good golf swing can't be faked, but then, you don't necessarily have to have one to be a great player. Case in point—Ray Floyd.

You're lucky they cast Matt Damon. It might have been Charles Barkley. I read the book, but I must admit I haven't seen the movie. I rarely go since I paid $7.50 to see *Ishtar*.

Mark Frost did a fabulous job on the Vardon story and I assume he was equally brilliant on the screenplay for the movie. Perhaps I'll rent it some Saturday night when I'm picking up a copy of *The Commitments*.

Maybe Mark will do a story about my golf career some day. We could call it *Bushmills: It's Not Just for Breakfast Anymore*.

Dear David,

I was on the ninth fairway Sunday at Congressional as the final groups were coming through. Peter Kostis came by with a contraption strapped over his back that allowed him to see the TV coverage. I thought to myself that it must be hard to carry that thing around for four-plus hours in the heat. You came walking up the fairway with the next group, and not only were you NOT carrying the contraption, but you had some hot babe lugging the thing on a monopod. How do you rate a slammin' babe carrying your junk while Kostis is relegated to schlepping it himself?

—S. Deering

S.:

Let me ask you something, Deering. If you could get your boss to assign you a slammin' hot babe to lug your contraption around, would you? I can't help it if Kostis hasn't figured this out yet. Thankfully he doesn't read this column. Keep your trap shut.

96

Feherty's Rants and Raves

Online—Published: October 21, 2007

Is it my imagination, or is golf being taken over by the anorexic? Of the entire field at the Mercedes, only Hal Sutton could be described as "not thin," and even he isn't close to fat. Why, even Mark Calcavecchia has gotten thin, the scoundrel. Davis Love has a little bit of a Nelly Kelly going on there, but he's still tall enough to look like a one-iron that swallowed a golf ball.

Where have all the fat guys gone? People like Tim Herron and Big John Daly are becoming an endangered species out there, so much so that I think we may eventually have to have them darted, crated up, and sent somewhere to see if we can breed them in captivity.

But really, Jack used to be tubby, Casper and Ed "Porky" Oliver were positively spherical, and Julius Boros and Lionel Hebert both loved their grub. There's five corpulent competitors off the top of my head. We had exactly none in the field last week. Maybe we should give everybody a cart.

Off and running would be a fair description of Sergio Garcia, I suppose, after his victory in the season opener. Running, jumping, skipping, gripping, gripping, gripping stuff. I'm led to believe the little ratbag may be scribbling in the mag too, along with that other sniper's nightmare, Charles Howell the third of my weight.

Just when they thought they were done with homework. We'll see how they'll shape up now that they're journalists. It's the first step on the slippery downward staircase toward stretch marks and mediastinal shift, let's hope.

Tiger's not exactly obese, but he's looking positively tubby by comparison to the new wave, most of whom would fall into their boxers if they lifted their arms over their heads. Something needs to be done before a caddie accidentally puts a headcover on his player, and sticks him in the bag beside the 3-wood. I'd write to the commissioner about it, if he didn't weigh 140 pounds with his glasses on. I think he's in on the conspiracy.

There is some kind of liposuction going on in the fitness trailer or something, which might be why they don't allow the media in there. (Of course, most of the media wouldn't fit in there.)

Thank God for announcers like Roger Maltbie, Peter Alliss, and me. Real men, with breasts, who have the decency to feel rotten most mornings, who always wear a shirt, and never, ever sunbathe. Just yesterday I took the skin off the roof of my mouth with a corn chip smothered with molten cheese. When was the last time David Duval did that? (Actually, one of the really annoying things about David is that he eats like a sea-gull, so he's probably not a great example, but no matter. I'm trying to piss off skinny people here.)

One of the great things about the game of golf, which sets it apart from other professional sports, is that the people who love to watch the game are still actually involved in playing it, so they can identify with the players. It used to be that in the galleries at PGA Tour events, the big guys wearing the chili dogs had someone to point at, and felt an affinity.

These days, they have to watch an LPGA event to get the same warm feeling, and I don't know what it is, but there's something not right about that. (Not that it makes them bad people, mind you.)

97

Flier Lies Risking My Dignity and My Lunch for a Good Cause

Golf Magazine, *10565493, November 2007, Vol. 49, Issue 11*

You couldn't get me on a roller coaster with a cattle prod, but I started the week of the PGA Championship with a flight in an F-16, courtesy of Class A PGA Professional and Oklahoma Air National Guard member Capt. Dan "Noonan" Rooney. The ratbag Rick Reilly had been up a few years back and wrote a hilarious piece for *Sports Illustrated* about it, but my jaunt was to promote the Fallen Heroes Fund, started by Capt. Dan just a year ago. The fund benefits the families of those who have been impacted by the war, so I immediately put my hand in the air.

Everyone who gets the privilege is given a call sign, and I remembered that Reilly's was "Two Bags" for the velocity and capacity of his hurlage, so I reckoned all I needed was "One Bag" to be one up on my more widely read hero. The flight and subsequent piece that aired on CBS created public awareness about Patriot Day, Sept. 1, when participating public golf clubs around the country donated $1 from every green fee and members of private clubs were encouraged to donate whatever they wished.

My day started with three hours of rigorous training on how to get in and out of the jet and how to kiss my ass goodbye if anything went wrong. Reilly had been advised to eat a preflight banana, but lunch for me was a double sweaty jalapeno cheeseburger, fries and a large chocolate malt because I hate throwing up on an empty stomach.

The plane, baking on the hot tarmac, looked like a hypodermic needle with razor blades for wings and a rocket for a plunger. Before I knew it I was strapped in, lit up, and screaming for my mommy as Desperate Dan launched down the runway, pointed the nose vertical, and shot to 30,000 feet in 40 seconds. I felt like I'd been fired out of a cannon with an elephant sitting in my lap. Then we leveled out, flew into Kansas, and Dan really started to tie my bowels into a sheepshank. Thank God for the G-suit, a plum-crushing harness and a pilot who knew what he was doing, or at least made me think he did. We did aileron rolls (whatever the hell they are, I think I've had them with red beans and rice), vertical swoopy things and plunging necklines before Dan gave me a few gut-churning banked dives that almost made me release a chocolate hostage I didn't know was a captive.

It was an unbelievable rush, and I wanted to go again right after we landed. I'd made it through 9g 3 times with no leakage north or south! Four hours later, still elated, and in 102 degrees, I took an ill-advised bike ride, during which two idiots speeding downhill around a blind corner on the wrong side of the path took me out, knocking me 20 yards down the hill and out cold, separating my shoulder and covering me in enough cuts and bruises that the next morning I had to wear my bedsheets into the shower to soak them off my oozing wounds. The front desk had to be informed that no murder had taken place in Room 506. For the four days of the tournament, the average temperature was about 2 degrees colder than hell.

Despite a strong challenge from "Woodrow the Weird" Austin, whose wheel is still spinning even though the gerbil has clearly left his cage, Tiger put his foot on the gas when it came to the crunch. You've got to love Woody, though. He'd make a cup of coffee nervous, but late in his career, he's taming his demons.

The week was a disaster for the weak, and I was weak all week. I decided to drive home to Dallas that Sunday night, drenched in sweat and Gold Bond powder. By the time I dropped my thunderbags in the bathroom, my nads had turned to limestone, a sight that gave She Who Must Be Obeyed quite a fit of the giggles. She suggested a small tap with a hammer to set the boys free.

But the important thing is this: Reilly can eat my perfectly stainless shorts! The call sign Dan gave me? "Spaulding!"

Wait a minute, didn't he hurl into a Porsche?

98

Feherty's Rants and Raves

Online—Published: November 16, 2007

I'm thinking that it's been ages since I picked a good nit, so here we go. I, like many of you, watch a lot of sport on TV, and if there is one thing that I cannot stand, it's when an announcer assumes that his or her audience is unable to identify the sport that he or she is watching.

Here's an example. I'm watching Green Bay and Dallas try to severely injure each other on a big strip of grass, which is marked off in five-yard increments, and there is a set of goal posts at either end. The players are wearing body armor and helmets, and most of the crowd are wearing big lumps of cheese on their heads. The announcer says: "Brett Favre [and if that's pronounced 'Farve,' then I've just fatred] is in complete control of this football game, and is throwing the football with deadly accuracy."

Now if I'm not mistaken, this is a GAME that is played with a BALL, and if there is anyone watching who has not yet noticed that it is a game called "FOOTBALL," then, to ensure the safety of us all, this person needs to be institutionalized as quickly as possible.

I of course use football as an example, but the problem is

even more widespread in golf. The terms "golf ball, golf swing, golf shot, golf club" are all equally acceptable when used without being preceded by the word "golf," unless of course we start playing the game on a football field, or a hockey rink, and I don't see that happening anytime soon. In fact, now that I come to think of it, hockey is thankfully one of the sports in which the announcers give the viewers the benefit of the doubt.

If Barry Melrose (who I think is the best analyst in any sport) ever says, "He shot that hockey puck so hard at Belfour," I shall feel as if someone has taken a swing at my balls. And I'm assuming you know which ones I'm talking about.

99

Good Pill Hunting

Golf Magazine, *10565493*, *December 2007, Vol. 49, Issue 12*

At last, the colder weather arrived in Texas, and my mind turned to the pursuit of quail, with the Tiger Woods of hunting hounds, Ziggy the beagle, at my side.

Ziggy spent the summer in air-conditioned luxury, his only exercise humping our other two dogs, Willard the Schnauzenwiener, and Scruffy, a Cairn terrier of dubious lineage. If a fart had hair, it would look like Scruffy, but probably smell better.

We set forth in the F-150 to my pal Eddie's ranch, 5,000 acres of quail paradise just north of San Angelo. Armed with my trusty Merkel side-by-side 28, double-tin Filson chaps and an Acme whistle, I'd packed a two-day food supply in a cooler, dog food for Zig, a good book, and my sleeping bag. I pulled into a Dairy Queen along the way, but forgot to relieve myself, so a covert roadside squirt was necessary just outside of town. By the time I got behind the wheel again, the mighty hunter had savaged my Beltbuster burger, paper and all, and growled his way so far through a chocolate Blizzard that I had to pull the Styrofoam cup off his nose.

We hit the ranch house about 9 p.m. With one eye on the cooler, Zig derisively sniffed the kibble, trotted over to the dumper for a drink, and was at the bottom of our sleeping bag snoring like a clapped-out Briggs and Stratton lawn mower before I had my pants off. It was like trying to sleep with an epileptic bush-pig, and within 20 minutes, after a battle that was not entirely one-sided, the hairy little bastard had farted and kicked me onto the sofa.

Next morning, I had the coffee on before I checked on Zig, who hadn't moved from the bottom of the sleeping bag. I reached in all the way, heaved the tricolor lump up the bag, and bade him a cheery good morning. Nothing. No movement. He didn't seem to be breathing, and when I pulled his eyelid up, it just snapped shut. For one horrible moment, I thought my beloved hound had been asphyxiated by the gaseous contents of his own bowels. Upon closer look, I noticed he was indeed breathing, but very shallowly. Then it dawned on me. I had left two wrapped Clif Bars and an Ambien on the nightstand before I abandoned ship for the sofa. The bars and the sleeping pill were gone—Ziggy was in a sugar-and-drug-induced coma. The hound was down, and now the man would hunt alone, which was problematic. Blues are different from bobwhite quail in that they won't hold for a pointer. You have to flush them first, and then go after pairs and singles fast and on foot. Ziggy might be the worst hunting dog in Texas, and the only thing he'd pointed so far was a thick milkshake, but I reckoned even he could accidentally blunder into a covey or two of blues.

That day, I made several trips back to the ranch house to check on Rip Van Beagle, and he was stone-cold out each time, but still farting, which I took as a good sign. I spotted several coveys of the crafty blue quail on my own, and each time tried in vain to make them fly by rushing into their cover—typically Ziggy's role in this opéra bouffe. This was not a good idea, as West Texas brush and cactus country is worse than the Devil's pubic hair. I spent the evening reading, tweezing my nads, and checking on my little pal. With a heavy heart, I slipped into our sleeping bag and spooned my little mound of hound, vowing that not even his poisonous flatulence would separate us that night. However, my beagle's bottom could violate the chemical-weapons clause of the Geneva Convention, and 10 minutes later I was on the sofa with a nosebleed.

At 2:30 in the morning, I awoke to a crash. I fumbled for the light switch, suddenly illuminating a rear view of a portly beagle, who with his nose had pried the lid off the cooler, jumped into it, and was now foraging like a hog, and mangling a packet of cooked ham. My boy was back! I told you, he's the canine Tiger Woods—he takes off whenever he wants and still comes up with the prize.

100

Give Till It Hurts

Golf Magazine, *10565493, January 2008, Vol. 50, Issue 1*

Christmas is upon us again, and I'm in my usual vile holiday mood. Everything has an acronym now, and I reckon I have SAHD (Seasonal A-Hole Disorder). It's not so much the holidays themselves that bring on SAHD, but rather the timing—I need either the warm sun upon my face or the cold, steel-toed boot of a West Virginia coal miner up my ass to remind me how lucky I am. Either would do, particularly when I'm confronted by charity panhandlers, some of whom end up being caught on the chin by the leading edge of my apoplectic mood swing.

Last year I gave away almost everything in my wallet on several consecutive days to a maniacal bell-ringer with a vacant, stitched-on grin who lurks just outside our local Tom Thumb grocery store for the whole month of December. Finally, I snapped. I'm all for charity, and believe me, I'm sure the guy was on the level, but he hit me upside the pocketbook every day on my way in, and then again on my way out, every time, as if it was the first time he'd ever laid eyes on me! I tried telling him I wasn't nearly guilty enough to be hosed like this on such a regular basis, at one stage dropping my pants and holding my ankles in front of him, only to be tapped on the shoulder by an elderly gentleman, who told me that the pharmacy was next door. (Apparently it's a full-service, compounding pharmacy.)

It's a funny old thing, charity. I've watched enough Animal Planet to know we're not the only mammals who practice it, but there is definitely something different about the scale on which it is perpetrated here in the United States. And Texas? Well, let me tell you pardner, this is a whole 'nother country. I'm convinced the people of the great state of Texas are the most generous in the world. When the PGA Tour's charitable giving is totaled up this season, it will have given away more than $100 million, and roughly 22 percent of it will have come from events played in the Lone Star state.

The Valero Texas Open distributed more than $8 million from proceeds generated largely by their Monday-after pro-ams, and that's in San Antonio, a relatively small market! The red-trousered, sweaty-nadded members of the Salesmanship Club at the Byron Nelson are the all-time champion wallet weasels in the history of the Tour, and when you toss in the Houston Open and the Champions and Nationwide Tour events held here, they just blow the rest of the country away.

Okay, so nearly everyone in Texas carries a gun, but I don't think that's it. No, I believe people in Texas just have a keener sense of how lucky they are not to be somewhere else. I'm taking a wild guess here, but I don't think there's a whole lot of charity going on in places like North Korea, Myanmar or Iran, to name just a few places where the authorities take a dim view of subversive activities like, say, reading about other places, or, God help us, women voting, you know, things that lead to the ultimate evil—education!

Texans, it seems to me, have a healthy disregard for what people from elsewhere in the world think of them. I like it, and in these times during which average Americans could be forgiven for thinking that there is something dreadfully wrong with their country, I think it's my duty as a registered fuzzy foreigner to state my opinion that the best Christmas present I can think of would be the right to live here, in the US of A. That's why I went to Baghdad at Thanksgiving with the USO, to do my part for the brave men and women who are fighting to look after my way of life. Granted, I was dragged there kicking and screaming, but hopefully as you're reading this, I've made it back in one piece, and right about now I'm trying to figure out a way to insert a turnip, or some similarly shaped tuber, into that damn Salvation Army bell at the grocery store. Hey, I'm sure the right to bury vegetables is guaranteed somewhere in our constitution.

101.

'08 Expectations

Online—Published: January 1, 2008

1. **Tim Herron** goes on my successful brussels-sprout-and-chickpea diet and emerges for the '08 season looking like The Rock, only to be DQ'd from the Sony Open for deliberately changing the direction of the Hawaiian tradewinds.
2. Poised to defend his Nissan Open title, **Charles Howell III** mysteriously goes missing when his dog accidentally buries him in the backyard.
3. **Camilo Villegas** withdraws halfway through the FBR Open and the EDS Byron Nelson for "scrotal exhaustion." Wilt Chamberlain is put on notice.
4. **Gary Player** again declares that the game is riddled with 'roids, and he appears at a Champions Tour event standing 6'2" tall. He says that if he'd known HGH was undetectable in his day, he would have won 26 majors, kicked sand in Tom Weiskopf's face, and given Arnold Palmer an "atomic wedgie."
5. **Greg Norman's** yacht sinks while Tiger Woods is spearfishing nearby. Nothing to see here, move along . . .

6. Steelers fan **Jim Furyk** buys Pittsburgh. (The city, because it was half the price of the football team.)
7. **Michelle Wie** puts her competitive career back on track after Britney Spears adopts her. (See, all the girl needed was a little parenting.)
8. Having completely run out of all other vices, **John Daly** enters rehab for his addiction to women who beat the snot out of him. He soon remarries, but his new bride turns out to be a member of the Taliban—and a guy.

102.

For Love of Country

Golf Magazine, *10565493*, *February 2008, Vol. 50, Issue 2*

I've been all over the world, and lived in a bunch of countries, and as I've said many times in this rag, I love this one the most. So every holiday in America is a thanksgiving to me, whether it's MLK Day, President's Day, Yom Kippur, Columbus Day or Super Bowl Sunday. In fact, before I got to be such a renowned expert on American sports, I thought Rashan Salaam was either Aladdin's best friend or another Jewish day off, and I was happy to celebrate either one. But I've come a long way from being that ignorant, so it is with a sense of great pride that I will set off for Iraq in just a few days. I'm writing my usual column before I go with no sense of what to expect—a literary experiment if you will—so that you can compare it with the feature that appears earlier in this issue. Like most of us, I have a political opinion of this war, but I will do my best to keep any such assholiness off these pages. I have a feeling, however, that my best is going to suck. Utterly.

Having grown up in the Margaret Thatcher era I do have a few opinions about how a war like this should be fought, starting with it might have been a good idea to shoot all the journalists (excluding sportswriters) first. My rules of engagement would be simple. See asshole, shoot asshole, rinse, and repeat. Tell no one! I have no idea who will be protecting us on this trip, but I honestly wouldn't have a problem if they were from Blackwater, which ironically is the name of a river that flows through Belfast. The difference between Baghdad and Belfast is when the Irish wanted to kill each other, we bombed the pubs. That way we could be sure of getting pretty much everybody on the other side. The pubs in Ireland are sort of like the mosques over there; the Irish get together at least five times a day, find the direction of the Guinness Brewery, thank merciful God, and later that day, they're usually on their knees begging forgiveness from whoever is actually in charge. So if you wanted to blow up anyone with whom you disagreed, you left a parcel, or smoked an RPG through the pub window. Having said that, there was a weird civility to the bombing campaign in Ulster. The bartender would usually get a wee phone call a while before the bomb was set to go off, so everybody knew how much time they had to finish their drink before they got out. It was only proper.

The main difference of course is that in Ireland, people never blew themselves up on purpose. Plenty of them did it by accident, but it was usually long before they got anywhere near anyone they didn't like, kind of like scoring on your own goal in soccer. We might be suicide drinkers, but we're not suicide bombers. Another thing I don't understand is the whole 72 virgins as a reward. I mean, what's in it for the virgins? And what happens if you get up there, only to find you've blown off your wobblies? You'd get 72 virgins pointing at you, laughing their asses off? Nope, not my idea of heaven. We Irish admit we're not the smartest nation on earth, but even we aren't dumb enough to fall for that one.

So, I set off on this mission, keenly aware of the golfing footsteps upon which I tread. Bob Hope, Bing Crosby, and Marilyn Monroe, to name but a few. What the hell did Marilyn Monroe have to do with golf, you might ask? Well, don't say you didn't ask, then, because you know she played a round or three with one very famous president. I'm not sure if we can bring that kind of relief to any of our soldiers in Iraq, but Tom Watson, Frank Lickliter, Howard Twitty, Butch Harmon, Joe Inman, Tom Lehman and I are honored to take a swing at the next best thing.

103.

Feherty's Tour of DUTY

Golf Magazine, 10565493, February 2008, Vol. 50, Issue 2

He came. He saw. He inhaled half the desert. David Feherty spent six days in Iraq & Kuwait on a USO tour. His mission: Make our brave troops laugh. This is his personal journal—both hilarious and heartbreaking—FROM THE FRONT LINES.

WHAT THE HELL AM I DOING GOING TO A WAR ZONE?

That's what I thought as I boarded a flight from Dallas to Kuwait City, and then to Iraq, where I would join Butch Harmon, Tom Lehman, Tom Watson, Howard Twitty and Joe Inman on Operation Links, a USO-sponsored visit to boost the morale of American servicemen and women. I grew up in Ulster, in Northern Ireland, in the 1960s and '70s, and the thought of being in a war zone never bothered me. So why did I feel uneasy this November morning? Perhaps because I was a child then, and now I had children.

On my flight out of Dallas, I examined the USO's press packet, filled with useful information about Arab culture, such as: Don't lean away if a man tries to embrace you, even if he's just farted—Arabs have little concept of "personal space." Me, I have a Heisman stiff-arm zone around me into which only freshly showered family members, friends, and beagles are allowed, so if I was to avoid an international incident, adjustments were in order. Before I knew it, we were wheels down.

DAY 1 THEY PAY HOW MUCH FOR GAS?

We landed in Kuwait City and were swept through immigration. Early the next morning, we set off for Camp Arifjan, comprised of 7,500 people on 64 square miles of powdered camel dung, and then Camp Beuhring, the major staging area for troops entering Iraq. Along for the journey were Capt. Trevor Garrett from the Pentagon's Armed Forces Entertainment Department and Scott Past from the Department of Defense, both packing heat. And, not for the last time, I wanted to shoot something. It was quail season back home, and we passed through scenery that makes west Texas oil country look like the snowcapped Tetons. Kuwait smells like a camel's arse. As we roll down the road in our bus, massive oil refineries loom to the left, and majestic white-stucco houses line the right. I can only assume that every time a Kuwaiti fills up his tank the government gives him a hundred bucks. (In fact—I'm not making this up—a gallon of unleaded goes for 78 cents in Kuwait.)

On both bases, our first stop was the D-FAC—the dining facility—where I ate seven scoops of Baskin-Robbins ice cream and a cheeseburger, in that order. We did our first meet-and-greets, signed golf balls, gave away goodies from EA Sports, Cobra, Titleist, Ping and Adams Golf, all while Butch offered tips to the boys hitting balls into a net. After shaking hands with about 200 Marines, my right hand was mangled. On the bus back to the hotel, I fell asleep on Twitty, who was very comfortable. Henceforth, we called him "The Desert Sofa."

DAY 2 TO THE THEATER, PRESIDENT LINCOLN?

En route to Al Asad Air Base, in western Iraq's Anbar Province, we were strapped into a C-130—a four-engine turboprop aircraft that roars louder than Roger Maltbie after two pushups. We wore heavy body armor and helmets, and as Kuwait slipped away behind us, visible through the open tail, a young Marine behind a jackhammer-sized machine gun scanned the desert floor for nasties. Harmon might have looked like a camouflage Teletubby, but he's been on these planes before, having served three years in Vietnam in the '60s.

Now run by the Navy, Al Asad was Saddam's main air base. One year ago, Anbar was considered unwinnable, a haven for car-bomb factories and Al Qaeda. But as of Thanksgiving, the base—which has two runways, thousands of troops and many locals—had not received incoming fire for several months. We went to our billets, known as "cans," dropped off our luggage, and hit the D-FAC (more ice cream for me). Then we met the legendary "SeaBees," Navy engineers who can build anything, anywhere—roads, bridges, fortifications, driving ranges—ahead of schedule and under budget (and can blow the crap out of anyone who tries to stop them). We hit balls, shook hands, signed autographs, and heard from the grunts. "Tell everyone at home we want to finish this," one of them said to me. "Give us the chance, and we will."

I thought to myself, At home, why is all the news bad?

Around the perimeter, we visited a Harrier Jump Jet squadron. They'd planted in their sandy range a 3-by-3-foot board bearing my smiling puss, which they use for target practice. "I can do you one better," I told one airman and ran to the 100-yard mark, dropped my pants, and gave them something to shoot for—a thin sliver of Arabian moon. But the hole was too tight, even for major champions Lehman and Watson. "I missed on purpose," Harmon said. "No one wants that kind of a lie for a second shot."

The base's hospital had hardly anyone in it. In one room lay a young Asian-American soldier who'd been electrocuted, his life saved by a female sergeant who kicked him off an electrified fence that was in the process of broiling him. Of the six patients here, two were insurgents, treated, I'm told, with all of the care and respect given to coalition forces. We weren't allowed to see the wounded insurgents, which is just as well, as Harmon or I might have "accidentally" stepped on an oxygen hose. In the next room, we visited a U.S. soldier, who, on his third tour, had been struck down by depression. I didn't have to ask what was wrong. I could feel it enveloping him, and trying to suck the air from my lungs, too. When I was researching my family history, to find the origin of my battle with mental illness, I discovered that my grandfather, David Weir, fought in the Great War, at the battle of the Somme, where more than a million men were killed or wounded. He did not speak a word for three years after he came back, one of the few in his regiment to survive. The horrors he witnessed in the trenches lingered for the rest of his life. While this young man had all his limbs, he might have been the most broken soldier in the hospital.

From Al Asad, we visited three Forward Operating Bases (FOBs), each closer than the last to Baghdad. Our first trip was to FOB Hit on a Marine Corps CH-53 Sea Stallion transport helicopter, which was dripping hydraulic fluid ominously onto its tailgate. I asked one of the crew if this was, umm, normal. He screamed over the roar of the rotor, "If it's not leaking, we don't fly, because that means it's empty!" Very reassuring. We make it, though, and meet Lieutenant Colonel Jeff Dill, one of many base commanders who explained eloquently why the Anbar situation has so dramatically improved. His men move freely among Iraqis outside the base's barbed-wire perimeter in the town of Baghdadi, where just a few months ago they regularly endured small-arms fire and IEDs (improvised explosive devices). The locals now have electricity and clean water. They no longer have to slaughter a goat every day for fresh meat. They have an optimism, thanks to the determination of Coalition forces and the bravery of locals, such as Colonel Shab'an B. al-Ubadi, the local police chief who has survived eight assassination attempts, seen family members killed and spurned countless bribes on his way to delivering the No. 1 insurgent into the hands of the Americans, precipitating the collapse of Al Qaeda in the area.

From FOB Hit, a V22 Osprey tilt-rotor Marine chopper (Watson, aka "The Desert T-Wat," reassuringly noticed that it wasn't leaking) whisked us away to Haditha Dam, the only operating hydroelectric plant on the Euphrates. A driving range has been fashioned atop the dam, where soldiers splash shots into the Euphrates some 300 feet below. It's a hoot, and one hulking Marine won the long drive with his first swing, smacking his drive a good 400 yards, 50 past Watson and Lehman!

It was back into the Osprey, westward, close to the Syrian and Jordanian borders to FOB Korean Village, named for the Korean workers who built Saddam's roads. The camp bears the scars of war. That night we visited the men who run the IED seek-and-destroy missions using a "Buffalo," a massive, blast-proof, Kevlar-reinforced vehicle with a pneumatic shovel arm designed to break away if a device explodes. The men were about to take it out to play. Walking past heaps of defused and exploded devices, we retired with a bunch of soldiers to the chaplain's quarters, and then to his rooftop range, where we broke open glow sticks, poured the chemicals over a bucket of balls, and lashed them like tracer bullets into the inky blackness of the Arabian night. One soldier caught a ball dead on the heel and gonged the chaplain's satellite dish, prompting a "Holy Crap! There goes my ESPN!" from the man of the cloth. I turned in early, my right hand crushed, a result of shaking the hands of thousands of muscular men—and two dozen women who could kick my ass. Ego deflated—sex life ruined.

DAY 3 "GOOD NEWS IS NO NEWS"

We were billeted together in a sand-bagged, cinder-block, 50-caliber-pockmarked fleapit. It turned out to be a riotous farce, with me playing the part of Rear Admiral Farting, Inman as Private Nothing, and Harmon as General Idiot. I peered out from under my blanket that morning to see Inman standing in the middle of the room like a mule staring at a new gate. "What's up?" I asked. He looked at me sheepishly. "I needed to pee so badly, I went to find the Port-O-Let and got lost. I peed myself before I found the toilet." I thought, Why would he tell me this? Doesn't he know I'm writing a story? Then Harmon stumbled in from the next room, rubbing his eyes, and in a moment of weakness said, "Yeah, I did the same thing!" This was too good. Now, along with the Desert Sofa, we had the Desert Sprinklers. I wasn't exactly innocent myself. Even a casual glance at any pair of my shorts would show that my talented-yet-noisy digestive system, fueled by mint-chocolate-chip ice cream and the vast amount of sand I'd swallowed, had turned me into "The Desert Fertilizer."

I soon hit the showers, where a G.I. was toweling off. I'm not one to strike up a conversation with a man with a visible willy, but it was cold, and I thought I'd seize the chance to see if I could get a negative reaction from someone about being stuck here, about how we're losing the war. This soldier had no idea who I was, so, as we stood side-by-side shaving, I said, "God but this sucks, doesn't it?"

"Maybe," he said. "But can you imagine how bad it would be if we weren't winning?" I told him who I was and asked why I hadn't seen another journalist. His answer: "You know that saying. 'No news is good news'? Well, it should be 'Good news is no news.' " Then he pointed at my groin and laughed.

Like I said—it was cold.

DAY 4 CALL ME FLORENCE OF ARABIA

En route to the former hellhole of Ramadi, nearer Baghdad, there was evidence that the trip was growing dangerous. Captain Garrett looked increasingly more alert as we lifted off in the Osprey, and two Cobra gunships rose menacingly alongside us, with Marines manning 120-mm machine guns jutting out each side. Even I, Florence of Arabia, felt safe surrounded by men packing this kind of heat. We'd gotten a close look at the Cobras minutes earlier, as each of us signed one of its missiles—just a polite message to our friendly neighborhood insurgents. I wrote " 'You're welcome" on mine. But Butch, who saw and lost the most in Vietnam, was less polite.

At the Ramadi base, we met Command Sergeant Major (CSM) Clarence Stanley, a bull of a man with a bristling military mustache. He was overjoyed to see us. While politicians and generals move their little chess pieces, it's the sergeants major who run and win wars, who get things done, who feel the sting when young people die. "I'm more like a parent," CSM Stanley told us. "My job is to ensure that my children get home safely to their families." He gave us a tour of the intel center, which was too intelligent for everyone except Watson. Between satellite images, stratospheric spy planes, human intelligence (squealers) and other top-secret sensors, if Bin Burpin lets out as much as a goat-falafel fart in the desert, coalition forces can have a laser-guided surprise up his mandress within minutes, provided the trajectory of same surprise is uninhibited by the presence of anything innocent or friendly. So if the Bearded One wants to launch a rocket at the base, he'd better do it from the hood—though the hood is now against him too. In February of 2007, the Ramadi base saw about 30 attacks daily. As of November, they'd had only one in the previous four months. Recently, the townsfolk even held a 5-K run and a parade with fire trucks to celebrate their freedom from Saddam and Al Qaeda.

Two more stops, the Ospreys replaced by a CH-46 Sea Knight tandem-rotor assault helicopter, with gunship outriggers. In the services, where everything has a code name, we were now "Watson's Wussies" (hey, Hogan had his heroes) and were headed for Fallujah, some 40 miles west of Baghdad, on the Euphrates. Just a year ago, Fallujah made '80s-era Beirut look like Miami Beach. We met a general who reported that violence is down and the troops are being welcomed. Politicians and TV talking heads arrive, see the difference, and forget it on their way home, he explained. The closer we get to Baghdad, the more I suspect that the smartest Americans are in Iraq, and they get progressively dumber the closer you get to Washington.

DAY 5 EXTREME MAKEOVER: SADDAM EDITION

The next day—shadowed by the Cobras that crisscrossed in our wake like hunting dogs—we bypassed Baghdad International Airport and landed at Camp Victory, where the second-ranking U.S. commander in Iraq, General Raymond Odierno, has thrown out Saddam's crap at one of the henchman's former palaces and turned it into his military headquarters. Saddam's old digs were impressive from a distance. But once inside, the place seemed to symbolize the cruel man who slaughtered his people. The marble interior is a thin veneer, held on by liquid nails; the massive chandelier in the entrance hall is made of Perspex. The place looks like Saddam sent a few of the Republican Guard down to the Home "Despot" to buy materials and do the job themselves. It's big, hollow, and falling apart on its foundation of camel dung. On the way up to the general's office, Inman had a senior moment and went up an extra flight of stairs, almost setting off a total lockdown. We put him on a leash for the rest of the visit.

Next, we had urgent business, the opening of a driving range dedicated to CSM Jonathan Lankford, much loved by his soldiers, and whose idea it was to give the troops somewhere to whack a golf ball. CSM Lankford died of cardiac failure at Camp Victory, leaving behind many broken hearts: his wife, 2-year-old daughter, and, judging by the turnout, hundreds of servicemen and women. Wherever we went golf was a common denominator. Our soldiers have covered Iraq with makeshift driving ranges. They hit balls off of roofs, into blankets, into rivers. Golf is a shared language here that helps ease the stress of being far from home and in harm's way. There was a huge turnout at the range, which backs onto the house where Saddam's two scallywag boys, Hooray and Poosay, or whatever their names were, practiced their favorite hobbies: rape, torture and murder. It seemed surreal to be out there watching Watson, one of golf's great champions, surrounded by American troops and whacking balls off a patch of artificial turf out onto a walled-in section of desert. Harmon and Lehman gave lessons, the Desert Sofa and Sprinkler hit balls, and I roamed the crowd pretending that I know Tiger. Operation Links was all but complete—but as it turned out, we had an unexpected stop to make.

DAY 6 THE LONG FLIGHT HOME

In all, we visited five hospitals, 11 bases, signed about 50,000 autographs—and I ate 14 gallons of ice cream and discarded seven pairs of underpants. We boarded the C-130 to go back to Kuwait, and that's when it happened. "We have to pick up HR," the brass told us. "HR" means human remains. We landed at Balad Air Base, about 40 miles north of Baghdad, at dusk. Our group walked off the plane and watched from a respectful distance as six Air Force airmen stood in double-line formation. A flag-draped casket was wheeled from an unmarked white van into their awaiting arms, and was carried to our plane with the delicacy of a funeral procession. In the background, a pilot taxiing his C-5 Galaxy transport plane saw the unfolding scene, stopped, and silenced his engines. Only the distant screams of F-16s that patrol the Iraqi skies 24/7 could be heard as the body of the fallen warrior was gently loaded onto the tailgate, slid into our aircraft, and secured to the deck, resting inches from our seats. As it should be. This wasn't cargo. This was another passenger. Moments later, we were wheels up, off on our 24-hour journey home. It was hard on Butch, who had seen this before, many years ago. I sat in a trance, staring at the gunmetal-gray casket for most of the trip, and the words of Baghdadi police chief Shab'an B. al-Ubadi came back to me. "The tree of freedom does not grow without the blood of sacrifice." Apparently, he had read Thomas Jefferson too.

I wish I knew who was in that casket—one of the 3,887 Americans killed in Iraq as of December—so I could write to the family to tell them what an honor it was to be on the same airplane as their son or daughter, and to thank them. I owe a debt of gratitude to the men and women of the U.S. armed forces, not just because of what they are doing in Iraq, Afghanistan, and elsewhere, but because of what they left behind. The insurgents they face have left one barren, theocratic hellhole to go fight in Iraq. Big deal. Americans leave behind America, the best place in the world to live. The message that Tom Watson, Tom Lehman, Butch Harmon, Howard Twitty, Joe Inman and I bring home is right from the lips of people who, thousands of miles from their families, lay their lives on the line every day to protect our way of life, and to improve it for the inhabitants of wherever they fight. The worst thing we could do is make them come home before they have had the chance to finish their job. I am proud to write their message.

The Troops First Foundation has become a huge part of my life. Go to troopsfirstfoundation.org for more details, or love a soldier, sailor, or marine today!—D.F.

104.

Feherty's Mailbag

Online—Published: February 26, 2008

Dear David,

As a huge Phil Mickelson fan, I was especially glued to my TV during the CBS coverage of the Nissan Open—I mean Northern Trust Open. As always, your commentary was both brilliant and eloquent. I saw a lot of Jeff Quinney, who I feel is on his way to career victory number one this season. After a little thought, my friend and I have come up with what we think is a fitting name for the young ASU grad: Pooh Bear. Like Winnie the Pooh, but without the Winnie. I think you should consider dropping this on the air next time he plays on the weekend.

—Brian "The Business" Karleskind

Brian:

"The Business," huh? OK. Usually that's the kind of thing that demands explanation, but the more I think about the possibilities, the less I want to know.

I think you're right about Jeff being on the verge of a win. He shows a lot of promise. He's 6 feet tall and 190 pounds, so I'm not so sure about the Pooh Bear thing. He does have a nice rack on him though. Maybe we could call him "Dolly" Quinney, or Quinney the Pooh?

Dear David Feherty:

For years now I have thought that Rory Sabbatini resembled a hobbit. Kind of a freaky-looking, bizarre-acting creature. I know that you and other commentators on Tour have a knack for bestowing nicknames on Tour players. If anyone could appropriately call Rory Sabbatini a hobbit, I feel it would be you. And I mean that in a good way. In any event, I just wanted to get this out there for your consideration.

—Mark Aumann

Mark:

If you're looking for a freaky-looking, bizarre-acting creature, you need look no further than Bobby Clampett. J.R.R. Tolkien modeled the Hobbits after Bobby. They met at a convention for the Terminally, Incomprehensibly, Totally Bewildered Half-Wits where Bobby was the keynote speaker. Compared to Clampett, Sabbatini is the voice of reason; a calm, sensible, reassuring dose of understated, rock-solid mother's milk.

Besides, I've sort of unofficially tagged Sabbatini with "Yosemite Sam." Since I don't think he knows who that is, my chances of getting him to talk to me after a bad round are a lot better.

Hi David,

I would love to see you write a column about nothing but the funny golf sayings you have come up with over the years. You and McCord crack me up. My favorite was when a player hit such a bad shot into the trees you said Lassie couldn't find the ball if it was wrapped in bacon.

—Tommy (The left-handed chop in Denver)

Tommy The Left Handed Chop:

I don't want to know any more about that name. You have a good idea there, my boy. The only problem might be that

McCord can neither read nor write. I basically have written everything funny that he's ever published. And he's never paid me a cent. So if I write a book, it'll be by me. And by the way, just so you know, all of McCord's lines come from somewhere else. His next original thought will be his first one.

Feherty,
    Where do you party during Masters week?

—Doug

Doug:
    At the Home for the Perpetually Incontinent on Washington Ave. Meet me there, Doug. You sound interesting.

105.

The New Rules

Golf Magazine, *10565493, March 2008, Vol. 50, Issue 3*

No matter how much you love golf, there are some things about watching it on TV that probably make you want to empty a full clip into your new flat-screen plasma. Like lines on the ball for a start. Who started that crap? I suspect one of those short-game gurus who convince players to approach every shot as if it were a blindfolded tightrope walk over a pit filled with runoff from John Daly's RV. In my thankfully rare tower moments, my nuts go numb watching players aim the line on the ball in the precise direction in which they want to start a putt. Then they step away and check it. Then readjust it. Then step away again and make sure it's right, by which time I'm drooling and delivering leg kicks to my cameraman like a dog chasing rabbits in its dreams. Then, and only then, do they remove the ball marker, my faithful spotter bludgeons me back to consciousness, and I witness thirteen practice strokes, one last alignment check and a putt that is invariably six inches short.

New Rule: No lines on the ball, unless it's a line of coke, which would at least get the bastards moving. And, of course, Tour officials and DEA agents could then swoop down on the players on live TV. I see great chase-scene potential, hopefully from the blimp.

Moving on to a related matter: At any given time there are several relevant shots a TV producer could show you at home, so as he scans the wall of monitors in front of him, he needs an innate sense of who'll pull the trigger first. Of course, once a decision is made and the director makes the camera cut, the chosen flaming slow-hole backs off his ball and three other shots that could have been shown instead (and will be shown later) are now in the air. This is how live golf becomes plausibly-live golf (that's actually what we call it), and announcers lose their hearing.

New Rule: A player may not address and then re-address his ball unless there is a major distraction. Major distractions are defined as follows:

1. A gust of wind in excess of 60 mph
2. A sonic boom
3. Elin Woods

New Rule: No more tapping down imaginary spike marks after a missed putt. Hey, Yippy, you missed an easy one because you suck. Deal with it.

From now on this will be a one-shot penalty, or in match play your opponent can deliver a free love-tap to your nads. That ought to do it.

New Rule: No more blaming the caddie after nuking a 9-iron into the skybox on 17 and sending shards of Miller Lite bottles and chunks of warm tuna salad into the hair of its occupants. This means no more slamming the club into the bag and berating the hapless guy, who, despite smelling like a Nicaraguan dope fiend, begged you to hit the gap wedge. Penalty: One shot, plus dinner tab for the caddie and his three favorite strippers.

New Rule: Read it quickly, and then weep. There are guys who have their caddie look at every putt from north, south, east and west, check the grain, slope, barometric pressure, Shotlink, write to Dr. Phil, and then crouch down behind them to make sure they're lined up correctly. Then, just before the player makes a stroke, the caddie walks away exactly four and a half steps diagonally and freezes like he just noticed his wife standing by the bag, holding up the panties she found in his glove compartment. Penalty: The player must tell Mrs. Looper the panties are his, and wear them for the rest of the season.

106

David Feherty Speaks: "I'm Lucky to Be Alive"

Online—Published: March 28, 2008
By Connell Barrett

Two weeks ago David Feherty was hit by a truck while riding a bicycle near his Dallas home. Golf Magazine *editor-at-large Connell Barrett caught up with the TV funnyman as he recuperates on his couch surrounded by candies and get-well cards.*

It's been two weeks since your bike-riding accident. How are you feeling?

Before the accident, I could ride 50 miles without breaking a sweat. Now, I can't get halfway up the stairs without breaking for a nap. I can't put enough weight on my arms to get out of a chair by myself, and I haven't voluntarily farted in 10 days. I can't cough, and a sneeze could be fatal. Otherwise, I'm peachy!

What are your injuries?

I have a torn bursa sac in my left elbow, a separated shoulder and three broken ribs, one of which is broken in two spots. That's called a "floater." I'm proud of my floater. Oh, and I have a punctured lung.

Tell us about the accident.

I adore riding. It's my therapy. Two weeks ago, I was riding my beautiful 6.5 Trek Madone—now mangled—on the right side of the right-hand lane on a road about a mile from my home in Dallas. I'd done about 45 miles. I can't go into detail about the accident due to legal reasons, but I was hit by a pickup truck towing a trailer as we both approached a traffic light. I felt a violent blow to my back, and I went flying through the air. I landed on my left side, on my left shoulder. I took a good crack to my helmet. It could have been much worse—the truck sort of pushed me off to the right, instead of sucking me underneath. Otherwise, I'd be roadkill. It was a slice—if it had been a hook it would have been fatal. So I'm lucky in that sense, but it was still a violent thud of a landing. It was Olympian. I got scores of 6.9 for artistic impression, but I couldn't stick the landing. *[After this interview, Feherty found out he had actually been run over by the trailer. —ed.]*

You hear about people seeing their life flash before their eyes. Did you experience any sensations like that?

No, I remember just trying to stay conscious. It was hard to breathe. I was lying there like a goldfish out of his bowl. As it turns out, I wasn't in grave danger lying there—you can breathe and survive with one lung, and I didn't have much internal bleeding. But, of course, I didn't know all that at the time. I was writhing around, unable to breathe. I said to myself, "If I pass out, am I coming back?" I remember feeling that if this is it for me, I'm not unhappy. I've done all right. I was ready to go, if it was going to happen. I wasn't afraid. I also remember a woman stopping. She came over and held my hand, asking, "Can you hear me?" She stayed with me until the paramedics came. I couldn't talk, but I could listen, and I remember her voice. I haven't been able to find out who she is yet. If you're out there, call me. I'd love to say thank you.

The paramedics came and put you in the ambulance. You were concerned about your riding clothes, right?

[Laughs] They strapped me to a board, put me in an ambulance, and we were off. It's funny how your mind works. Under my outer clothes I was wearing this skin-tight riding suit. It has a chamois that protects your ass from a bike's razor-blade saddle. This is a $400 skin-suit. They had to cut my clothes off in the ambulance to check for broken bones. They're ripping and tearing, and I'm tallying up the total in my mind, thinking, Hey, easy! This is a $400 suit! Of course, I couldn't really talk. I was too busy yelping like a coyote on acid. I remember thinking, "I wonder what my manhood looks like." There's a compression issue with clothes that tight, and sometimes it makes your member look like a button mushroom. No, guys, it's normally bigger than this, I swear!

You were in the hospital for four days. Did you get an outpouring of support?

It was incredible. I want to offer a class-action "thank you" to everyone. I'll be writing about this in *Golf Magazine*. Jack Nicklaus, bless him, called and made me laugh hardest. I had to cancel plans to go to The Jake, Jack and Barbara's pro-am benefiting their efforts to fight childhood illnesses. I really wanted to be there, and Jack said, "Hey, don't worry about it. We might actually make some money now that you're not coming." I laughed so hard I almost broke another rib. Johnny Miller called to wish me well. That fat bastard [Roger] Maltbie at NBC suggested on the air they take up a collection to buy me training wheels. Like training wheels are so expensive? If he really cared, he'd have splurged and bought them himself.

Have you heard from your CBS cohort, Gary McCord?

McCord calls me twice a day. He loves other people's misfortune. But if I have to tell one more person about what happened . . . I've now explained it so many times in calls and text messages that it would be less painful to go back to the scene, build some bleachers, invite all my ghoulish friends, and have the guy hit me with his trailer again. That would save me some time. [Laughs]

Sounds like laughter is not the best medicine when you have broken ribs and a punctured lung.

I almost didn't survive the Eliot Spitzer story. That nearly killed me! But people have been fabulous. I've injured my thumb sending out so many BlackBerry messages. I've written over 80 thank-you notes. I've got more flowers here than a funeral home, and I've been eating about 800 boxes of Easter candy people have sent me. It's been wonderful and heart-warming.

You'll be at the Masters, we hope?

Oh yeah, I'll be ready. I'll weigh about 800 pounds, but I'll be there.

107.

Offended Behavior

Golf Magazine, 10565493, April 2008, Vol. 50, Issue 4

In my very first event as an announcer—the Johnnie Walker World Championship on the USA Network—Loren Roberts bounced a shot off a coconut floating in a pond and onto the edge of a green. I rushed over and retrieved the helpful husk, which upon examination showed clear dimple prints. I felt this was newsworthy, and convinced the producer to put me on camera. My first words to an American TV audience were, "I'm standing here, nursing Loren Roberts' bruised nut." Thankfully, I had the evidence to explain the words, but in retrospect, it was an uncalculated gamble, particularly in light of the reaction to Kelly Tilghman's spontaneous crack about opponents lynching Tiger Woods.

I've been blessed by two things my whole life. First, I find something to like in everyone I meet (even the complete a——holes) and second, I'm just plain, ordinary lucky. There's no other way to explain why I still have a job in sports television. There seem to be different sets of rules for sports announcers, comedians and political satirists. David Letterman can say things on his show that would probably get me fired in a heartbeat, although I'm not sure why.

I don't like being nice; in fact it makes me feel kind of nasty, or at least disingenuous. I only have one life to live, and I've no patience or time to waste on social posturing. I've always found the quickest way to get to know someone is to poke them where it's uncomfortable, and watch how they react. The key is not to stand back, but to stay within the critical poke-back zone. This gives the pokee the usually correct impression that the poker has no intent to inflict insult or pain, but rather the opposite, i.e. to offer the pokee an opportunity to show that he or she is already past something that might still be a problem for others. The result is dignity, and, I believe, the evolution of our species. The people who don't get uncomfortable, or figure it out quickly and take a poke back, usually turn out to be my favorites. Payne Stewart and Tiger Woods are two perfect examples. Payne was poke-proof, and lethal on the counter-poke. It was no coincidence that he and Tiger got along so well. Tiger loves the intellectual stimulant of the well-timed jab, and he's quick to recognize the difference between stupid words chosen by a good person, and the genuine intent to be hurtful from a narrow-minded bigot. The truth is, unless there is reason to suspect someone is actually dangerous, it's always best to completely ignore the imbeciles, for in so doing you can retain your dignity. It's a damn shame there are intolerant idiots out there, but it's also disappointing that there are people who seize any and every opportunity to be offended, and use them as a vehicle to promote their agenda.

Kelly Tilghman is a good person, and she's almost always clever. Okay, so she wasn't a genius when, in response to Nick Faldo's joke about the young players on Tour having to gang up on Tiger, she suggested with a laugh that they "lynch him in a back alley." But her career doesn't deserve to be defined by one innocent blunder. Nobody is clever all the time, not even me, and this piece is proof. Hell, it might even get me fired.

108.

David Feherty Reflects on the 2008 Masters

Online—Published: April 15, 2008

A few notes from David Feherty on the new Masters champion, Tiger's trying Sunday, and sucking face (almost) with Verne Lundquist.

—**Trevor Immelman** played astonishing golf Sunday. If you have the lead at Augusta on Friday or Saturday, the green jacket feels like it's made of lead. On Sunday? It's so heavy, you can barely walk. It wears on you. He handled the pressure that wrecked everyone else, including Tiger.

—**Immelman's biggest shot** was his 20-foot par putt on 11. What a 4! It was gigantic. And he followed that by holing a bowel-liquefying bogey putt on the par-3 12th. If he misses that bogey putt, he could be looking at a triple. With these greens, if the ball lips out, you're not left with a tap-in; you have three or four feet. You could see Trevor's hair turning gray with each hole.

—**We saw the perfect storm** of conditions at Augusta on Sunday. The course couldn't have played harder, with the speed of the greens, the softness of the fairways and the howling wind. It's too bad the gusts were so great. A calmer day could have produced some back-nine fireworks. But the wind took an already difficult course right to the edge.

—**Tiger's defining moment** came on 13, when he missed his short birdie putt. The stage was set. He'd birdied 11, and if he birdies 13, he hangs six under on the board, and we might have seen Trevor Immelman become *Tremor* Immelman. But for all the money he has, Tiger couldn't buy a putt. You could see the frustration bubbling up. It's a testament to his greatness that he still finished second. When he plays well, everyone else is finished. When he doesn't, they have a chance.

—**You'd think Immelman's** six-shot lead with three holes to play would be safe, and then on 16 . . . bingo! Double-bogey. There's no other course where six shots can vanish so quickly. It shows you what Augusta can do to these players. But Trevor's poor tee shot was not due to nerves. I watched his swing from my position in the CBS tower at 15, and it appeared his alignment was off. He hit it dead square. That swing is something— so efficient and reliable. He's lucky it hasn't been kidnapped by the Swiss. But his alignment appeared a bit off on 16.

—**If you think** the tee shot on 16 is frightening, I've got something much scarier: Verne Lundquist tried to kiss me! We were in the CBS Masters house. He was reading the newspaper, and I was eating a bowl of cereal. Ever since I broke some ribs in a bicycle accident last month, sneezing has become indescribably painful. It feels like getting shot in the heart. I tried to fight it, but I let loose a big one. A mouthful of All-Bran shot across the room, and I dropped to the floor—the pain was that bad. Verne jumped up and rushed over. He couldn't tell if I was breathing, and I was in so much pain that I couldn't talk. I looked up to see Verne coming toward me, bending down, and I realized, "Oh, god! He's going to give me the kiss of life." So I did the only thing I could to avoid mouth-to-mouth: I kicked at him like a bronco. Phew! That was close. Verne, I appreciate the thought, but I don't kiss on the first date.

109

I Have a Scream: Or, How Grunting Like a Rutting Bull Moose Can Save Golf

Online—Published: April 16, 2008

Other than chess players and scuba divers, Tour players are probably the quietest sportsmen around. Yeah, sure, there's an occasional outburst of profanity (not to be confused with the amateurfanity you hear in your foursome), but otherwise the game is a regular shhhh-fest.

The other day I was watching a National Geographic show about screaming and its ability to make people stronger. (Think karate chops, or 1,000 hairy Scots with their bums painted blue charging down the glen into battle with the English.) Apparently there is evidence that if you're in the mood to break several blocks of masonry with your forearms, and you let out your best primal gulder (an Ulster yell) before and during the act, you develop measurably more kinetic energy than if you attempt such demolition gulder-free. Nat Geo had the brain images, stress monitors and numbers to prove the theory, but She Who Must Be Obeyed and I are building a house, and have watched in agony as the stonework in our kitchen was butchered and torn down three times in a row by an elderly white man who labored to the mercifully quiet sound of some really dreadful country music.

Still, screaming has definitely made its way into sports, probably starting with competitive cave-farting before creeping into ancient martial arts, and then weightlifting, all of which I understand. But how the hell did it start in tennis? I seem to remember Monica Seles squeaking like an acid-crazed gerbil every time her strings met the fuzz, but now everyone with a racquet seems to be making a racket. It makes me want to break out the duct tape. How can any umpire say, "Quiet please," and then in good conscience have some poor drunk in the crowd ejected, when the contest on the court sounds like it's between a pair of howler monkeys in the mating season?

It's the women in tennis who scare me the most. They start their scream on the backswing, change the tone and volume at impact, and let it subside on the follow-through: "Aaaaaa-WEEEEEH-gaaaaah!" Some of the men are in on it too, but not at the same level as the women, who are just plain better at screaming in general, even if a male lion's territorial call can be heard for miles.

All the yelling has made tennis almost unwatchable with the volume up, which is a damn shame, because John McEnroe might be the best analyst in sports (and is probably tied with me for Most-Likely-To-Get-Fired-For-Saying-Something-Insulting), so I hate not to hear him. It all makes me wonder how long it will be until we have a giant Neanderthal in bad plaid pants teeing it up on Tour, with a pre-shot routine like a rutting bull moose making some kind of primal bugling noise on the downswing, and caving in the face of his 50-inch driver in the process. It doesn't sound pretty, and I reckon golf's governing bodies should put some noise restrictions in place before it's too late. A simple decibel limit would do it, but as the game's self-appointed mental hygienist, I feel there should be a cutoff after the swing, at which point a player can make as much noise as he wants. I mean, let's be fair—it's one thing to mute players before a shot, but if we mandate that they have to be silent after the ball is gone, we'll lose some of the color in the game, and might even cause a head injury due to pressure build-up. I've never felt the urge to scream at the ball before impact, but if I have to watch that rotten, little black-hearted swine of a sphere fly out of bounds, I reserve the right to yodel obscenities louder than I do at a digital prostate exam. I'll go blue in the bum before I give up that inalienable right.

110

Pro-Am Purgatory: My Seven-Step Plan to Pro-Am Happiness Will Ensure a Good Time Is Had by All

Online—Published: May 1, 2008

Much has been written about the attitude of Tour pros to the ubiquitous Wednesday pro-am. The difficulties of concentrating on the day before the tournament while playing with nervous amateurs are many.

However, no one seems to offer these quivering victims any advice. Well, here are my "Seven Steps to Pro-Am Heaven"—for pro and amateur alike. A few dos and don'ts of playing with the pro—a road map through the purgatory of the pro-am.

I always try to imagine what it would be like for me if I were plucked out of my comfort zone and thrust into the spotlight, say, on stage with Bruce Springsteen or into the boardroom with Bill Gates, and told not to make an idiot of myself. The truth is that neither Bruce nor Bill would expect me to be any good at all. I, on the other hand, would still like to give a decent account of myself, or at least limit the damage.

The first thing to remember is that your pro requires one thing from you—that you enjoy yourself. The reason we play for so much money these days is that you do enjoy the game, you do buy the equipment that you don't need, and you do love to watch us on television. So, don't be overawed: Chances are you do something for a living that we would be completely use-less at. A good pro will always do his or her best to put you at ease on the first tee, so when you make your first swing that makes contact with the planet nine inches behind the ball and measures 4.8 on the Richter scale, you can at least have a laugh at it, too.

Some of the best fun I've had on a golf course has been with complete hackers who have had enough confidence in what they do in other walks of life to laugh it off without self-consciousness, while enjoying the walk and the banter.

So, here are a few guidelines that will help both you and your pro enjoy the day:

1. Get a Caddie. It's the only way to play the game. You can walk free of hindrance and have the club handed to you clean and dry. If possible, get one of the Tour caddies whose man isn't in the pro-am. For $100, you can have someone who is used to being screamed at, blamed for the weather, the rate of inflation, and some of those hard-to-explain skin rashes.

Mind you, he won't be able to club you because you don't know which part of the club the ball is about to bounce off of. However, he will be able to regale you with stories on and off the course to which most people are never privy.

2. Be ready to hit. Even if it isn't your turn. Discuss with your partners the concept of "ready golf" before you tee off. This means forgetting whose honor it is—if you're ready, just go. Pro-am play is hideously slow at the best of times and your pro will really appreciate it if you make the effort to keep it going.

There is nothing sadder than watching a finely tuned athlete walking slowly into the woods to whack his forehead on a Scotch pine just to relieve the pain of watching a 23-handicap account executive from Sheboygan agonize over whether to miss the green by 70 yards with a heavily disguised 11-wood or a very fat 4-iron. It makes me droop just thinking about it.

3. No cellular phones. At the very least turn them off. The surgical removal of a cellular phone from certain regions of the anatomy is painful and, to the best of my knowledge, is not covered under most company health insurance plans.

4. Get a yardage book. And ask a Tour caddie how to use it. This will make the pro very happy. Contribute to your pro's mental well-being by being the first "ammy" in the history of his pro-am career not to ask the question: "How far have I got from here?"

There are only a certain number of times in your career you can be asked this question before your spleen bursts. Mine burst six years ago.

5. Out of the hole? Pick it up. And, be sure to tell your pro when you have done so. Not only will you contribute to the pace of play, but you will avoid the awkward situation of having the pro wait, expecting you to hit, while you are rummaging around in your bag looking for that three-year-old stick of gum that's making everything sticky.

In this category, there is only one thing worse than waiting around for no apparent reason, and that is waiting around for a very bad apparent reason; i.e., holing out for a 9, net 8.

6. Forget about score. And, don't be upset if your pro doesn't know how your team stands. Remember, it's a Wednesday. He probably doesn't even know his own score.

7. Watch your feet. Be very, very mindful of the line of your pro's putt. Look at television coverage of a golf tournament and watch how respectful the pros are of each other's lines. Quite often a player walks 60 or 70 feet around another player's marker just to avoid stepping over it.

There's no need to take it to these extremes, but ask your pro where his line is and he or she will show you where to step over. Remember, this is our office. How would you feel if you were in the process of finishing a very carefully written letter to your boss and I came in wearing a pair of golf shoes and did a Highland fling all over it? I thought so.

Finally, if any of you are still interested in playing this game with anybody ever again, try not to give the pro any advice on how to play the course, even if it is your home course and you've been a member for 75 years. Trust me, he knows more about it than you do just by looking at the yardage book.

It's a question of knowing what to look for. Even giving the occasional line off the tee can be dangerous because you don't normally play two club-lengths from the back edge of the back tee. I don't know how many times I've heard, "Oops, I could have sworn you could have carried that bunker!"

If you follow those rules, you should have a great day. Remember, there is no other sport where you can play alongside the pros in such close proximity without being injured.

Despite what you've read, we can have fun on a Wednesday, too. And, as I said, thanks for the prize money!

111.

Naked Submission

Golf Magazine, *10565493, July 2008, Vol. 50, Issue 7*

By the time this issue hits the newsstands, a few brave men on
the PGA Tour are likely to have whipped out their wedding-
tackle in front of keen-eyed observers and handed over warm
little bottles of their wee-wee for drug testing. Such drastic
measures are the result of abiding by the WAD of A (World Anti-
Doping Agency), whose regulations athletes have attempted to
circumvent in every conceivable manner, including, by at least
one cyclist, filling a condom with a relative's urine and stashing
it under his armpit. Frankly, I doubt that I could hide a condom full of family pee and make a dry backswing, and if I took
a shot at it they'd probably tell me I was clean, but pregnant
with twins.

Many players have serious issues with the observation procedure. The golfer has to drop his pants to his ankles, roll up
his shirt and hold it under his chin, and squirt. I'm not kidding!
Believe me, if I had to pee in front of someone, I'd toss down a
dose or three of Cialis and Viagra, and maybe call Dick Vitale
during the performance, just to make sure it took four hours.
I'd make the observer hold the bottle in one hand and his
umbrella in the other. I imagine some idiot will eventually get

caught for smoking dope, or some other recreational substance, but as I've said before, none of that crap helps you get a little white sphere into a hole in the ground in less swipes.

I don't see steroids enhancing a golfer's performance either. If being bigger and stronger is enough of an advantage to compensate for a scrotum the size of a seedless raisin and a temper like Rasputin, why don't we have gorilla-sized players getting shot outside of strip clubs or tossing their wives off balconies by now? Sure, HGH is a drug that helps the body recover from injury, but the side effects are either unknown or not good, so taking it for performance enhancement is an idiotic personal risk. If you want to hit it ten yards farther and don't mind having a prostate the size of a bagel, have at it Einstein, and while you're at it, wash it down with a cup of Liquid Drano. And what about beta-blockers? Anyone with a tame doctor (which would be everyone I know) can get an excuse note for those. Hell, just reading this column sends the collective blood pressure of about 50 percent of you through the roof, and there are so many people on prescribed amphetamines like Adderall and Ritalin who have to take a beta-blocker to counteract the resulting rise in their blood pressure that we can effectively kick those out, too. An amphetamine might work for a player who wasn't nervous enough, but I don't think I've ever met one of those.

But say a player does get tossed for being amped-up—do we give his son an F in remedial quilting for taking the same pill?

Fortunately, the PGA Tour has had the good sense to implement a set of measures that give a player who has made an innocent mistake the chance to prove it, and they have ensured that all proceedings will be kept confidential until the entire process is over. But get this: The WAD of A regulations actually require a player to submit to testing in his own home! I have advice for any tester who's thinking of trying this in the great state of Texas, where our law overrides the WAD of A. In Texas, if there is anyone on your property who is acting as though they might be a threat to you, your family, or even your beagle, you are allowed to give them a sample of lead, which, in a magnificent irony, is in exactly the same category as the drugs they're looking for. It's toxic, and it definitely won't help your golf game. Thanks for calling 'round, pardner, and have a nice day!

112.

Old Golfers Don't Die—They Just Keep Going, and Going . . .

Online—Published: August 1, 2008

Judging by some of the commercials aired during golf telecasts, you'd think that every golf fan is an erectionally challenged male in his late 50s looking for a retirement community in Florida, where he can spend his days playing unlimited bad golf on 6,000-yard courses and his nights square dancing with covens of blue-haired old trout who've killed off an average of 2.7 husbands apiece.

So I got to thinking, maybe the next generation of golf TV ads could be two-minute product-placement sitcoms. Try to picture a foursome of sixtysomething men at The Ditherage, the happiest retirement community in Florida, when one of their carts veers off into the woods.

"What's up, Bob?" asks Dave.

"Very funny," replies Bob, as the cart skids to a halt on the pine-straw. "But you know I can't make a backswing for 36 hours if I've popped a Rectoris. I need to hang out the hose."

"Again?" says Dave.

"Bob, you piss on the bushes more often than the *New York Times*. You should try Plumsadrainin, you know, or maybe Gonax? It'll straighten you right up. Just look at old Ronnie over there on the green, he's only been taking it for two weeks, and just the other day he pitched a two-squirter from the Acid Reflux tees." (Ronnie makes a six-footer, high-fives Edgar, bends down to pick the ball out of the hole and falls in a heap.)

"Sure," says Bob, easing himself out of the cart. He unzips behind a tree, flexing his knees. "But every time Ronnie picks his ball out of the hole, he has a sudden drop in blood pressure and faints. Look at him, he just went down like a f——ing deck chair. Damn lucky he's developed that big old set of man-hammers. They cushion his fall every time!"

And back to golf . . . shot, shot, shot, leaderboard, "And we'll be right back after these messages and a word from your local station."

Bob is still behind the tree, and Dave is becoming impatient. "Anything?" he says. . . .

"Damn it, Dave, I was this close to getting started, and you ruined my stream of consciousness." Bob zips up and gets back in the cart. "I'll just have to wait until the next PJ."

"That's okay," says Dave. "Here at the Ditherage, you're never more than a hole from your next opportunity to make one—or, for that matter, two. Good thing, too, because since Marge has been putting that LavaFart stool-softener in my oatmeal, I could lay a length of cable across the Atlantic. She says her last husband died from food-poisoning, but I'm beginning to wonder if he didn't just crap until his head caved in."

"Speaking of Marge," says Bob, "how are the two of you getting along now that you've decided to entrust your bedroom karma to Big Pharma?"

"Oooh, now you're talking," Dave says. "A gentleman doesn't tell, but suffice to say I timed one just right the other night, and it's been a while since Marge's dentures have fallen out for that particular reason. And it was thirty minutes before we were done."

"Really?" says Bob, surprised.

"Oh, yeah—they went under the dust ruffle, and I put my back out trying to reach them."

Dave suddenly slams the steering wheel as they screech to a halt outside the porta-potty. "Damn it—the trouser-turtle beat me to it again!"

"Too bad, Dave," says Bob. "I sure hope you're wearing your Dampers with Wings, or should I move to the upwind passenger seat on the special E-Z-FLO cart they provide for us here at The Ditherage?"

And back to golf . . . or maybe not. I mean, who knows what will happen next at The Ditherage, the General Hospital of golf. . . .

113.

An Ode to Sir Charles

Online—Published: May 1, 2009

Basketball is a sport I don't play and barely understand because the damned hole is in the air, yet I adore Charles Barkley as an announcer. Like John McEnroe, Sir Charles has the ability to open his mouth and allow whatever is in his massive, shiny cranium to fly out, unfiltered by thought of consequences. This is a beautiful thing, and long may it continue for both of them, the two best announcers in sports.

Believe it or not, despite the well-documented point that Barkley's golf swing is as painful to watch as four women screaming simultaneously, otherwise known as *The View* (I'm not hammering a CBS show, even though I completely agree), I actually admire the big man's golf game, and for once I'm being sincere. Toward the end of last year George Lopez and I were hosting our annual pro-am at Vaquero Club in Westlake, Texas, when Sir Charles hit the range for a lesson with Hank Haney. Accompanied by a Golf Channel crew, student and teacher made a show of attempting to banish the infamous spasm that occurs in the middle of Charles's backswing, an unnatural phenomenon that has made him an interesting case study in teaching circles, and the subject of many lame jokes like the one above. And frankly, *nothing* is as painful as watching *The View*. Dear god, if they'd put that show on a loop in the cells at Gitmo when they opened it we'd have had all the confessions we needed within 15 minutes. Hell, a photo of Barbara Walters on her own might have done it.

Meanwhile, back at Sir Cumference . . . Here's a man who doesn't need to be doing this in public, who has accepted all of the abuse thrown his way with grace and good humor, who clearly loves the game of golf, and makes a constant effort to get better, undeterred by what seems to the rest of us an impossible goal.

I further admire Charles because I *know* the yips eventually get to all of us, no matter who we are or what we do—life yips, relationship yips, job yips, public toilet yips. (Okay, that last one might just be me.) In golf, the yips affect fine motor skills, resulting in skinny wedge shots, pathetic stabs with the putter and/or drives that only gravity keeps on the planet. Here's what happens: You set out to make a swing or a stroke, but your mind tells you that you are a dilwad and that something that feels this bad can't possibly work and you don't have a change of underpants so you had better make seventeen minor adjustments on the fly to limit the damage that is about to occur and oh holy shit what the hell was *that*? SOILAGE!

Admit it, you're more than familiar with that sequence. And here's the thing, Sir Charles is not alone in having this happen to him in the middle of his full swing. Off the top of my head I can name three major champions who definitely had more than a few full-swing yippity-do-dah days, starting with my old cobber on the CBS crew, Ian Baker-Finch, who at one point by his own admission couldn't have hit the Gulf of Mexico off an oil rig. Finchy hit it OB off both the first and 18th tees at St. Andrews, which would be pretty hard to do, even if you were trying it deliberately. Then there's Seve, bless his lion heart and pray for his wounded head. At times golf's greatest magician hit it so far off line that Lassie wouldn't have found it if it had been wrapped in bacon. And lest we forget, after winning the Open Championship David Duval needed Google Earth to locate his pill.

So give Sir Charles a little slack and a lot of credit. Just like the three champions I've just mentioned, his only mistake is caring too much. I may not be much of a coach, but I've been to a few psychiatrists, and the trick is this: You have to find a way to take your mind off what *might* happen, and pay attention to what *is* happening. Look inward, Charles, deeper and deeper. George and I saw you on that practice tee with Hank, smoking them 300 yards down the range, and you were *smooth*. Swing like Hank has shown you, and then don't think at all. Let the club go where it wants to go, just like the words do when you open your mouth on TNT. That way you'll find out where the ball goes when you make a comfortable swing, and all Hank will have to do is get you pointed in the right direction.